Black Motherhood(s)

T0307239

Black Motherhood(s)
Contours, Contexts and Considerations

EDITED BY
Karen T. Craddock

DEMETER PRESS

Funded by the Government of Canada
Financé par la gouvernement du Canada | Canadä

Demeter Press
140 Holland Street West
P. O. Box 13022
Bradford, ON L3Z 2Y5
Tel: (905) 775-9089
Email: info@demeterpress.org
Website: www.demeterpress.org

Demeter Press logo based on the sculpture "Demeter" by Maria-Luise Bodirsky <www.keramik-atelier.bodirsky.de>

Front cover artwork: Theresa Craddock, "Sowers," 2015, watercolour, 11x14.

Printed and Bound in Canada

Library and Archives Canada Cataloguing in Publication

        Black motherhood(s) : contours, contexts and considerations / editor, Karen T. Craddock.

Includes bibliographical references.
ISBN 978-1-927335-25-3 (paperback)

        1. Motherhood. 2. Women, Black. 3. Mothers.
I. Craddock, Karen T., 1965-, author, editor

HQ759.B63 2015   306.874'308996   C2015-906376-0

To Clark Craddock-Willis and Coleman Craddock-Willis,
my sun and moon ... lights of my life, thank you for blessing me
with this most Divine gift of motherhood.

To Minnie Canty Platt, Theresa Platt Hayes,
Jessie Hammond Gough and Elizabeth Gough Craddock
in honor of these grand women — my grand mothers who are the
daughters of mothers that expand the globe ...
your voices encourage and your hands usher me forward.

For my mother, Theresa G. Craddock
in deepest gratitude for her optimally resisting and
life-affirming model and aphorism ... "I am here."
This proclamation of beingness and purpose has been
both root and wing for my journey.

Table of Contents

CONTENTS

There is nothing like a mother's love.
—Roland Lee Smart (1956-2015)

Kinsman Redeemer and Beloved Man...
rest in power, rest in peace.

Mother Maya...
In remembrance and rejoice of Marguerite Annie Johnson

Vibrant light illuminating ourselves to ourselves,
You entwined our hearts around the strength of your fore-arm
    and lifted us high enough
to see over the wall of doubt and despair.

There, you unfurled us atop your brilliant hills of lush words and
    wisdom
And we danced into knowingness to the beat of your lyrical prose
    and sang ourselves
out of cages and into our promise.

We, the lovely birds, with clasped hands and faces turned upward
    to the One
lovingly smile and celebrate you ... Phenomenal Woman.

—Karen T. Craddock (May 2014)

Acknowledgements

It is with great appreciation and admiration for the contributors to this volume that I acknowledge them for their sustained engagement, poignant individual transdisciplinary offerings, and collective participation in exploring Black Motherhoods. Though singularly crafted, their essays resound remarkably among and across one another, which delightfully informed the thematic editing process and provide rich opportunity for further collaboration. I am also thankful to Dr. Saundra Nettles and Dr. Nicole Banton for their editorial contributions in the early stages of this project.

I am forever grateful for my sister-scholar, Dr. Tracy Robinson-Wood, for her brilliant scholarship and creative salience that inspire innovative expansion in the academic arena and social impact in the fields of practice.

Thank you to Dr. Sara Lawrence-Lightfoot and Dr. Layli Maparyan whose work has provided personal illumination and robust possibilities for integrating the self, the story, and the spirit into the scholarly with a visionary approach and contextual application that uncover and elevate the complexities and intersections of the human journey, especially that of black women.

And with profound acknowledgment of all of the mothers and mothering worldwide — the elemental bedrock on which we all stand and a timeless source of how we make meaning in the world.

Black Motherood(s)

Introduction

KAREN T. CRADDOCK

B LACK WOMEN LIVE THROUGH a complex array of realities
that intersect and amplify the human experience in distinct
and unique ways. As Black mothers, we encounter and
confront barriers of race and gender-based hegemony that are
intertwined with strong holds around notions of motherhood.
These entrenched social constructions are elemental to societal
and relational systems that are in operation globally and hold
tremendous power with how Black mothers experience themselves
and the world around them. Black motherhood also encompasses
and carries strengths that are culturally informed and embedded
in generational narratives of womanhood, exemplifying rich and
varied textures that are reflected in countless scholarly works,
creative expressions, activism, advocacy, caretaking/help-seeking
practices and spiritual beliefs. Using a primary lens of womanism to
review and reflect, some dynamics emerge in the contours, contexts
and considerations of Black motherhood that can be explored for
further illumination.

BLACK MOTHERHOOD, WOMANISM AND
TRANSCENDENT RESISTANCE

The discourse on Black women, social activism and reconceptualization of the institution of motherhood in both praxis and
scholarship can be grounded in Patricia Hill Collins' seminal
work *Black Feminist Thought: Knowledge, Consciousness and
the Politics of Empowerment*. Collins' body of work challenges

stagnant and static definitions of Black female identity and motherhood revealing the marginalizing limitations drawn in the hard lines of the American psyche and represented across a range of subordinating media archetypes and manifest throughout civic and educational policy that minimizes Black women and mothers by reinforcing deficit ideologies that are anchored in the troubled socio-historical context of the U.S. In addition, Collins framed and offered strength-based paradigms and pathways of Black mothering reflective of the creative, cultural and communal ethos of empowerment and love held among and enacted by Black women, as indicated in her epistemological construct of "standpoint theory" or in the Black feminist concept of "other-mothering" (Collins 172-180). These ideas are robustly discussed in Kalia Story's *Patricia Hill Collins: Reconceiving Motherhood*, amplifying the fundamental role of Collins in our understanding Black motherhood in a multifaceted way through interdisciplinary and intersectional vantage points that push scholarship and practice to engage race, gender and power in essential and innovative ways (2-9).

Building on Collins' central conceptualization of Black motherhood through a lens of Black feminism incorporating the power of self-definition, advocacy, resistance and resilience, we can further traverse the breadths and depths of Black motherhood through a womanist understanding specifically around the definition of womanism, according to Layli Maparyan, as "spiritualized politics that encompasses humans, the environment/nature and the spiritual realm" (xii). At the cornerstone of this definition is her vision for LUXOCRACY "rule by Light," referring to the Inner Light, Higher Self, or Soul that lies within, encompasses, and transcends all aspects of Creation (3-4). According to Maparyan, this emphasis on recognizing Inner Light and how it relates to broad spiritual realities is inherent to the womanist idea and how womanists recognize the Innate Divinity in all forms of life and uphold principles of non-violence, interdependence and interwoven connectedness (7).

Maparyan delves into and offers a profound and innovative reading and interpretation of womanism as a "thoughtform" in operation across multiple sites and with spirituality, not necessarily organized religion, as the foundation of a social change and activism. She suggests, "Such is the power of the womanist idea to gather us together and transform, even transport us beyond this curious historical moment in which we are living" (xii). Noting its roots in Black feminism predominant in the mid 1980s to early 1990s, Maparyan remarks that womanism was submerged in these earlier notions and reemerged in the mid-2000s with new momentum notably in *The Womanist Reader* covering the history and trajectory of womanism with womanist offerings across an array of disciplines and fields. Acknowledging the widely known understanding and definition of *womanist/womanish* by Alice Walker, she clarifies that the act and spirit of womanism even predates Walker and that the very nature of womanism "resists definition at the same time as it invites embodiment and engagement" (xiv). The thrust of this work then is to construct, articulate and offer an understanding of the womanist idea as a social and ecological change modality through the centrality of spirituality, thus providing a framework for understanding theory and activism from a womanist standpoint. This expansive framing opens the aperture for seeing and capturing Black motherhood in diverse ways.

Motherhood metaphors are used extensively in womanist works both descriptively and methodologically in reference to social change and transformation. Maparyan reminds us that the mother construct in the context of womanism is especially suitable in its facile ability to connect diverse attributes—such as in physical and emotional nurturance, conscious and moral leadership, creative and equitable approaches to conflict resolution and distribution of resources, or in the unique dynamic relationship between self-care and self-sacrifice (62). Reinforcing an understanding that the idea and ideal of *mother* then holds the ability to simultaneously supersede and unify varying ranges of differences, Maparyan underscores the power of *motherhood*:

Motherly power evinces from a combination of love, caretaking, and authority; perhaps most importantly, it is tethered to a sense of the unbreakable ties that bind a group of people, however different they each may seem or be. This is why motherhood serves as a trope of womanist social and ecological transformation methodology, and this is what distinguishes it from other forms of social change praxis that are willing to countenance various kinds of fissure in the social fabric. (Maparyan 62)

This lens at the intersection of motherhood and womanism is particularly palpable for reflecting on Black Motherhoods, which draws on African ethno-cultural tenets of interrelated communal sensibilities and inherent strength, which do not fall into predominant Western patriarchal ideas of frailty and subordination that are presented in association with mothers. At the same time, West African cosmologies are exemplar archetypes of motherhood as social transformation change agents through leadership that are transcendent and can be embodied by anyone regardless of gender, thereby reinforcing the model of motherhood as an activist role detached from biological confines (Maparyan 62). So the womanist idea at its core is applicable to people of all backgrounds, while also especially expressed and disseminated by and through Black women given a derivation from Black women's religious thought, histio-cultural traditions, social change leadership and spiritual practices grounded in African and African-American roots. The conflation of an African ethos of motherhood and newly emerging womanist ideologies proposes a way to explore Black Motherhoods along the lines of past and future trajectories for Black women, as well as through a paradigm for broader engagement with diverse communities toward ideals of overarching freedom, equality and unity.

As we move in and through this twenty-first century still challenging globally existing constructions that constrict us, such as those around race, gender, sexual orientation and class, an invitation is presented to broaden our discourse and actions at this nexus using Maparyan's womanist framework and guided by the manifesto "rule by Light." In this way, to explore Black motherhood as a reimagined idea, space and energy for transformative social change and liberation embraces the possibilities for a "luminous revolution" (14) that honors the historical struggles, vital contributions and significance of Black women and mothers while also elevating the visionary truths, ancestral traditions and universal spiritual insights that can boldly lead and tenderly nurture our collective wellbeing.

CONTOURS, CONTEXTS AND CONSIDERATIONS

While reading this volume, you are invited to reflect on the dynamics of Black motherhood, womanism, relationship and resistance through a three-point prism of inquiry to enlighten and enliven our discourse and understanding.

Contours

The *contours of Black mothers' hearts* represent the abundant *emotions and affective dimensions that overarch and undergird the experience of Black motherhood.* Whether the unimaginable pain of separation from your child during the insidious and perverse occurrences during the slave trade across Africa, the Americas, Europe and the Caribbean to the triumphant pride and joy in our youth as they continue to breakthrough and ascend externally placed barriers or uncover their internal gifts and abilities. The social-emotional and relational health for Black mothers is a critical component to understanding the Black mothering experience and it is fundamental to exploring intersectional platforms of race, class and gender across multiple fields.

Contexts

The *contexts that Black mothers embody and encounter* represent the *behaviors, actions and the body itself as locations of the Black motherhood experience.* From caretaking tasks that reflect traditions passed down across the African diaspora or parenting practices that are deliberately aimed to incorporate cultural pride and knowledge, as well as the necessary survival skills to counter and buffer against race-based biases and threats. It encompasses Black mothering "sites" and activity such as neighborhood mobilization, fight for education equality or battle for reproductive rights. The socio-political and medical advocacy, family engagement and community work of Black mothers has been and will continue to be bedrock of action for defining and shaping 'ourselves for ourselves' while resisting demeaning societal designations.

Considerations

The *considerations of Black mothers' minds* represent the *multifaceted thoughts, contemplations, intellectual, and expressive conflicts and contributions of the Black motherhood experience.* Inclusive of the range of strategic agendas and plans Black mothers have designed and employed over centuries as a matter of survival for themselves and their family, alongside the varying depths and diversity of resourcefulness and creative offerings that Black mothers manifest in celebration, protest, instruction or to counter narrow and monolithic interpretations of what it means to be a Black woman and mother. The socio-psychological expressions and inner work of Black mothers is vital to understand and uphold as it can convey the vast differences across while also outlining a more broadly defined unification among Black mothers.

CONTOURS, CONTEXTS AND CONSIDERATIONS
IN THE FRAME OF RESISTANCE

To openly excavate the ongoing contours, contexts and considerations of Black motherhoods is to move toward an exploration of "beingness," an ontological approach to understanding the experiences of Black women and mothers that defy the hegemony of race and gender, the limitations of scripted popular tropes and the harness of widely expected norms of Western academic thought. Case study research to explore how young Black mothers resist marginalization (Craddock *Mother to Mother*) used qualitative ethnographic methodologies to analyze and create a coding schemata from personal narrative data based upon the Affect, Behavior, Cognition Framework of Resistance (Robinson; Craddock "Paths"). My research revealed a co-existence of both optimal and suboptimal strategies of resistance integrating affective, behavioral and cognitive modalities used among the sample of Black mothers that resulted in distinct "Profiles of Resistance" reflecting specific pairings of optimal and suboptimal strategies used to push back against their marginalization (Craddock; Chapter 2 of this volume). The layered and interwoven realities of their motherhood experiences were captured in stories and accounts of both being a mother and being mothered. Across the affect, behavior and cognition (ABC) framework of resistance I find ripe comparisons within the contours, contexts and considerations (CCC) of Black motherhood. In the contours of their hearts (affect) expressions such as pride and pain were uncovered, in the context of their embodiment (behavior) activities including goal setting and isolation were observed, and in the considerations of their minds (cognition) thoughts of self-determination and self-negation among others also emerged. Ongoing analysis of the Profiles of Resistance reveal that the most adaptive profiles that aligned with better overall health and achievement outcomes for the mothers were those that incorporated aspects of healthy relationships and some form of spiritual beliefs or faith-based practices (Craddock *Mother to Mother*). This emphasis on relatedness, connection and transcendence comes forward within the dually existing optimal and suboptimal resistance strategies that Black mothers operationalize in the face of marginalization across varying modes. This extant and emergent research provides confirmation, rich fodder and a sturdy platform to further explore the dynamics of the Black mothering experience in more nuanced and illuminating ways that I am believe will offer transdisciplinary insight and action.

Ultimately by exploring and integrating constructs like the ABC of psychological resistance to marginalization with the CCC of Black motherhoods, I perceive a quilted scaffold of understanding that comes into view stitching together the fabrics of our individual and collective experiences and identities as Black women and mothers. We are able to counter false fragmentation by embracing authentic connectedness to self, to others, to Earth and to Spirit. And in so doing, we see resistance to marginalizing forces that occur across affective, behavioral and cognitive strategies shaping the contours of our hearts, the context of our actions and the considerations of our mind. Thus, a womanist ideal of mothering in all its forms and facets holds the power to radically emote, create and reimagine a world through a "luminous revolution" that can effect social change and have global impact for generations to come.

ESSAY OVERVIEWS AND ABSTRACTS

While this volume is not an exhaustive treatment or overview of the complex construct and realities of Black motherhood, nor could it ever be, it is a diverse offering of voices to add to an ongoing discourse with aims to potentially disrupt placid understandings of the Black maternal experience, as well as to reengage established theory and catalyze new ideas about the rooted yet ever evolving experience of Black motherhood from multiple viewpoints. The following essays provide provocative and rich material on varying contours, contexts and considerations of Black motherhood.

NARRATING BLACK MOTHERHOOD — TELLING BLACK MOTHERS' LIVES

In this section the power of storytelling is explored as a vehicle to understand identify and resistance in analyses of the Black maternal voice in literary fiction as well as personal narrative accounts.

In Helen Crump's essay, "'Mother's Voice' — Having Her Say: Storytelling in Articulating Black Women's Diaspora Identity" she explores the theoretical potential of examining diaspora identity through a Black feminist literary and diaspora analysis. Using a close reading of three examples of diaspora fiction—Sandra Jackson-Opoku's *The River Where Blood Is Born*, Dionne Brand's *At the Full and Change of the Moon*, and Maryse Condé's *Desirada*—she focuses on the maternal narrative of "mother's voice" (mothers' stories and storytelling) as a critical lens for examining the diversity of Black women's identity. Centering Black women's voices—both what they tell and how they tell it—suggests agency in articulating the self, particularly as it allows maternal figures to think through and/or create a sense of identity in relation to, outside of, and/or not only associated with motherhood. This examination of Black women's diaspora fiction then emphasizes reclamation of Black women's voices through the act of storytelling, becoming yet another means of telling the diversity of Black women's lives and experiences across the African Diaspora.

The premise of my essay, "Pushing Back with our Souls Intact: Young Black Mothers' Psychological Resistance to Marginalization" focuses on how Black mothers face marginalizing societal stressors deriving from oppressive discourse, actions and ideologies around race, gender, class and power, while navigating complexities associated with Black female identity, as well as practices and beliefs about motherhood. A theory of psychological resistance to marginalization addresses optimal (long term; liberation focus) and suboptimal (short term; survival focus) forms of resistance that Black women and mothers engage in to push back (Robinson & Ward, 1991). My ethnographic case research using personal narrative for data collection explored psychological resistance resulting in the *Profiles of Resistance* framework capturing specific patterns and combinations of optimal/suboptimal resistance reflected in affect, behavior and cognition. This essay discusses dynamics of more adaptive profiles that emerge, such as the "Purposeful Resister" profile anchored in cognitive awareness and determination, yet also reflecting social-emotional strain of the mother. Implications for maternal depression, social isolation, child impact and the relational-cultural context are discussed along with directions for potential support strategies, future research and assessment.

MOTHERLAND MOTHERS—EXPERIENCING AFRICAN MOTHERHOOD HOME AND ABROAD

Perspectives on the African mothering experience are provided in this section with essays that explore dynamics and complexities of African mothering from abroad as well as through a biographical lens amplifying African mother empowerment.

In Florence Kyomugihsa's "Transnational Mothering: The Meaning of African Immigrant Women's Lives" she notes that the rationale of choice is damaging when it obscures the needs of women who are essentially choice-less because they are situated outside of the mainstream. On a daily basis, African immigrant women in the United States who left their children in Africa negotiate their family life, their work life and their freedoms, which are all the choices that most people in Western society take for granted. The distances in space that separate these mothers from their children contrast sharply to ideal Western model of the exclusive bonded dyadic relationship of mother and child.

9

The caring and nurturing African immigrant mothers provide for their children is defined within the context of extended family and kinship networks that invoke the interdependence and collective responsibility of raising children. The study utilized interviews among twenty-one African immigrant mothers who lived on the West Coast of the United States. Mothers' narratives described: (1) their reasons for migrating to the United States; (2) alternative child rearing arrangements that the mothers negotiated; (3) how mothers define their mothering along African ideological norms of raising children; (4) the social and emotional challenges of being separated from young children and the strategies they employ to accommodate the spatial separation from their children; and (5) the meaning and value they attribute to their to their lives in the United States, that help them to deal with western societies' contradictions and expectations.

Delphine Fongang's article, "Motherhood and Empowerment in West Africa: The Case of Buchi Emecheta," focuses on West African women's empowerment, especially as it relates to their pro-natal ability and construction of subjectivity. African women define their subjectivities in relation to mothering, and West African women in particular, celebrate motherhood and mothering as a conceptual space in which they find solace and peace from stifling environments characterized by tradition and patriarchal culture. The preoccupation with motherhood is central in Buchi Emecheta's autobiographical account, *Head Above Water*. Emecheta's experience as a mother opens up possibilities for reinventing herself beyond the circumscribed gender roles. Her achievement of empowerment strategically progresses, moving from victimhood to subjecthood and power. Motherhood becomes a powerful source of strength and inspiration that drives Emecheta's desire for self-definition and agency. For Emecheta, becoming a mother is an achievement sine que non to attaining the full development of a complete person to which many African women aspire. Emecheta pushes that feat further by connecting motherhood to other aspects of her life such as gaining an education, and becoming a writer. Seeing motherhood beyond the boundaries of the private sphere is an important step towards African women's empowerment and agency.

MUSING BLACK MOTHERS—REFLECTING BLACK MOTHERS IN POETICS AND LITERATURE

The rich array of Black motherhoods has been displayed across a range of creative expressions and literary works. In this section, essays discuss Black mothering in novels, poetry and historical fiction. In "Everybody's Mama Now: Gloria Naylor's *Mama Day* as Discourse on the Black Mother's Identity," RaShell Smith Spears describes that Miranda Day, the title character of Gloria Naylor's *Mama Day*, illustrates the struggle that underlies the book as a whole and the struggle with identity of Black women, particularly mother-figures, in America: Miranda is given her identity both by the community and because of her relationship to the community. This connection to the community, serves as a boon to Miranda in that she becomes the matriarch that they need, ultimately functioning as a messiah figure for the community. On the other hand, this identity robs her of her own desires and individual opportunities as a woman. This article explores this "self" created by the community and the "self" manufactured by the individual, asking: What effect does this double consciousness have on Miranda, and what effect does it have in the actual world on Black women who are asked in their own small but myriad ways to be salvific figures in their communities?

Celeste Doaks' "Re-envisioning Black Motherhood: The Performance Poetics of Gwendolyn Brooks and Lucille Clifton" examines the poetic performances of Black Motherhood in the works of Lucille Clifton and Gwendolyn Brooks. Doaks notes that employing the ideology that all texts operate as a body, both Clifton's *Blessing of the Boats* and Brooks' *The Selected Poems of Gwendolyn Brooks* must also perform, as their poems defy conventional constructs of Black Motherhood. The essay shows their innovative redefinition in Brooks's and Clifton's work exploring rare aspects of Black Motherhood that are often overlooked by mainstream culture. Black Motherhood is inextricably tied to both gender and race, and this paper illustrates how both poets resist stereotypical notions of Black Motherhood.

In "Mothering, Mothers and the Historic Representations of Black Motherhood in Fiction: Barbara Chase-Riboud's *Sally*

Hemings," Lisa Elwood emphasizes the importance of examining American literature within the historical context pointing out that novelists seek to write in the histories that have been neglected so that we can acknowledge and celebrate previously devalued history. In revisiting many alternate forms of documenting history, many writers have used fiction-writing as a legitimate form of expressing and critiquing historical representations for women of color. Elwood remarks that in a close examination of the notion of motherhood in American history, one very important mother has become the newest sensation: Sally Hemings and the debate surrounding her relationship with Thomas Jefferson. Elwood's interest focuses on how the fictional form represents historical truth in Barbara Chase-Riboud's Sally Hemings. In this paper, she examines notions of fictional form to present what we know and understand about the historical treatment of Black motherhood in American history.

BODY AND SOUL—INTERPRETING BLACK MOTHERHOOD IN REPRODUCTION AND RELIGION

Black motherhood and the "black body" has been long intertwined in the psyche and experiences of Black mothering mingling with notions and constructs related to sexuality, reproductive policy and identity with major implications for Black women's health equity and wellness. Similarly, and often related, interpretations of motherhood within religious doctrine and tradition have held a prominent role in shaping societal views of and activity surrounding women in general. For Black motherhood, these ideologies are conflated with specific race-gender beliefs that have played out globally in religious practices.

Tyralynn Frazier's "Birthing Black Mothers: A Short History on How Race Shapes Childbirth as a Rite of Passage" seeks to examine how Black woman's relationship with technocratic rituals of birth are grounded in histories of social and political contexts that have limited the sphere of choices for many Black women. In her essay, she addresses the tensions between lay practitioners and medical professionals that reflect a broader problem framed by how birth attendance situates the birthing process. She posits that locating birth within a highly technocratic paradigm of care disconnects this transition into motherhood from the contextual factors that have substantive meaning within this process. In this chapter she examines how this disconnect has emerged and how this substantive orientation could help the obstetrics community better address racial inequities in birth outcomes.

Emilie Gangnat explores notions of Black mothering and missionary practice in Africa in "Black Motherhood as a Metaphor of Christianity in Missionary Photography." Gangnat comments that since the nineteenth century, African women have become major figures of missionary iconography. Appearing in different media, they mostly presented in housework and as mothers. This phenomenon could be explained by the purpose given to images: they must encourage donations in order to maintain missionary activities. Motherhood is then a major Christian iconographical theme because it permits missionary organizations to connect African women to Christian values. Motherhood is also used as a metaphor of the work made by missionary organizations among African people: in the same way than African women, the Christian missions are the mothers of new generations of African. African women and Black motherhoods are thus used as signs of Christianity in missionary images. From the analysis of some photographs produced in Gabon and Zambia by missionaries of the Société des missions évangéliques de Paris, this paper aims to present how Christian missionary organizations have used Black motherhood to present their activities and their proclaimed "success" among African people to Western audiences.

WHAT WE SAY, HOW WE DO—INTERACTIONS BETWEEN BLACK MOTHERS AND DAUGHTERS

Central to any discourse on Black motherhood is the core relationship between Black mothers and daughters, inclusive of generational mothering/daughtering connections and the host of othermothering relationships between and among Black women. In this section, dynamics between Black mothers and daughters are explored in the context of daily parenting practice and socialization messages elemental to shaping psycho-social and sexual identity.

In "Getting the Parts Straight: the Psychology of Hair Combing Interaction between African-American Mothers and Daughters," Marva Lewis notes that the daily task of combing hair offers multiple opportunities for African American mothers to interact with their daughters. From birth to middle child hood the texture of African American hair requires daily styling that has evolved into a routine and ritual for young girls rising to womanhood. Research on the task reveals that a series of relationship based activities occurs during this brief, daily ritual and routine between African American mothers and daughters. A brief summary is presented of research that determined four different perceptions of the task of combing hair in a study of African American moms. Finally, the stages of interaction that occur between a mother and daughter are described.

In Tracy Nichols and Regina McCoy's "Black Mothers' Messages of Independence, Pride, and Gendered Behaviors to their Adolescent Daughters," they discuss Black mothers' socialization of their daughters noting that it has been portrayed as focused on self-reliance and strength yet few studies exist on Black women's perceptions of mother-daughter relationships. It has also been suggested that Black mothers have a unique influence on their daughters' expectations of gender roles and sexuality. For this study, semi-structured interviews were conducted with ten Black mothers. Narrative profiles were constructed to identify participants' perceptions of their daughters, their relationships and their parenting strategies. Profiles were crystallized into poems and compared and contrasted across participants. Analyses reveal how mothers balanced contradictory messages of independence and self-sufficiency with "being a lady" and controlling sexuality. Mothers' personal experiences, as daughters and as partners within heterosexual relationships, shaped the messages they gave their daughters. Findings are discussed within the extended literature on Black motherhood and mother-daughter relations and current societal messages on Black girls' sexuality.

The contours, contexts and considerations of Black motherhoods are fluid in depth and breadth. In keeping with this evolving reality, the sections of this volume, and the essays therein, easily flow and overlap. Cross-sectional reading and discussion are highly encouraged to catalyze deeper feelings and innovative ideas that can be translated into meaningful action by and about Black motherhoods.

WORKS CITED

Craddock, Karen T. *Mother to Mother: Profiles of Psychological Resistance in Young Black Mothers and Models of Mother Involvement in the Relationship with Their Mothers.* Diss. Tufts University, Medford, 2007. Print.

Craddock, Karen T. "Paths of Resistance: Exploring Strategies of Psychological Resistance Among African-American Young Mothers." Unpublished Manuscript. Tufts University, Medford, 2005. Print.

Collins, Patricia Hill. *Black Feminist Thought: Knowledge, Consciousness, and the Politics of Empowerment.* 1990. New York: Routledge, 2002. Print.

Maparyan, Layli. *The Womanist Idea.* New York: Routledge, 2012.Print.

Robinson, Tracy L. "The Intersections of Dominant Discourses Across Race, Gender, and Other Identities." *Journal of Counseling and Development* 77.1 (1999): 73-79. Print.

Story, Kalia, ed. *Patricia Hill Collins: Reconceiving Motherhood.* Bradford, ON: Demeter Press, 2014. Print.

Walker, Alice. *In Search of Our Mothers' Gardens: Womanist Prose.* Boston: Houghton Mifflin Harcourt, 2004. Print.

Narrating Black Motherhoods:
Telling Black Mothers' Lives

1.

"Mother's Voice" – Having Her Say

Storytelling in Articulating
Black Women's Diaspora Identity

HELEN CRUMP

Yet so many of the stories that I write, that we will write, are my mother's stories. Only recently did I fully realize this: that through years of listening to my mother's stories of her life, I have absorbed not only the stories themselves, but something of the manner in which she spoke, something of the urgency that involves the knowledge that her stories—like her life—must be recorded.
—Alice Walker (*In Search of Our Mothers' Gardens* 240)

Remembrance, or historical memory, is a creative act of diasporic longing, if not the actual recovery of a lost ancestral African homeland, yet it remains a necessary creative act.
—Jana Evans Braziel (*Diaspora: An Introduction* 17)

IN THE FIRST EPIGRAPH, Alice Walker suggests the value and influence of the mother's voice, the mother's stories, and, to an extent, the function of those stories and their telling on the listener (or daughter) and her sense of self or identity. Additionally, Walker speaks to the need to document and take notice of the mother's stories—which include the mother's life experiences, thoughts, creativity, the wording and topics of her narratives, as well as the way she tells her stories and what she knows and relays in them. Thus, attending to the mother's voice and/or herstory (literally, her story about her life) is about fully acknowledging the person and the voice with which she speaks. In the second quotation, Jana Evans Braziel expresses the intertwining of memory and diaspora (defined here as the dispersal of a group of people from a central location to diverse parts of the world and the subsequent formation of related groups based on the integration into the new cultural and geographical spaces)—as in one being fundamentally linked to the other and the importance of both in forming diasporic identity. Both Walker and Braziel's statements speak to the need to seek out and recover voices and experiences, histories and creativity in the diaspora and to allow for the necessary act of expression.

For this essay, I draw on black feminist literary and diaspora literary critical analyses, and I center a discussion of identity across diasporic locations and within black women's diaspora fiction. Specifically, I explore the maternal narrative of "mother's voice" as one that articulates an intersection of gender, race, and diaspora as a means of exploring the concept of black womanhood and/ or black women's identity. In this examination of Sandra Jackson-Opoku's *The River Where Blood Is Born*, Dionne Brand's *At the Full and Change of the Moon*, and Maryse Condé's *Desirada*, each positioned specifically as diaspora fiction, I contend that, within each novel, the narratives and the use of storytelling as agency in crafting voice and articulating self ("mother's voice") allows the maternal figures to create a sense of identity. As such, black women's fiction demonstrates a reclamation of black women's stories (and the diversity of their lives and experiences) through women characters and their storytelling. Through their writing, novelists like Jackson-Opoku, Brand, and Condé emphasize the need to record black women's experiences, to write them as fuller stories than simple footnotes that do little to express black women's subjectivities.

In each of the primary works discussed in this essay, storytelling is important and is carried out in several ways. Angelita Reyes suggests, "Storytelling is one way of accessing the memory sites" (132), of recovering past events, histories, ancestry. Referring to "mother's talk," a passing on of stories (one's own and those of foremothers) to descendants, Trin T. Minh-ha states, "To (re) tell stories is 'to enter into the constant recreation of the world, of community, of mankind'" (28). This is important not only in the retrieval of black women's narratives, but also of their voices—not only their experiences, but also *their* expressions of those lives. Illustrated in women characters in *River Where Blood, At the Full,* and *Desirada,* numerous factors contribute to making identity. The various "textures of memory refer to the multiplicity of ways...the different layers of remembering the past [occur] in storytelling" (Reyes 132). In writing such layered cross-cultural, matrilineal stories, Jackson-Opoku, Condé, and Brand engage in recreating the varied ways of telling story and their effects on the generational relationships through which women characters establish and assert agency.

The acts of telling and listening to stories are integral means of sharing family histories. Recognizing that women are considered first teachers who initially share cultural and familial histories with subsequent generations (Collins 54), Karla Holloway notes that "African-American and African history document that the tellers were women and their stories and songs were the oral archives of their culture" (24). Similarly, the idea of women characters telling their stories represents a continuing of traditions and a reclaiming of voice. It is a regaining of their ability to speak *for* and *of* themselves and to reveal aspects of their lives that have otherwise been hidden, ignored, negated, or marginalized—as have many black women globally.

For the women characters in these novels and the Diaspora context in which their lives are situated, having voice is equivalent to making the "self" visible. It is also comparable to demonstrating agency in the construction of identity and the relating of lived experiences. Through the process of storytelling, identity formation is based on actual events and/or the author's adjustments during the telling. This does not mean that the narrative is necessarily inaccurate; however, it might include exaggerations, restructuring of memoried information, or reinterpretations based on hindsight or temporal distance that influences one's perception. Similarly Reyes comments, "Many women writers ... create new ways of *interpreting* history and culture" (6 *emphasis mine*). Storytelling, and the agency involved in it, is an example of this reinterpreting of black women's experiences across cultures within the Diaspora. "For many of us, memory through storytelling is what inscribes our history" (Reyes 129) whether that be personal history told

through stories between mothers and daughters or narratives
shared on a broader cultural, national, and/or racial history.

Drawing on Holloway's critical analysis of voice in black wom-
en's literature, I position the Diaspora novels of Condé, Brand,
and Jackson-Opoku as "works that claim the texts of spoken
memory as their source and whose narrative strategy honours
the cultural memories within the word" (25), as well as honours
the speakers of those memoried texts.[1] The speakers are multiple,
ranging from characters who speak to the authors who write out
of their own diasporic realities—their identities, experiences, and
cultural backgrounds and other diasporic influences, such as other
writers and scholars.

The sharing of personal life-stories emphasizes and is a part of
the process of forming subjectivities. The women characters in
each novel move throughout their matrilineal narratives, seeking
signs of their family histories and connecting (or not) with various
maternal figures. These multiple movements and interactions assist
the women in their journeys toward self and include "three essen-
tials: the decision to explore history, the absorption of heritage,
and [the] interpretation of the past's uses in the present. The her-
oines' historical exploration generally centers on female ancestors,
particularly mothers and grandmothers, with storytelling as the
primary means of discovery" (Kubitschek 22). This is demonstrated
in interactions between Jackson-Opoku's Big Momma and Alma
and Condé's Marie-Noëlle and Nina or Reynalda, yet it resonates
within other mother-daughter-like relationships throughout the
primary novels.

Speaking to articulations of black women's diasporic voices in
black women's fiction, Gay Wilentz echoes the idea of women as
first educators of cultural, social, and gendered behaviours. This
coincides with Patricia Hill Collins and Missy Dehn Kubitschek,
who perceive this matrilineal heritage as a key source of knowledge
and knowledge itself. Continuing, Wilentz points to the importance
of voice, of women's stories for black women and the African
Diaspora community in general, commenting,

> What we see from the voices of these Black women writers
> is that their concerns ... address the formerly unvoiced

members of the community—the wife, the barren woman, the young child, the mother, the grandmother. They look at their existence as a continuum, an invisible thread drawn through the women's stories to women readers and the men who will listen. Through their alternative, mothering practice, these writers (re)construct residual herstory as emergent culture. (xxxiii)

Significantly, Wilentz posits black women's voices in relation to the maternal, as does Kubitschek. And although it has the potential to appear as enforcing the intersection or, more problematically, the conflation of womanhood and motherhood, key here is the suggestion of "alternative mothering," which reflects the idea or potential of "mother's resistance" to normative ideas of woman-hood and motherhood.

While stories and storytelling are prevalent within the novels analyzed, I limit the ones centered in this work to those that either directly or indirectly indicate the woman-as-also-mother or mother-figure character speaking for herself. For instance, I analyze stories and storytelling moments where the maternal characters speak in a first-person perspective or where the narrator specifically indicates that the maternal figure speaks. This includes monologues, letters, and conversations or any combination of these. The "mother's voice" is one of the ways that women's resistance to certain or normative gender roles and expectations is revealed. In such narrative formats, black women gain the opportunity to speak for themselves, to tell their *own* stories of their experiences, and thus to claim them in a way that could be impossible (or limited) if revealed through a daughter's or someone else's perspective and re-telling.[2]

REMEMBERING IN *THE RIVER WHERE BLOOD IS BORN*

Among her characters, Sandra Jackson-Opoku stresses remembering the ancestral past as key to a more developed sense of self. In addition, the storytelling that takes place between characters, such as between mothers / mother figures and daughters, expresses the link between identity and memory. This is illustrated specifically in Callie Mae's letter to her daughter Alma, which I elaborate on below. Jackson-Opoku's highlighting of the mother's telling emphasizes the link between identity and voice. This storytelling takes place in several capacities. While several prominent characters provide examples of this "mother's storytelling," I focus on one that I perceive as representative of the significance of "mother's voice" in black women's fiction.

Callie Mae: Remembering / Telling Her Story

Callie Mae draws on memory in writing a letter about her life to her daughter Alma. In the letter, Callie Mae recalls her years as a young woman, meeting Benjamin Peeples (her first husband and Alma's father) and working as a nanny for a wealthy white family (Jackson-Opoku 206-13). The letter provides an opportunity for the mother to have and use her voice, to engage memories, and to share her life with her daughter in a way that hasn't been available to her throughout their mother-daughter relationship and in a way that seems limited to this particular opportunity for telling.

In telling her story, Callie Mae expresses the impact motherhood has had on her life, on the kind of person she has become. Specifically, she states, "Motherhood turned me into somebody I didn't like" (210), especially in terms of her relationship with her husband—it made her "[a] prying, jealous, hateful somebody" (210). In addition, Callie Mae acknowledges the complications that her life has created for Alma: working at least two jobs, she depended on Alma to help her around the house and with Alma's mentally challenged older brother; in marrying second husband Otis and having to deal with his overbearing behaviour, she further disrupted her already tenuous relationship with daughter Alma and had even less time mothering. Callie Mae notes too that, since her own dreams of travel and experiencing the world were deferred, she has wished that Alma would have opportunities to pursue her own dreams and to travel the world, consequently, allowing Callie Mae to live vicariously through her daughter's encounters.

Callie Mae continues speaking of motherhood as limiting and as stifling her identity: "But don't a day pass when I don't wonder what I would have done and where I would have gone if I'd lived my whole life as a free woman. With no babies to keep me home" (211). Thus, she contemplates how different her life would have been had she chosen to "live" her life for herself instead of becoming a mother and having others depend on her. Callie Mae's questioning her choice and her life demonstrate a resistance to the heteronormative gender expectation that all women are "made to mother," that it is a natural and desirous identity for all women. And even for women who appear to take on motherhood more readily—for example in regards to the difference between Callie Mae's approach to being a mother and that of her cousin Lola, who hands over the raising of her daughter to her husband Clyde—Jackson-Opoku's novel demonstrates that acceptance of the role is not without critique, concerns, or regrets.

Furthermore, the idea of the "mother's voice" as her own is emphasized in the example of Callie Mae's letter as well. In writing to Alma about a contest that asks contestants to write stories about "My Most Unforgettable Character," Callie Mae, admitting that she isn't the best writer, suggests to Alma, "Maybe you could write it up for me" (207); later, she writes, "So you take it and fix it up, make it so it reads right" (213). Retaining claim to her story, Callie Mae passes the narrative along to her daughter, implying a kind of "giving permission" for Alma to "speak for" her on this occasion. Additionally, it reflects the inter-generational story-sharing between mother and daughter that typically includes passing along advice about developing into womanhood or identity, which Callie Mae's narrative becomes when given over to daughter Alma.

Still, the understanding is that the mother's voice—her telling, her thoughts, and her experiences—are given rather than the daughter deciding what to share of the mother's narrative. Callie Mae's story is very specifically delineated in the novel (in a letter from mother to daughter), suggesting a link between Jackson-Opoku's work and Alice Walker's assertion that the mother's voice needs to be noted and recorded, heard for itself. Thus, Callie Mae's narrative allows the mother to be positioned as an active subject, and so, as an individual outside of other associated identities of mother, employee, or wife, despite those being the main roles mentioned in her letter.

VOICING SELF IN *AT THE FULL AND CHANGE OF THE MOON*

Like Jackson-Opoku, Brand employs story to reveal identity, and with certain maternal characters, she emphasizes the value of memory through storytelling in constructing identity. Briefly, Brand employs a number of examples of memory as functional to characters' development and individual narratives. Eula, a descendent of Marie Ursule, the matrilineal foremother who initiates the family line situated at the center of the novel, uses memory to reflect on her life experiences and to talk to her mother through a "blue airmail letter" addressed to Dear Mama. Then too, she uses storytelling in her letter to confront the traumatic moments of her life, such as the sexual abuses at the hands of her older brother Priest, experiences that leave an oppressive psychological mark on Eula. However, those recollections demonstrate a sense of self-empowerment also in that they allow Eula to confront and, consequently, to resist her past.

Brand uses multiple narratives—letter writing, character reminiscence, or character imagining—to express the significance of voice in constructing identity. While the first-person voice of mother figures "telling" their own stories isn't prominent in *At the Full*, Brand attends to the experiences of key maternal characters. Most relevant, she uses the narratives and the lives of maternal figures in relation to, outside of, or in opposition to motherhood to explore the linkages between voice and identity. However, in the context of maternal narratives and examinations of identity via black women's voices and stories *within* fiction, I elaborate on the example of "mother's voice" expressed through the character Eula.

Eula: Letter to Mama, Letter to Self

Although positioned more as a daughter than a mother, mainly because her story is written as a daughter speaking to her mother, Eula's reflections on motherhood and her choice not to mother her child allow her to be taken up simultaneously as an example of "mother's resistance" and "mother's voice," expressed via a letter she sends to her mother (Brand 227-58). She reveals, "I thought that I had come here [to Canada] to be independent" (232), to be separate from the life and problems of her family in poverty-driven

26

Terre Bouillante that previously limited her self-development. And in this act of recalling her experiences growing up, her relationships with her mother and other family members, and her experiences away from home, Eula gets to tell her story using a voice *not* silenced by familial, cultural, or societal gender expectations.

Then too, the letter—addressed to Dear Mama—is a reflection of Eula wanting to be important, to be missed and noticed by her mother. She writes, "I wanted to think of you quarrelling with some small child for misplacing my letter, as if it were so necessary for you to have it and to have some sign of me that was close" (229). In part, Eula constructs her identity in response to her relationship with her mother. Specifically, she determines her sense of self in resistance to what she witnesses as her mother's life in Terre Bouillante and in opposition to her own childhood experiences. She chooses to be independent and separate from her past to the point that she severs ties and communication with her family / her mother. That is, until she writes this letter, which minimally reconnects her to her mother. Yet even this brief attempt to reconnect seems impossible (futile) at this point since Dear Mama is deceased. Eula, then, can seek only a spiritual, memoried relationship created from memories of her mother, her mother's actions and reactions, smell, weight, body type, and movements. However, the significance here is the act of storytelling, of using one's own voice to reveal and reflect on one's sense of self, of development, of maternal thinking (resistance and/or acceptance).

Eula (as both daughter and mother) writes to explain certain choices and aspects of her life and her absence, things she might not have shared had Dear Mama been able to read her daughter's thoughts and experiences. But knowing that her mother is not present to read the letter, and possibly to chastise, question, or even be disappointed in her, allows Eula license to speak her mind.[3] Eula comments, "I would not tell you this if you were here or able to read this" (228). She reveals, "I am writing you this letter because I have no ordinary things to tell you. No things we share now and are used to. I am writing only to imagine you reading it with children around your bed. I recognize this fantasy because of course there are no children and no bed. I am writing to no one. You are dead" (236). Thus, Eula writes the letter with a certain uninhibited license in claiming her life and experiences, from the good to the bad. Consequently, the letter is more about Eula expressing herself, releasing the past and others' judgments, and saying goodbye to her mother.

Similar to Jackson-Opoku's Callie Mae, Eula acknowledges that motherhood / mothering would have changed her, would have limited her life. By sending her daughter Bola, named after Eula's grandmother, to Dear Mama, Eula "felt all new again.... I hated the child. She was an intrusion" (Brand 243), a hindrance to Eula's attempt at independence and self-discovery. And unlike Callie Mae who acquiesced to motherhood, Eula rejects it.

Here, as in Jackson-Opoku's novel, the letter is an interesting piece, an inspirational site of storytelling: it allows Eula to "talk" to her mother, to contemplate her past and her past actions and to express herself on several issues, including her response to maternity. Yet, it gives her the peace of mind of not worrying about whether she has offended or burdened her mother. This letter lets Eula work through and reconcile her choices and accept herself. Previously, she'd defined herself against her mother, stating, "I always waited for you to wake. So my life would continue" (258). This telling, then, provides a kind of catharsis that allows Eula to create her identity as separate from her mother. This "erasure of the mother—the attempt to position the mother as object and not subject...—serves as a means by which theorists both argue a discontinuity with past ideas of femaleness and hypothesize the burgeoning presence of an autonomous female persona" (McGill 34). In Brand's novel, it serves as Eula's opportunity to define herself away from the social and cultural expectations of womanhood and motherhood that had directed her mother's life.

STORYTELLING / TRUTH-TELLING, IDENTITY IN 'DESIRADA'

Nina: Same Circumstances, Different Stories

Maryse Condé uses a kind of "her story" in structuring *Desirada*, and voice and memory are prominent factors in both the telling and in the stories told. In search of the truth about her parentage, protagonist Marie-Noëlle gathers information from and engages numerous sources, including her mother and her grandmother.

She expects that knowing of her heritage will give her a better understanding of her past and allow her to move forward in constructing her own identity. Because Marie-Noëlle's relationship with her mother Reynalda has never been one of effective, or even prolonged, communication and active engagement, she seeks out her grandmother Nina, a woman whom she has never met yet whom she believes can fill in the details and provide insight regarding Reynalda.

As the grandmother attempts to assist Marie-Noëlle with her quest, she tells a story that sits in opposition to that of her daughter Reynalda. Discussing past events that impact current relationships, the stories and storytellers demonstrate an intersection between memory and storytelling (questions of truth and fiction) that Reyes mentions and storytelling as a way to recover the past that Kubitschek addresses. Yet, as Nayana Abeysinghe indicates, the narratives in *Desirada*, specifically those associated with Reynalda's experiences, "are rife with contradictions, ambiguities, and gaps.... The inaccessibility of the truth about the past, and the ensuing impossibility of reconciliation with the past and self, perpetuates the fracturing of the selves of the three women" (324)—grandmother, mother, and daughter. Furthermore, she contends, "Not possessing the knowledge of their experience, each generation of mothers recreates this lack [of resolution] and subjects its daughter to the same suffering that was inflicted on them" (Abeysinghe 324). Therefore, while Nina and her daughter Reynalda have the opportunity to use their voices and tell their stories, their understanding of those experiences is clouded by conflicting family histories; the women are unable to overcome their contradictions enough to assist Marie-Noëlle in forming her own story.

However, instead of viewing this as necessarily hindering the women, I suggest that understanding that their narratives will never sync allows them to move forward, not remain entangled by contradictions. For Nina and Reynalda, a collaborative resolution of the past is not necessary because both women claim to "know" the family history—at least the version that has affected their lives and which they choose to accept. Set on their versions of the past, the "truths" they know, they refuse to be swayed. Still, acknowledging the impossibility of gaining *one* truth from Nina or

Reynalda offers some resolution for the daughter who needs them more than the mother figures themselves. As such, Marie-Noëlle is the only person in this matrilineage who questions the past and seeks closure. Eventually, she acknowledges there can be no *real* "truth" beyond that which one is willing to believe. In creating identity, then, Nina's narrative isn't so much about reclaiming voice as demonstrating her ability to use her voice as she chooses.

In considering the benefits of black women's storytelling in the selected texts—such as an emphasis on voices that are often over-looked or silenced and a diversity of views on historical events from personal, social, and political perspectives—the characters demonstrate that not all herstory, or rather the ability to tell or recall, is available to the tellers. On one hand, this could be the result of re-writing the narrative and purposeful omission of certain details, or it could be the effect of traumatic events and temporal and/or spatial distances that make it difficult to recall past events. Often, the reality or "truth" of a situation is dependent upon the perspective and intent of the storyteller / witness.

Keeping this in mind, remembering can be disconcerting to the storyteller, especially if it requires the individual to recall tragic and/or oppressive situations, because it requires a re-living of those moments or because it might be viewed as a passing on or endorsing of negative histories and representations as exemplified, for instance, in Gayl Jones's *Corregidora*. Reyes notes that not everyone wants to remember or to pass along stories of an enslaved or oppressive past; therefore, people practice what she refers to as a "deliberate amnesia" (130), a purposeful forgetting. The same goes for experiences with any form of personal, familial, or communal trauma. Passing along the trauma passes along an unbearable weight that potentially presses upon future generations who haven't experienced the trauma directly but encounter it indirectly through the re-telling—possibly what Marie Ursule witnesses when she looks into the future and sees her descendants prospective lives (Brand 18, 49), or it might be compared, as Nayana Abeysinghe suggests, to Nina, Reynalda and Marie-Noëlle's experiences of abuse, betrayal, and loss that are integral to their family history.

In a comparison of Reynalda's story to "Nina's Tale" and supporting information from other characters, Reynalda integrates a combination of forgetting, re-writing, and suppressing of past, possibly traumatic, events in recalling her earlier years (generally those prior to Marie-Noëlle's birth). The multiple perspectives result in diverse ambiguous narratives, which make "truth" unachievable. Through her analysis of Condé's novel, Abeysinghe explains, "Aside from [a few] accounts, all other narratives in the story are rife with contradictions, ambiguities, and gaps.... The inaccessibility of the truth about the past, and the ensuing impossibility of reconciliation with the past and self, perpetuates the fracturing of the selves of the three women" (324). In addition to these multiple uses of storytelling, there are several other prominent issues. The question of "truth" versus fabrication is raised in the re-telling of events that have affected Reynalda, Nina, and Marie-Noëlle's lives; the concepts tend to be inextricably linked. These central matrilineal characters engage the past in an attempt to put it behind them and to move forward with their lives. Marie-Noëlle's grandmother Nina shares this advice with her, commenting, "I can only give you the *truth*. I can only tell you what happened.... If you want my advice, *forget all of this and go back where you came from*.... There's no place for you here.... You've got schooling.... education.... good health. *Live your life*. What more do you need?" (184, *emphasis mine*). Thus, truth becomes a relative term among this matrilineage.

Moreover, telling "truth" is associated with a kind of cathartic release for the maternal characters. For example, in observing Nina at the end of the telling of her narrative, Marie-Noëlle notes, "As if she were *draining herself of this past*, retched up from the very depth of her being *for her own sake*" (186, *emphasis mine*). The telling, which began in an attempt to provide her granddaughter with basic details about her origins and Reynalda's life, turns out to offer Nina a sense of release as well. As the entirety of "Nina's Tale" demonstrates, Nina suffered several traumatic events—from the loss, at an early age, of her grandmother and her parents to the loss of her home, the loss of her innocence through being raped by her cousin and rejected by her aunt, which precipitated her life in poverty, from being accused of abusing and mistreating her daughter to experiencing an unrequited love. Nina compares her childhood beginnings of working in cotton fields to slavery (Conde

166-67), and she describes the oppressive expectations put upon her because of her gender and race quite vividly, highlighting the lasting impressions of such experiences.

Overall, storytelling allows Nina to empty herself of the past and once again to be comfortable with herself and isolation, in her cabin on the island of Désirade. Analyzing "Nina's Tale," Abeysinghe comments, "The return to the land where her life began … enables Nina to come to terms with the traumatic events of her past …, all of which were played out on la Désirade. By giving voice to her experiences, including her lack of love for Reynalda, she confronts herself, performs the act of witnessing, albeit belatedly, and restores historical continuity to her life" (325). Emphasizing the importance of the mother's story and voice in *Desirada*, grandmother Nina's narrative provides background of the family heritage and, via the act of storytelling, gets passed along, transmitted from "mother" to "daughter." It provides a story of matrilineage previously un-available to Marie-Noëlle because Reynalda is limited her sharing. However, Nina's story, in addition to telling her *own* life, challenges Reynalda's accounts of her childhood, providing an alternative nar-rative. The contradictory narratives raise questions regarding the notion of "truth" and the knowability of "truth," especially when memory is required in determining and relating that truth. And in situations like those of Nina, Reynalda, and Marie-Noëlle where secrets are used to protect or forget or even to avenge a perceived wrong, memory in storytelling can be even more subjective.

MY VOICE, MY WORDS …

Voice and story give insight into a person's identity, which covers a range of thoughts, experiences, expectations, and more. When an individual's voice is eclipsed or a person is unable to share her/his story, is unable to access subjectivity in personal expression, the whole being is simultaneously unavailable. However, the invisibility of the individual is more oppressive and tragic when that voice is silenced, not by choice but by force. Such conditions speak to a greater need for society to respond, to make spaces and opportunities for those neglected, negated, and quieted voices to be heard, to be allowed to sound out. In doing so, we gain a greater chance to understand the world around us, especially because the un-silenced voices and the finally told stories tend to provide us with information, perspectives, and experiences of which we have been unaware. It gives us access to a broader view of our history. For this essay, that history involves black women's experiences in the Diaspora and across diverse times and cultures, demonstrated in *River Where Blood, At the Full*, and *Desirada*. It is "[t]he female character's ability to construct and tell her own story, in a version that she can bear to speak [or write] and to finish, [that] is frequently the measure of her wholeness" (Kubitschek 181). While Kubitschek's focus is in providing a critical analysis of African American women's novels and history particularly, her point is relevant to this discussion and to the intent of this analysis of diaspora and identity.

Several stories and storytelling in Jackson-Opoku, Brand, and Condé's diasporic novels relate to maternity. The maternal narrative of "mother's voice" offers a means of exploring black women's identity within a Diasporan context. Such narratives highlight black women who are (or are positioned as) mothers using their own voices and telling their own stories in regards to identity formation. These "voices" challenge, accept, reconstruct, and resist, thus expanding the idea of maternal narratives, black mothers' stories and storytelling and, consequently, black women's identity. Black women characters' telling their own stories reflects a self-awareness that includes an ability to remember and acknowledge a past that has kept them silent. In *At the Full and Change of the Moon, The River Where Blood Is Born*, and *Desirada*,[4] the women characters analyzed here, and therefore the authors, emphasize the value of the past, either to the character herself or her descendants. Thus, the women find agency in recalling their pasts and/or in telling their own stories, which provides a cathartic release for the storytellers and for the listeners, ultimately signaling a personal and communal empowerment.

[1]By "memoried text," I mean simply that the speakers' stories draw on their memories or that the memories inform the stories and their telling.

33

[2]The "mothers" still speak through their daughters in that the authors act as both/and literary and Diaspora daughters while also being positioned as mother figures telling stories of Diaspora. [3]Although Callie Mae's letter is from mother to daughter, the disclosure is similar to Eula's comments to her mother in that Callie Mae shares diverse aspects of her life with Alma that she might not have done otherwise. [4]While the first two novels demonstrate an intentional passing of information between generations, in Condé's text, sharing family history serves a different purpose than that associated with the mother-daughter dyad. Yes, Nina passes family history to Marie-Noëlle, one she would not have gotten from Reynalda—even if Reynalda knows it. However, Nina's intent in telling her story is directed toward contradicting Reynalda, providing an "accurate" account of Reynalda's early life, and so "clearing" her own name rather than sharing family history and contributing to Marie-Noëlle's self-development. Still, hearing "Nina's Tale" alongside Reynalda's allows Marie-Noëlle to realize that the "truth" about her parentage has become somewhat subjective, based on the point-of-view of the person telling the tale.

WORKS CITED

Abeysinghe, Nayana P. "Shattered Pasts, Fractured Selves: Trauma and Memory in *Desirada*." *The Romantic Review* 94.3,4 (2003): 319-27. Print.

Brand, Dionne. *At the Full and Change of the Moon*. New York: Grove Press, 1999. Print.

Braziel, Jana Evans. *Diaspora: An Introduction*. Massachusetts, Oxford, and Victoria, Australia: Blackwell Publishing, 2008. Print.

Collins, Patricia Hill. "The Meaning of Motherhood in Black Culture and Black Mother-Daughter Relationships." *Double Stitch: Black Women Write About Mothers and Daughters*. Eds. Patricia Bell-Scott, et al. New York: HarperPerennial, 1993. 42-60. Print.

Holloway, Karla. *Moorings and Metaphors: Figures of Culture and Gender in Black Women's Fiction*. New Jersey: Rutgers University Press, 1991. Print.

Jackson-Opoku, Sandra. *The River Where Blood Is Born*. New York: One World, 1997. Print.

Kubitschek, Missy Dehn. *Claiming the Heritage: African American Women Novelists and History*. Jackson and London: University Press of Mississippi, 1991. Print.

McGill, Lisa D. "Thinking Back Through the Mother: The Poetics of Place and the Mother / Daughter Dyad in *Brown Girl, Brownstones*." *The Black Scholar* 30.2 (2000): 34-40. Web. 17 Sept. 2004.

Minh-ha, Trin T. "Mother's Talk." *The Politics of (M)Othering: Womanhood, Identity, and Resistance in African Literature*. Ed. Obioma, Nnaemeka. London: Routledge, 1997. 26-32. Print.

Reyes, Angelita. *Mothering Across Cultures: Postcolonial Representations*. Minneapolis: University of Minneapolis Press, 2002. Print.

Walker, Alice. "In Search of Our Mother's Gardens." *In Search of Our Mother's Gardens*. San Diego, New York and London: Harvest/HBJ Book, 1983. 231-43. Print.

Wilentz, Gay. *Binding Cultures: Black Women Writers in Africa and the Diaspora*. Bloomington and Indianapolis: Indiana University Press, 1992. Print.

2.
Pushing Back with Our Souls Intact

Young Black Mothers' Psychological Resistance to Marginalization

KAREN T. CRADDOCK

At the core of life is a hard purposefulness, a determination to live.

—Howard Thurman

THE EXPERIENCES OF YOUNG African-American mothers in North America, specifically in the United States, are influenced by socially constructed discourses about race, gender, class and power (Cole; Collins, "Sexual Politics," "Shifting Center," "Fighting Words," "Meaning of Motherhood," "Intersections," "Black Feminist Thought"; Lawson). As a group, Black[1] women have higher rates of poverty, are occupationally segregated, and have poorer access to healthcare, as well as unhealthy outcomes, compared to other race and gender groups (Harris; Gee and Sturges; Lipscomb, Gotay and Snyder). The marginalization of Black women within society reflects their membership in groups that are perceived as having less worth and are construed as being lower in status. As with all social groups, social views and discourse have an impact on Black women, and how she derives meaning about herself has implications for overall health. Black women contend with this ongoing tension and related issues of psycho-emotional health in a society that has harshly denigrated their immutable characteristics, constructing them as inferior. Therefore finding ways to push back against the societal stressors occur at an elemental level as identities are being formed (Craddock, "Paths of Resistance," "Mother to Mother"; Moradi; Robinson; Robinson and Kennington; Robinson and Howard-Hamilton; Shorter

Gooden; Robinson and Ward "African American Adolescent," "A Belief in Self").

A theory of psychological resistance suggests that in the presence of an oppressive context or circumstance, a person may resist in ways that defend against the oppression in both optimal and suboptimal forms (Myers and Speight; Robinson and Ward "A Belief in Self"). These forms of resistance can manifest in behaviors and attitudes used as life management strategies that push against marginalization. Optimal resistance (long term, liberation oriented) and Suboptimal (short term, survival oriented) are not bifurcated; they can and often do co-exist within the array of a person's response (Robinson and Kennington), although one form may tend to dominate over the other. Suboptimal forms of resistance can also serve as an immediate coping mechanism and an eventual bridge to the healthier optimal form of resistance. The complex way that resistance emerges is heavily influenced by the social context in which the individual is living. One population for whom resistance is particularly central is Black adolescent or young mothers.

Teenage motherhood among Black youth continues to be an area of focus and concern in the fields of public health and social services, and while researchers address the educational, physical, health and socio-economic implications of young parenthood still more attention must be paid to the psychological dynamics of young motherhood among African-American females. Specifically, how do issues of race, gender and class affect the young Black mother's understanding of herself and her ability to negotiate such aspects of her identity in a society that relegates them to lower status? Moreover, how do young Black mothers confront and cope with the marginalized status associated with these issues of race, class and gender? This question is even more compelling and less understood.

WHY RESISTANCE AND BLACK MOTHERHOOD?

An exploration of psychological resistance to a marginalized status in the context of Black mothering reveals some central tenets that anchor the discussion, and provides a basis for its essentiality in the consideration of race, gender and class. The three domains of significance are history, validation and voice.

History

Historically, the concept of mothering in African communities and throughout the Black Diaspora has had a broad impact, described by some as "the entire way a community organizes to nurture itself and future generations" (Reagon 80). Mothering, as a key tenet of the African worldview, comes to the fore in discussions of resistance to oppression in the Black community and is often the forum through which collective responsibility and accountability is enacted. This concept of collective responsibility within the community is most notably documented by the way unrelated children in the community have often been mothered by other women in response to circumstances that would have otherwise left them alone or neglected (James). The term *othermothering* encompasses this concept and has been used to describe the mothering that grandmothers and other women in the community do to assist or replace blood mothers in the responsibilities of childcare, nurturance and more. Thus, they serve not only as help to mothers, but also as additional role models for children and in the community at large (Collins, "The Meaning of Motherhood in Black Culture"; "The Social Construction of Black Feminist Thought").

This concept and practice of *othermothering* with roots firmly planted in the traditional African worldview can be traced prior to and throughout the institution of slavery and well beyond. Well documented, this act of mothering is a pivotal Black feminist link to the development of new models for social transformation in the twenty-first century and a central construct to newly emergent womanist theory and practice (Maparyan).

Within Black communities, the act of mothering incorporates an undercurrent that suggests both survival and liberation. Providing care for the next generation of African-Americans reaffirms the need to secure the existence of a people who were subject to the oppressive institution of slavery and subsequent marginalization that threatens survival. Nurturing and socializing the future generations establishes possibilities not only to survive, but also to resist marginalization through increased growth, and through the self- awareness that leads to liberation. This *motherwork* (Collins "Black Feminist Thought") is at the base of many sociological studies examining social movements and community activism in Black communities (Collins " Fighting Words"; Gilkes; Lawson; McDonald; Naples).

The practice of community mothering is noted as a central experience in the lives of many Black women, and mothering has been characterized as a key form of emotional and spiritual expression in societies in which Black women are marginalized (Lawson). Thus, mothering in the Black community is a site for women-centered bonds that build upon emotional and spiritual connections, as well as a site for "community economic survival and political expression among Black women" (Lawson 27). Historically, it is in these forums that Black women are able to exercise influence and power in their lives whereas they often face inaccessibility to mainstream institutions of power. Critically illustrated in this research is the historical power of mothering as a form of resistance among Black women as well as a forum for connectedness and support within extended family and kin networks, blood related or not. These two points are central and serve as the basis for the rationale to examine resistance in the context of Black mothering.

Validation

The experience of mothering has also served as a validation of womanhood for Black women in their identity development (Jenkins; PerrymanMark). Scholars have addressed the links between Black motherhood and validation within the larger theme of resistance in a societal context that marginalizes Black women on the basis of race, gender and class (PerrymanMark). Specifically, she discovered as a young Black single woman that the prevalent perspective was that motherhood became a significant vehicle of resistance and self-validation:

> My motherhood, then, has come not only as a vocation, as in raising my child as I do with my partner but also a lifeline, a resistance, an activist work that may not be recognized on a large scale, but one that I do with all my heart, ensuring (in my own small way) that Black mothers

are out putting an end to the 'assumption of deviance' that, unfortunately is often internalized by young, Black and pregnant (single) women. (PerrymanMark 132)

These assertions of self that go beyond the individual reflect the power of motherhood among young Black women who have found themselves cast as deviant members of society when racist, sexist and classist ideology may deem them "not good enough" because they are Black, poor and a "teenage mother." Motherhood in this context has been for some a "triumph of self-discovery and a chance to challenge people and systems in their beliefs" (PerrymanMark 132). Research with young mothers has established the centrality of mothering as resistance and validation; they view mothering, not teen pregnancy, as an honor and a passage into womanhood. PerrymanMark aptly suggests that mothering built a bridge from Black woman as "Other to Mother" (132). The role of motherhood among Black women has two contrasting qualities: a resistance to oppressive ideologies about what it means to be Black, a woman and a mother, and an essentialism that views motherhood as a definition of what it means to be a woman (PerrymanMark). The strong link between motherhood and affirmation that is contextualized in resistance makes the construct of *validation* a critical component in the rationale for exploring resistance within the Black motherhood.

Voice

Closely aligned with validation is the notion of *voice* that is giving empowered expression to one's experience. Motherhood may often become the vehicle through which Black women find a voice. Upon becoming mothers, Black women often feel an increased or new sense of empowerment to express resistance to their marginalization. This voice is not only due to a new-found and validating identity, but most often reflects a purpose: to protect and advocate for their children in a society that relegates them to inferior status. The metaphor of becoming a "lioness," noted in the literature describes this powerful sense of protection and purpose (Thomas). In research with young Black mothers, Thomas found specific themes that showcased their voice via mothering. These included an expression of the complexity of mothering that encompasses both joy and struggle, the determination to set a good example for their children, the way motherhood expanded their sense of self and spirituality, and the specific needs of Black mothers that range from the practical to the spiritual. The power of voicing experience intertwined with motherhood and marginalization is essential in the discussion of and rationale for exploring psychological resistance among Black mothers. This is especially true in examining the lives of young or adolescent Black mothers who are often further stifled in voicing their experience because their age and social stereotypes constrain their identity (Stevens). Black adolescent girls develop skills that often manifest in an expressive and assertive style to guard themselves and negotiate with this perceived hostile environment (Stevens). Stevens posits that hegemonic effects from the stereotypes and social stigmas that impact their social identities help determine to how Black adolescent girls evolve "smart and sassy identities to resist controlling racist definitions of them" (Stevens 61). A form of "voicing" their discontent, these smart and sassy identities are derived and linked to a form of psychological resistance. For Black adolescent mothers, the importance of voice becomes further heightened because of the protective quality mentioned earlier and the intensity of the stigmatized social identity placed upon her as the "Black teen mother." Black mothering, particularly for the population of new mothers under the age of twenty, is a pivotal moment in personal identity development and for understanding and using one's voice to resist the imposed definitions of their lives.

All three areas—history, validation and voice—are grounded in an exploration and often an experience of resistance. Examining young Black mothers' resistance activity as it manifest in the domains of affect, behavior and cognition towards an overall "profile" help to convey how she has understood and experienced marginalized status and how she responds to it.

PSYCHOLOGICAL RESISTANCE TO MARGINALIZATION THEORY

At the core of this theory is the premise of resistance theory. The theory developed out of a consciousness of the socio-political context in the United States, where those who are marginalized resist their circumstances in both optimal and suboptimal ways. As noted before, we all have multiple identities and the confluence of socially constructed identities (race, gender, class) become the arenas where oppression occurs and resistance happens. These interlocking identities and the resulting "isms" are upheld by the overlapping discourses about such identities in the dominant culture. Robinson describes this process, "Those who deviate from an established and preferred standard are often devalued, and discourses help to maintain the allegiances of those who allegedly are valued by maintaining the status quo with punitive gaze" ("Intersections" 75). African-American women find themselves under this "punitive gaze" within the dominant culture. In turn, they incorporate strategies to resist its impact in their lives, both functionally and psychologically. How African-American women navigate and manage this state of marginalization has been well researched.[2]

Some researchers have examined this marginalization through a resistance framework. Robinson and Ward ("'A Belief'") developed the Resistance Modality Model based on optimal psychological theory. Their model addresses the oppressive assaults by society that African-American women contend with using strategies of resistance. They state that for African-American women the key to healthy identity development is in employing resistance strategies. They distinguish between optimal resistance and suboptimal resistance. The literature notes that historically, African-American females have been seen as resilient and strong in spite of oppressive circumstance, implying that they have been survivors. Yet, as Robinson and Ward ("A Belief") reveal, survival-oriented resistance is not enough for complete and whole identity development and health (Watt). In line with Optimal Conceptual systems theory, the optimal way to resist is to employ strategies that transcend survival and incorporate empowerment and liberation at their core.

Based on research and analysis with African-American teenage girls, Robinson and Ward ("A Belief") examined the impact of the negative images and messages that bombard these young women. More recent studies of Black women, culture and the media continue to show how Black women have been represented over the years (Emerson). They may be active participants in popular culture in ways that impact their sense of self-esteem and self-image if they let the media construct meaning in their lives. As they participate in pop culture either they connect with and identify with, or else reject and disregard the representations of Black femaleness, especially of sexuality, that they consume (Emerson).

Moreover, the socio-political context in which young Black women develop influences the multiple aspects of their identities. Research addressing the community/family context and the role of the media in this developmental trajectory considers how specific elements of each context shape African-American female identity and outcomes.[3] As noted in the psychosocial development literature, the social environment is critical to psychological growth and development. In adolescence, the primary task is to achieve "ego identity" (Erikson) and while primarily internal, it requires the collaborative processes that occur in the family system. The family system has been considered an important predictor of psychological adjustment (Minuchin and Fishman).

The conceptualization and frame of "Black feminist thought" (Collins "Black Feminist Thought") and other scholarly considerations of Womanist identity (Maparyan; Moradi; Walker) amplify the construction of Black female identity at its core. Indeed, Collins' ("Intersections," "Black Feminist Thought") seminal works centrally informed the development of the Resistance Model in which the reconceptualization of race, class and gender helps Black women to resist the "matrix of domination" and become empowered as "agents of knowledge" (Collins "Black Feminist Thought").

For African-American adolescent mothers, stress related to the stereotypical societal image of their group ("the Black teen mother") may elicit resistance responses that are both, optimal and suboptimal. Within this nexus of race, gender and class, they must also navigate multiples notions of motherhood that compound the stress. Indeed, early parenthood can be a response to societal stress; some teens have children to provide purpose in their life in a society that has deemed them valueless. Then early parenthood can bring about even more stress in a society that already expects early parenting of them, and has low expectations for their ability to parent well. Thus, being a young or adolescent African-American mother can co-align with many hardships. Previously noted, perspectives on Black motherhood have been largely shaped by socially-constructed ideas of race and gender perpetuated by the media. Given the socio-historical ideologies of Black female identity, the Black mother has had to address many negative assumptions about her ability and efficacy as woman and mother, in society as a whole and sometimes even within her own community. Understanding and coping with external definitions of self as parent and individual have become a central part of resistance for the Black mothers.

In these circumstances, the way they choose to resist has significant implications for the young women. The surrounding context of social support could affect the strategies they employ; which strategies they employ can affect the child's development. To examine resistance strategies, it is helpful to identifying significant stressors and embedded social network dynamics. The resistance model addresses the multiple identities of race, gender, class and even age. It contrasts the resistance strategies of Suboptimal (survival) with Optimal (liberation). Distinct attributes of each strategy mark their definitions and offer a frame for analyzing the experiences and coping mechanisms of African-American women dealing with their life stressors within the layers of identity. Suboptimal Resistance is characterized as: isolated, individualistic, and externally defined, seeking immediate gratification, and placing an emphasis on the present. In contrast, Optimal Resistance is captured as: unified, self-determining, collective, purposeful/future oriented, and faith-based (Robinson and Ward "A Belief"). A central tenet of resistance theory posits that Optimal resistance implies a cognitive awareness of the socio-political context of the oppression. Thus, the cognitive domain is critical. Theoretically, how a woman thinks about her circumstances and the challenges of marginalization reflects her belief system. Her belief system in turn affects her emotions and behaviors. Therefore, the resistance model is useful as it maintains that Optimal and Suboptimal resistance modalities, or strategies, can be observed and are behaviorally, affectively and cognitively different from one another.

Subsequent research of resistance theory and development of resistance paradigms reinforced the non-bifurcated nature of Optimal and Suboptimal resistance modalities and thus emphasized the dialectical nature of resistance (Robinson and Kennigton). This literature specifically addressed how a resistance model has implications for counseling applications and applicability to a wide array of people.

PROFILES OF RESISTANCE: CASE STUDY REVIEW

Building on the extant research emerging from original resistance theory and subsequent resistance paradigms, an expanded construct of resistance emerged.

A qualitative case study using a small sample of Black young mothers, explored their psychological resistance to marginalization and factors contributing to their resistance strategies in a relational context. Data was collected from in-depth ethnographic participant interviews, reflective notes and observations that were analyzed using key emerging constructs as conceptual frames including the *Profiles of Resistance* (Craddock *Mother to Mother*)—specific patterns and combinations of optimal/suboptimal resistance reflected in *affect, behavior* and *cognition*. Review and analysis of the data led to increased understanding of how these resistance forms co-exist and emerge into profiles.[4]

Five specific profiles emerged each profile with a distinct manifestation of both Optimal and Suboptimal forms (Craddock, *Mother to Mother*):

The *Purposeful Resister* exhibited specific awareness of her marginalization and was very determined in Optimal Cognition to push back against them. This acute awareness also appeared to manifest in some form of Suboptimal Affect, as noted in depression among some.

The *Quick-Fix Resister* showed Optimal Behavior in goal setting activity but also Suboptimal Behavior in her a lack of follow-through on these identified goals and plans often linked to needs for immediate gratification.

The *Up-Hill Resister* exhibited Optimal Affect through a positive emotional outlook despite unsupportive home or social environs that present personal barriers that also made her susceptible to Suboptimal Behaviors used to the dull the harshness such as overeating.

The *Tacit Resister* used understated yet concrete Optimal Behavior strategies to steadily pursue goals, but also engaged in Suboptimal Behaviors that externalized her power to others.

And lastly, the *Individually-Driven Resister* showed a lack of awareness of or denied her marginalization altogether, so she did not represent the classic Optimal Cognitive category; still, she exhibited individually driven "optimal- like" strategies to improve her life. However, what did emerge and coincide with this thinking were Suboptimal Cognitive patterns that reveal a subconscious internalization of negative messages about her personal identity, specifically attached to negative socially constructed definitions around race and gender.

The development of these Profiles has contributed to the model of resistance theory and provides a robust framework for further inquiry into these patterns. Of the profile patterns that were revealed in the analysis, the Purposeful Resister emerged as one of the most adaptive strategy patterns albeit complex, and particularly ripe for further interrogation of how external stressors related to race, class, gender intersect with a psycho-social response to marginalization.

PURPOSEFUL RESISTANCE

Resisters in this profile have an overt consciousness of their marginalized status and use many of the strategies in *optimal cognition,* but they often find themselves struggling with *suboptimal affect* as they try managing their lives (see Figures 1 and 2).

Optimal Resistance—Cognition

As noted in the literature, a cognitive orientation to marginalization is a cornerstone to optimal resistance; overall these young mothers captured more cognitive optimal resistance strategies than affective and behavioral strategies in their narratives. The most prevalent cognitive strategy was in the instances of *Parenting Awareness,* noted in all but one of the young mothers. This high representation confirms the connection between psychological resistance and mothering among Black mothers. Nearly as prominent across the sample are strategies that focus on future outlooks; most mothers made comments coded as *Belief in One's Dreams and Goals.* A self-reflective type of resistance was captured in the

Table 1 – *Profiles of Psychological Resistance Overview* (Craddock, *Mother to Mother*)

Purposeful Resister	Resisters in this profile have an *overt consciousness of their marginalized status* and use many of the strategies in *optimal cognition,* but they often find themselves struggling with *suboptimal affect* as they try managing their lives.
Quick-Fix Resister	People who fit this profile use significant numbers of *optimal behaviors around goal-setting.* Thus they are aware of strategies to counter their marginalization, but they often fail to follow through, because *immediate gratification is another mark of suboptimal behaviors.*
Up Hill Resister	In this profile, *contextual challenges such as prevailing socio-economic stress and unsupportive environments create a climate of overt personal barriers* that these resisters must manage while resisting the broader array of marginalization using *optimal affect.* Still, they are susceptible to using **suboptimal behaviors** *to dull the harshness* of their situation.
Tacit Resister	People in this profile use *understated yet concrete optimal behavior* strategies that allow them to steadily pursue their goals that resist the marginalized circumstance, but they also engage in *suboptimal behaviors that can externalize the resisters power* and allow others to direct or dictate their choices.
Individually Driven Resister	In this resister model, people may *deny their marginalization* while engaging in strategies for personal advancement. *Suboptimal cognitive behaviors take the form of self-negating thinking patterns* that may compromise whole identity development.

categories of *Constructive Self-Critical Thinking*, *Confront Oppressive Circumstances through Constructive Self Definition* and *Maintaining Life-Affirming Thinking Patterns*; more than half of the sample of young mothers made relevant comments in these categories. Half of them were using cognitive strategies anchored in a positivist perspective with *Belief in Self Agency*, *Belief in the Goodness of Others* and *Conviction* as ways to push against the marginalization they face.

Suboptimal Resistance—Affect

Among the suboptimal forms of affective resistance that emerged, three stood out: *Hopelessness*, *Cynicism*, and *Insecurity* each appeared in the narratives of a little less than half of the young mothers. These affective responses were largely fueled by their overwhelmingly stressful context and a mounting frustration with trying to push against it. Fewer noted *Chronic Pain* in their narrative text and only one case captured *Inferiority*. These more internally located affective elements presenting in the face of marginalization were less widely represented across the sample, yet when noted they described very profoundly impacting emotions and incidents. Closely related to elements of the suboptimal resistance affect were suboptimal resistance behavior aspects most apparent in *Isolating Self from Others*, which has particular significance for examining resistance strategies in the context of the social network.

TINA'S STORY

Tina's narrative provides an example of the Purposeful Resister who exhibits the seemingly dialectical pattern of optimal cognition and suboptimal affect.

Tina's Background

Tina was a deeply reflective and focused young woman who had become a mother at 18. At the start of the study she was living at home and then in a shelter program for teen mothers. Tina was very determined to be a good provider and mother to her son; she was constantly working to manage his health challenges and secure resources and support. She had a somewhat strained but close relationship with her parents who were active in her life and provided support when asked or needed. Tina was very independent and was finishing high school while in the shelter. She had deep admiration for her mother who worked hard and sacrificed a lot for her and her sister while they were growing up to ensure that they had what they needed or desired. Battling a race discrimination suit as well as a severe illness that left her depressed for a period of time during Tina's early adolescence, Tina's mother was a source of great pride, but also pain for Tina who felt somewhat guilty and frustrated with the effects the illness had on their lives.

The father of her son was a much older man who did not live in the region and was not very active in their lives. Tina had entertained the idea of dating someone she had met later, not only to provide her companionship but also to be a role model for her son. Tina eventually graduated from high school and obtained an apartment through a subsidy program while looking for work. The isolation and challenges of managing her life circumstances created intense stress for Tina who sought out some professional counseling. At the close of the study, Tina was enrolled in classes at a community college while working part time.

Tina, the Purposeful Resister

Tina's narratives reveal both breadth and depth in her resistance strategies. Grounded in her beliefs and thoughts, Tina exhibited both self and communal awareness that informed her actions and emotions. Across her narratives, each of the indices for optimal thinking was noted, including some transcendent qualities of resistance coded in the *Goodness of Others,* as well as some level of *Conviction* (Optimal Cognition). Also noted was a type of transcendent quality to her resistance approach as she discussed her son's future and potential partners; she said that while some will judge him on his race, their love and respect for him were far more important than the race of the other person. She revealed her sense of conviction when she said that motivation to improve oneself and one's situation must come from within or spiritual sense. She referred to something larger than simply a practical outside source offering instructions.

Another Optimal Cognitive strategy used was *Confronting Disempowering Messages with Self-Constructed Knowledge*, which appeared in more than half of the documents in her case. She also revealed her understanding of race marginalization in her parental awareness. This understanding in her discussion of godparents for her son: she was looking for someone who would love and support him as their own, and who was aware of the challenges he faced as a Black male. She wanted someone who would encourage him to strive despite the reality that the "majority of Black men are behind bars, and that's not where you belong. You belong out there in the world, proving to all those people who said that you couldn't make it, proving them wrong." Elaborating on this sentiment, Tina describes her desires for her son to have pride in his ethnic and racial identity through role models,

> Yeah. I need positive people. I need people who he's going to look at and be like, "Wow, you know, these people are really trying to get somewhere," or "Wow, these people as African-Americans have really struggled to get what they have, and they did a dag-gone good job at it." I want him to look at his people, also to be for friends, whoever you want to be friends with, but to look at your race and just be like, "Wow, we've come a long way," or "These African-Americans that I'm around have really struggled so I choose to follow behind them," or "I choose to follow behind my mother...."

This keen determination, which showed in her *Strength* and *Confidence*, was also obvious in her emotional expression, which involved both *Anger* and *Sadness* as optimal means of release that propelled her forward (Optimal Affect). One of the few young mothers in this sample who exhibited an *Entitled* disposition and gave *Hopeful* comments throughout our time together, Tina's actions mirrored her consciousness as she revealed every attribute of optimal activity (Optimal Behavior). Tina mentioned *Asking for and Giving help*, which also underscores her communal orientation. Her self-awareness shows in her ability to *Delay Gratification*, and her *Spiritual Development* was central for her. Her goal activity was closely linked to her parenting resistant activity; she was one of half the mothers in the sample to *Accomplish a Goal* she had set, despite the challenges.

Alongside these attributes, subtle expressions of *Unworthiness* and *Subconscious Demeaning Self-Images* (Suboptimal Cognition) were noticed, as she discussed how she might have been viewed. In one instance, she reported feeling she behaved "too Black," to the disapproval of some extended family members. *Isolation*, due somewhat to circumstances and at times to choice, often amplified these thoughts (Suboptimal Behavior), but she desired community and was aware that she needed to be connected. She struggled with some of the suboptimal resistance strategies, most often in the area of emotional management where *Hopelessness, Depression* and *Insecurity* were especially noteworthy (Suboptimal Affect). With a well-developed socio-political awareness and the determination to resist hegemonic stressors, Tina modeled the range of resistance in her efforts to cope. Given the intensity of her societal awareness, her desire to achieve her goals as woman/mother and to be connected to others--as well as her dip into loneliness, self-doubt and isolation--appear consequential. Tina clearly reflects the tension and emotional consequences of coexisting in the broad optimal and suboptimal range.

Because Tina combines these patterns of resistance she best exemplifies being aware of issues of oppression and determined to make choices to resist it. She showed her awareness when she was asked what it meant to her to be a 19-year-old Black woman in American right now. She responded:

A statistic ... because its just like, "Here they go again! Reproducing like cats!" But, I think that me being a "statistic" is good for me because it gives me even more reason to prove to you that I am not a statistic and that I'm more than that, I am a 19-year-old Black woman that is trying and will make it to where I want to be and to let people know that I did work. I worked very hard to get where I am right now and it's just like, call it what you want, but I am not gonna live in this for the rest of my life, I'm gonna have something, I will have a college degree and I will be somebody.

The quote encapsulates both Tina's awareness of how the world has relegated her to an inferior status, and her passion and persistence to define herself for herself and prove them wrong. The orientation of the purposeful resister incorporates elements of self-reliance and connection with others. This is a central tenet of optimal psychology and resistance. The profile also reflects the particular tension that arises between optimal and suboptimal resistance. As noted earlier, an individual is not entirely optimal or suboptimal in her overall resistance; often people use both strategies, with one dimension dominating. For the purposeful resister, the strong base of hegemonic awareness motivates a wide range of optimal coping strategies; however that same awareness appears to take its toll as it is suboptimally manifested, most often in Suboptimal Affect. In this case, Tina suffers from some chronic pain and despair fueled by her weariness in having to resist and combat the negativity of her life circumstances.

Just being Black is already one strike against you. Being a woman is another strike against you. So you have two strikes against you and you may have to work ten times harder than an average white person ... but you take it in stride ... that's the only way you're ever gonna get by, you will say finally, "I've achieved what I wanted to" ... guess its just me for me, it hurts but I can't let them know that....

IMPLICATIONS AND IMPACT: SOCIAL-EMOTIONAL WELL-BEING, SUPPORTS AND STRATEGIES

As noted in the case study, hallmarks of the Purposeful Resister include suboptimal affect and behavior resistance attributes that centrally defined their social-emotional well being often noted in the coded narrative as *Depression* and *Isolation*. These findings highlight the growing attention to implications of maternal depression and social isolation, particularly among mothers who find themselves marginalized and confronted by multiple societal stressors.

Maternal Depression and Social isolation

Not surprisingly, according to a report tracking maternal depression among diverse demographics, mothers living in poverty are over three times more likely to have depression than those in higher socio-economic brackets (SAMHSA). The report also showed that although rates of depression are higher among white, non-Hispanic mothers, African American and Mexican American women have higher rates of dysthymic disorder—a chronic form of depression that is present for at least two years and which can have a significant impact on a mother's livelihood and mental health, thus consequently effecting the well being of their children. Also underscored was the critical role of the social context on maternal depression highlighting the social, economic and physical environments as key factors of mothers' lives that can impose significant barriers to her well being. Specifically addressed were social norms about help-seeking that may prevent some mothers from accessing treatment early and contribute to isolating behaviors. Other deterrents include the high cost of care and lack of health insurance that can also impede mothers from getting the care they need. Neighborhood factors such as lack of transportation services and healthcare providers in their area can also obstruct the ability to access care (SAMHSA). Alongside these factors is the role that culturally informed beliefs about depression, particularly among communities of color, might play in identifying and seeking support for depression. Therefore, in addressing maternal depression, it is important to consider the multiple and broad array of contextual circumstances in the lives of mothers.

Salient Factors and Issues

In light of the aforementioned and overarching issues, three areas emerge most salient in review of Purposeful Resistance as it relates to maternal depression and social isolation, especially among African-American mothers—implications for birth and child outcomes, economic and neighborhood factors, and issues related to treatment.

A growing body of research points to deleterious birth and child outcomes for pregnant Black women who experience stress and depression. One study reported that higher levels of stress may have contributed to greater incidence of prematurity and low birth weight neonatal outcomes among depressed mothers and may explain higher rates of prematurity and low birth weight among Black women compared to white women (Field et al). Other studies cite a correlation between high rates of stress among socially isolated Black mothers living in poverty and child behavior issues. Conversely, it also indicated a correlation between mothers with higher educational attainment and self-efficacy with fewer child behavior problems (Jackson). In another study examining the role of parenting, family routines, family conflict and maternal depression in predicting social skills and behavior problems among low income African-American preschool age children, they found that mothers utilizing positive parenting practices and with lower levels of maternal depressive symptoms was predictive of children with fewer external and internal child behavior problems (Koblinsky, Kuvalanka and Randolph).

Closely aligned with the child outcome data is the community and economic context within which the mothers are parenting. Issues linking stress levels, isolation and depression to neighborhood safety have been well documented (Ceballo and McLoyd; Hill and Herman-Stahl). Reports of neighborhood safety were linked with maternal depressive symptoms in one study that also reported depressive symptoms as mediating the relation between neighborhood safety and inconsistent discipline, which according to the researchers suggest that the influence of safety on inconsistent discipline of children was due to its impact on maternal depression (Hill and Herman-Stahl). Another study explored how stressful environments influence the relation between mothers' social supports and parenting strategies. Ceballo and McLloyd found that as neighborhood conditions became worse the positive relation between emotional support and mothers nurturing behaviors were weakened. In addition, as the context became more dangerous and increasingly constrained economically, the positive influence of social and instrumental supports were also strained and diminished. These studies underscore the power of the community context on mothers' parenting practice, available supports and social-emotional status all of which directly impact their children.

The pervasive impact on both mothers and children from maternal depression and isolation, which is heightened in stressful contexts, provides ample motivation for exploring effective treatment options, especially for those mothers particularly marginalized. As seen in the Purposeful Resister profile, those mothers who engage in adaptive optimal strategies to push against their marginalization such as awareness of their parenting role, self-agency and forward thinking, are also highly susceptible to social-emotional challenges such as depressive symptoms and isolating from others. Studies addressing issues of maternal depression and isolation point to some of the challenges and potential treatment strategies for Black mothers, in particular.[5] In a study of major maternal depressive disorder across a range of socio-demographic patterns, researchers found that only half of depressed mothers received services for their depression, and Black mothers were most likely to experience multiple adversities in association with their depression and less likely to receive services than white depressed mothers (Edwards et al). The study asserts that maternal depression is a major public health problem in the United States citing that one in ten children experience a depressed mother in any given year. The findings suggest that Black mothers are especially susceptible to being depressed and most at risk for not receiving services. Another study of depression among a diverse sample of mothers, showed that ethnic minority patients were less likely to receive "guideline concordant care" for depression which may in part be do to service delivery and racial/ethnic differences in beliefs, attitudes and preferences for treatment (Cooper et al.). Results of the study reported that African-Americans had lower odds compared to Whites of finding antidepressant medications acceptable suggesting need to for comprehensive socio-cultural exploration and education about depression among African-Americans for both the caregivers and community.

RESISTANCE AND RELATIONSHIP IN CONTEXT: NEW DIRECTIONS

Recent research exploring the interplay of mechanisms of risk for young children's emotional and behavioral health touch upon all three of the key areas discussed in relation to maternal depression and social isolation: child outcomes, economic context and implications for mental health treatment (Rijlaarsdam et al.). Findings showed that both internalizing and externalizing behavior problems among children were influenced by underlying mechanisms effecting economic disadvantage which included maternal depressive symptoms, parenting stress and harsh parenting strategies. Rijlaarsdam et al. suggest that interventions must not solely focus on raising income levels among economically disadvantaged parents, but must also involve the issues in family processes that emerge as a result of economic stress.

This approach is in line with findings from the *Profiles of Resistance* case analysis wherein young African-American mothers exhibited multiple resistance strategies to their marginalizing circumstance manifested psycho-socially in both optimal and suboptimal ways through their parenting, relationships and in the context of their environment. Both program and policy level interventions must include assessing and addressing the mental health of mothers with young children, as well as their home or neighborhood environment as a key factor in supporting overall family health and well-being.

While the effects of marginalizing societal stressors for young Black mothers living in economically disadvantaged settings is most pronounced, stressors associated with race and gender persist for Black mothers across a range of age and socio-economic lines. Some research documents the persistence of low-birthweight and infant mortality even among college-educated Black women in comparison to their white counterparts (Alexander et al.). Preterm delivery is often cited as factor in infant mortality among Black women, and in another study results showed a linkage between a mother's exposure to racial discrimination their pre-term births (Rich-Edwards et al.). The report specifically addressed the failure of socio-demographics to fully explain the differences in birthweights among Black and white mothers also pointing to evidence that the gap persist among college educated Black and white mothers, possibly even widening as Black women climb the socio-economic ladder. Suggesting a "toxicity" of growing up a woman of color in the United States due to a hostile context laden with racism and sexism, and thereby the associated stressors, the report points out higher birth rates and overall better health ratings of recently immigrated mothers as compared to US born Black women (Rich-Edwards et al.). Further accentuating this point are studies that reveal a decrease in maternal health outcomes for immigrant populations the longer they live in the United States (Gopal et al.). The marginalizing stressors of racism and sexism in the United States therefore emerge to the top as critically influential factors for the physical, emotional and mental well being of Black women. These multiple and complex factors associated with race, gender and class impact the pregnancy and parenting among African-American mothers with well-documented implications for the health outcomes of their children and themselves (Gay "Stress Kills," "Racial Discrimination" ; Ahmad and Iverson).

Additionally, it is important to continue research that investigates and documents the range of strengths and optimal strategies that Black women and mothers use regularly, especially from a culturally informed and empowered position. Research that builds on a growing literature examining relational-culturally based protective factors that Black women employ to mitigate societal stressors is essential to growing the knowledge base for prevention and intervention efforts.[6] Specific examination of Relational Cultural Theory—RCT (Miller *Toward a New Psychology*) and the *Profiles of Resistance* are revealing complimentary aspects of the most adaptive Profile types and core tenets of RCT, which is anchored in the understanding that people grow through and toward relationship and that culture informs relationship in powerful ways (Jordan, Hartling and Walker; Miller *Toward a New Psychology*; Walker and Rosen). Recent explorations of RCT informed relational neuroscience (Banks "Four Ways to Click") and the *Profiles of Resistance* have uncovered specific areas of optimal and suboptimal resistance strategies in relation to how they map to innovative discoveries in brain science, which has implications on understanding depression and social isolation among Black women and mothers (Craddock and Banks).

Equally important to ongoing theoretical exploration is the development of diagnostics, tools and practices to more accurately understand and assess the psycho-emotional wellbeing and resistance to marginalization among Black women and mothers which is necessary for improving equitable, effective programs, treatment and optimal health outcomes. Banks' C.A.R.E. program ("Four Ways to Click") is a guide and tool based on relational neuroscience research to assess the quality of relationships in one's life and can strengthen neural pathways toward connection. The attributes grounded in neuroscience most indicative of healthy connection are Calm, Acceptedness, Resonance and Energy (C.A.R.E.). This innovative research and program offers new and emerging ways that we can counter marginalizing disconnections and stimulate inclusive connections by examining overlapping physiology and relational psychology. The Resistance Modality Inventory – RMI (Robinson-Wood) is a research instrument currently being used to gather empirical data on African-American women to assess psychological resistance to marginalization, stress and racial identity development (Mirkin, Suyemoto and Okun; Robinson-Wood). One of the more groundbreaking and critical contributions of using the RMI has been in uncovering often masked or misdiagnosed depression among highly educated, highly functioning, middle class African-American women who are struggling with an depression due to chronic societal stressors (Martin et al.). Both the C.A.R.E. program and RMI are providing opportunities for action research using the *Profiles of Resistance* to gather more meaningful data that can be applied to therapeutic and programmatic strategies to foster healthy connections within and across maternal, familial and communal networks, all with implications for parenting practices, early childhood learning and health outcomes, as well as relational well-being and safety for women and mothers. Using the resistance and relationship lens to affect change at the policy level also centrally includes creating strategic partnerships across reproductive and economic justice advocates, mental health practitioners, action research scholars, community-based and peer driven social support networks who would be encouraged to meet the ever-increasing needs particularly facing women of color by honoring and making space for the "growth-fostering" connections and practices that can optimally impact physiological and psychological health. This approach combining resistance and relationship exemplifies the very root of Black womanhood

Figure 1: *Purposeful Resister: Optimal Resistance*

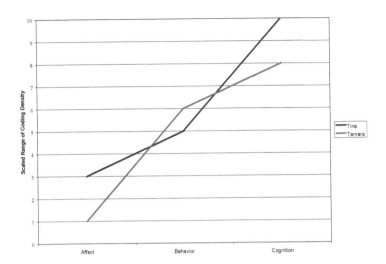

Optimal Resistance – Affect, Behavior and Cognition scaled range of coding density for Purposeful Resister cases (Tina – featured in this essay). Optimal cognition scores highest.

Figure 2: *Purposeful Resister: Suboptimal Resistance*

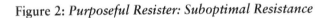

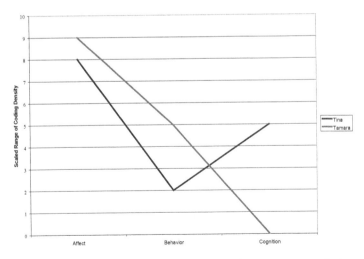

Suboptimal Resistance – Affect, Behavior and Cognition scaled range of coding density for Purposeful Resister cases (Tina – featured in this essay). Suboptimal affect scores highest.

reflecting deeply embedded African/African-American cultural worldviews and practices that Black women manifest in daily living and that have been drawn upon for large scale movements over the course of human history.

With further investigation of the *Profiles of Resistance* framework and with the emergence of its assessment tool, there is an opportunity to expand the discussion around and treatment of depression and social isolation for a wider array of ethno-culturally and socio-economically diverse women. This interrogation and expansion will provide more robust understanding of the construct, the dynamics and effects of marginalization in its many forms including microaggressions and blatant practices. This resistance framework also provides ample opportunity to deepen exploration of multiple resistance strategies that are employed to counter health-diminishing hegemonies, and gives insight into how to improve and implement program, practice and policy that strengthen and sustain the social-emotional health for women and mothers across diverse communities, thereby purposefully catalyzing social justice for all.

[1]The terms "Black" and "African-American" are used interchangeably throughout the essay.
[2]See, for example, Collins "Sexual Politics," *Fighting Words, Black Feminist Thought*; hooks *Feminist Theory*; Jarrett-MacAuley; Lorde; Watt; Watt, Robinson and Lupton Smith.
[3]See Brooks-Gunn and Paikoff; Furstenberg; McLloyd et al.; Pittman and Chase-Lansdale.
[4]*Data Collection and Analysis summary.* Qualitative case study data was collected and analyzed from a sample of African-American mothers who also participated in an evaluation of the Massachusetts Healthy Families Program and in the ethnography portion of the evaluation study. All were first-time mothers under the age of twenty-one. All names used in the study were changed to preserve anonymity. Each self reported as both African-American and a U.S. citizen. Following qualitative methods of ethnographic data collection and analytic techniques (Miles and Huberman; Spradley), the sample of African-American mothers was interviewed

over a period of two and half years (1999-2002). Visits included in-depth observations and field notes documenting mother-child interactions, home environment and activities. Informal conversation, naturalistic observation and semi-structured interviews to capture dimensions of parenting, help-seeking, and family and program perspectives, as well as questions addressing race socialization messages, using an adaptation of Ward's interview protocol and schemata to elicit personal narratives noting experiences and beliefs about the constructs of race and gender. Data was transcribed and analyzed from each mother meeting using the QSR NVivo07 (Gibbs "Qualitative Data Analysis") software to catalogue, index and analyze the qualitative data. Including Optimal and Suboptimal resistance strategies using the Affect, Behavior and Cognition (ABC) resistance framework (Craddock, "Paths to Resistance"). Analysis of the data utilized phased process grounded in the principles of Resistance Theory (Robinson, "The Intersections"; Robinson and Ward, "'A Belief'") and Miles and Huberman's conceptual approach to qualitative analysis. Four specific aspects of the Miles and Huberman approach to "data chunking" and "data reduction" were used in the phased analytical process for this study and blended the NVivo coding framework: Free Node and Structure Coding (Clustering), Embedded Coding of Tree Nodes (Partitioning Variables), Node Reports and Matrices (Counting/Matrices Displays), and Profiles (Factoring Patterns).
[5]See Ertel, Edwards and Koenen; Cooper et al.
[6]See Greer; Martin et al.; Pittman; Stevens-Watkins et al.; Szyzmanski; West, Donovan and Roemer.

WORKS CITED

Ahmad, Farah, and Sarah Iverson. "The State of Women of Color in the United States." Center for American Progress, 24 October 2013. Web. April 2014.

Alexander, Greg R., et al. "Racial Differences in Birth Weight for Gestational Age and Infant Mortality in Extremely-Low-Risk U.S. Populations." *Pediatric and Perinatal Epidemiology* 13.2 (1999): 205-217. Print.

Banks, Amy. *Four Ways to Click: Rewire Your Brain for Stron-*

ger, More Rewarding Relationships. Westminster, UK: Penguin, 2015. Print.

Brooks-Gunn, Jeanne and Roberta Paikoff. "Sexuality and Developmental Transitions During Adolescence." *Health Risks and Developmental Transitions During Adolescence* Ed. John Schulenberg, Jennifer L. Maggs, and Klaus Hurrelmann. New York: Cambridge University Press, 1997. 190-219. Print.

Ceballo, Rosario and Vonnie C. McLoyd. "Social Support and Parenting in Poor, Dangerous Neighborhoods." *Child Development* 73.4 (2002): 1310-1321. Print.

Cole, Elizabeth R. "Intersectionality and Research in Psychology." *American Psychologist* 64.3 (2009): 170-180. Print.

Collins, Patricia Hill. "The Meaning of Motherhood in Black Culture and Black Mother-Daughter Relationships." *Toward a New Psychology of Gender.* Ed. Mary M. Gergen and Sara N. Davis. *Toward a New Psychology of Gender.* New York: Psychology Press, 1997. 325-340. Print.

Collins, Patricia Hill. "The Sexual Politics of Black Womanhood." *Violence Against Women: The Bloody Footprints.* 1 (1993): 85-104. Print.

Collins, Patricia Hill. "Shifting the Center: Race, Class, and Feminist Theorizing About Motherhood." *Mothering: Ideology, Experience, and Agency.* Ed. Evelyn Nakano Glenn, Grace Chang, and Linda Rennie Forcey. New York: Routledge, 1994. 45-65. Print.

Collins, Patricia Hill. *Fighting Words: Black Women and the Search for Justice.* Vol. 7. Minneapolis: University of Minnesota Press, 1998.

Collins, Patricia Hill. "Intersections of Race, Class, Gender, and Nation: Some Implications for Black Family Studies." *Journal of Comparative Family Studies* 29 (1998): 27-36. Print.

Collins, Patricia Hill. *Black Feminist Thought: Knowledge, Consciousness, and the Politics of Empowerment.* New York: Routledge, 2002. Print.

Collins, Patricia Hill. "Black Feminist Epistemology [1990]." *Black Feminist Thought: Knowledge, Consciousness, and the Politics of Empowerment.* New York: Routledge, 2002. Print.

Cooper, Lisa A., et al. "The Acceptability of Treatment for Depression Among African-American, Hispanic, and White Primary

Care Patients." *Medical Care* 41.4 (2003): 479-489. Print.

Craddock, Karen T. *Mother to Mother: Profiles of Psychological Resistance in Young Black Mothers and Models of Mother Involvement in the Relationship with Their Mothers.* Diss. Tufts University, Medford, 2007.

Craddock, Karen T. *Paths of Resistance: Exploring Strategies of Psychological Resistance Among African-American Young Mothers.* Unpublished Manuscript. Tufts University, Medford, 2005

Craddock, Karen T. *Resistance Theory Data Collection Protocol/ Analytical Construct – ABC Framework.* Research Protocol. Tufts University, Medford 2005

Craddock, Karen T. "Moving from Social Exclusion to Inclusion–Models of Resistance to Marginalization" JBMTI Wellesley Centers for Women, Wellesley College. Web. November, 2014

Craddock, Karen T. and Banks, Amy "Stopping the Pain of Social Exclusion: Everyone Needs to STOP the Pain, Everyone Needs the Pain to STOP." *Psychology Today,* "Wired for Love," September 2015. Web. September 2015.

Emerson, Rana A. "'Where My Girls At?' Negotiating Black Womanhood in Music Videos." *Gender and Society* 16.1 (2002): 115-135. Print.

Ertel, Karen A., Janet W. Rich-Edwards, and Karestan C. Koenen. "Maternal Depression in the United States: Nationally Representative Rates and Risks." *Journal of Women's Health* 20.11 (2011): 1609-1617. Print.

Field, Tiffany, et al. "Depressed Pregnant Black Women Have a Greater Incidence of Prematurity and Low Birth Weight Outcomes." *Infant Behavior and Development* 32.1 (2009): 10-16. Print.

Furstenberg, Frank F. *Managing to Make It: Urban Families and Adolescent Success.* Chicago: University of Chicago Press, 1999. Print.

Gay, Elizabeth Dawes. "Stress Kills: Economic Insecurity and Black Women's Maternal Health Outcomes." RH Reality Check. March 2014. Web. December 2014.

Gay, Elizabeth Dawes "Report: Racial Discrimination Severely Undermines Black Women's Health." RH Reality Check. August 2014. Web. December 2014.

Gee, Gilbert C., and Devon C. Payne-Sturges. "Environmental Health Disparities: A Framework Integrating Psychosocial and Environmental Concepts." *Environmental Health Perspectives* (2004): 1645-1653. Print.

Gibbs, Graham. *Qualitative Data Analysis: Explorations with NVivo (Understanding Social Research)*. Buckingham: Open University Press, 2002. Print.

Gilkes, Cheryl Townsend. "Going Up for the Oppressed: The Career Mobility of Black Women Community Workers." *Journal of Social Issues* 39.3 (1983): 115-139. Print.

Greer, Tawanda M. "Coping Strategies as Moderators of the Relation Between Individual Race-Related Stress and Mental Health Symptoms for African American Women." *Psychology of Women Quarterly* 35.2 (2011): 215-226. Print.

Hill, Nancy E., and Mindy A. Herman-Stahl. "Neighborhood Safety and Social Involvement: Associations with Parenting Behaviors and Depressive Symptoms Among African-American and Euro-American Mothers." *Journal of Family Psychology* 16.2 (2002): 209-219. Print.

hooks, bell. *Black Women and Feminism*. Boston: South End, 1981. Print.

hooks, bell. *Talking Back: Thinking Feminist, Thinking Black*. Boston: South End Press, 1989. Print.

hooks, bell. *Outlaw Culture: Resisting Eepresentations*. Routledge, 1994. Print.

hooks, bell. *Sisters of the Yam: Black Women and Self-recovery*. Boston: South End Press, 1993. Print.

hooks, bell. *Feminist Theory: From Margin to Center*. London: Pluto Press, 2000. Print.

Jackson, Aurora P. "Maternal Self-Efficacy and Children's Influence on Stress and Parenting Among Single Black Mothers in Poverty." *Journal of Family Issues* 21.1 (2000): 3-16. Print.

James, Stanlie M. "A Possible Black Feminist Link to Social Transformation?" *Theorizing Black Feminisms: The Visionary Pragmatism of Black Women*. Ed. Stanlie Myrise James and Abena P. A. Busia. New York: Psychology Press, 1993. Print.

Jarrett-Macauley, Delia. *Reconstructing Womanhood, Reconstructing Feminism: Writings on Black Women*. New York: Psychology

Press, 1996. Print.

Jenkins, Nina Lyon. "Black Women and the Meaning of Motherhood." *Redefining Motherhood: Changing Identities and Patterns.* Ed. Sharon Abbey and Andrea O'Reilly. Toronto: Canadian Scholars' Press, 1998. 201-213. Print.

Jordan, Judith V., Linda M. Hartling and Maureen Walker, eds. *The Complexity of Connection: Writings from the Stone Center's Jean Baker Miller Training Institute.* New York: Guilford Press, 2004. Print.

Koblinsky, Sally A., Katherine A. Kuvalanka, and Suzanne M. Randolph. "Social Skills and Behavior Problems of Urban, African American Preschoolers: Role of Parenting Practices, Family Conflict, and Maternal Depression." *American Journal of Orthopsychiatry* 76.4 (2006): 554. Print.

Lawson, Erica. "Black Women's Mothering in a Historical and Contemporary Perspective: Understanding the Past, Forging the Future." *Journal of the Motherhood Initiative for Research and Community Involvement* 2.2 (2000): 21-30. Print.

Lipscomb, Joseph, Carolyn C. Gotay, and Claire Snyder, eds. *Outcomes Assessment in Cancer: Measures, Methods and Applications.* Cambridge: Cambridge University Press, 2004. Print.

Lorde, Audre. *Sister Outsider: Essays and Speeches.* New York: Random House, 2007. Print.

Martin, Agnes, et al. "Applying Resistance Theory to Depression in Black Women." *Journal of Systemic Therapies* 32.1 (2013): 1-13. Print.

McDonald, Katrina Bell. "Black Activist Mothering: A Historical Intersection of Race, Gender, and Class." *Gender and Society* 11.6 (1997): 773-795. Print.

McLoyd, Vonnie C., et al. "Unemployment and Work Interruption Among African American Single Mothers: Effects on Parenting and Adolescent Socioemotional Functioning." *Child Development* 65.2 (1994): 562-589. Print.

Miles, Matthew B., and A. Michael Huberman. *Qualitative Data Analysis: An Expanded Sourcebook.* Thousand Oaks, CA: Sage, 1994. Print.

Miller, Jean Baker. *Toward a New Psychology of Women.* Boston: Beacon Press, 2012. Print.

Miller, Jean Baker. *The Healing Connection: How Women Form Relationships in Therapy and in Life*. Boston: Beacon Press, 2015. Print.

Minuchin, Salvador, and H. Charles Fishman. *Family Therapy Techniques*. Cambridge: Harvard University Press, 2009. Print.

Mirkin, Marsha Pravder, Karen L. Suyemoto, and Barbara F. Okun, eds. *Psychotherapy with Women: Exploring Diverse Contexts and Identities*. New York: Guilford Press, 2005. Print.

Moradi, Bonnie. "Advancing Womanist Identity Development Where We are and Where We Need To Go." *The Counseling Psychologist* 33.2 (2005): 225-253. Print.

Myers, Linda J., and Suzette L. Speight. "Identity Development and Worldview: Toward an Optimal Conceptualization." *Journal of Counseling and Development:* 70.1 (1991): 54. Print.

Naples, Nancy A. "A Socialist Feminist Analysis of the Family Support Act of 1988." *Affilia* 6.4 (1991): 23-38. Print.

PerrymanMark, Crystal'Aisha. "Resistance and Surrender: Mothering Young, Black and Feminist." *Journal of the Motherhood Initiative for Research and Community Involvement* 2.2 (2000): 130-138. Print.

Pittman, Chavella T. "Getting Mad But Ending Up Sad: The Mental Health Consequences for African Americans Using Anger to Cope with Racism." *Journal of Black Studies* 42.7 (2011): 1106-1124. Print.

Pittman, Laura D., and P. Lindsay Chase-Lansdale. "African American Adolescent Girls in Impoverished Communities: Parenting Style and Adolescent Outcomes." *Journal of Research on Adolescence* 11.2 (2001): 199-224. Print.

Reagon, Bernice Johnson. "African Diaspora Women: The Making of Cultural Workers." *Feminist Studies* 12.1 (1986): 77-90. Print.

Rich-Edwards, Janet et al. "Maternal Experiences of Racism and Violence as Predictors of Preterm Birth: Rationale and Study Design." *Pediatric and Perinatal Epidemiology* 15.s2 (2001): 124-135.

Rijlaarsdam, Jolien, et al. "Economic Disadvantage and Young Children's Emotional and Behavioral Problems: Mechanisms of Risk." *Journal of Abnormal Child Psychology* 41.1 (2013): 125-137.

Robinson, Tracy L. "The Intersections of Dominant Discourses Across Race, Gender, and Other Identities." *Journal of Counseling and Development* 77.1 (1999): 73-79. Print.

Robinson, Tracy L., and Mary F. Howard-Hamilton. "An Afrocentric Paradigm: Foundation for a Healthy Self-Image and Healthy Interpersonal Relationships." *Journal of Mental Health Counseling* 16.3 (1994): 327-339. Print.

Robinson, Tracy L., and Patricia Anne Davis Kennington. "Holding Up Half the Sky: Women and Psychological Resistance." *The Journal of Humanistic Counseling, Education and Development* 41.2 (2002): 164-177. Print.

Robinson, Tracy L., and Janie V. Ward. "African American Adolescents and Skin Color." *Journal of Black Psychology* 21.3 (1995): 256-274. Print.

Robinson, Tracy and Janie Victoria Ward. "'A Belief in Self Far Greater Than Anyone's Disbelief': Cultivating Resistance Among African American Female Adolescents." *Women and Therapy* 11.3-4 (1991): 87-103.

Robinson-Wood, Tracy. "Measuring Resistance in Black Women: The Resistance Modality Inventory." *Journal of Systemic Therapies* 33.2 (2014): 62-77. Print.

Shorter-Gooden, Kumea. "Multiple Resistance Strategies: How African American Women Cope with Racism and Sexism." *Journal of Black Psychology* 30.3 (2004): 406-425. Print.

Spradley, James P. *Participant Observation*. Belmont: Wadsworth, 1980. Print.

Stevens, Joyce West. *Smart and Sassy: The Strengths of Inner-City Black Girls*. Oxford: Oxford University Press, 2002.

Stevens-Watkins, Danelle, et al. "Racism and Illicit Drug Use Among African American Women: The Protective Effects of Ethnic Identity, Affirmation, and Behavior." *Journal of Black Psychology* 38.4 (2012):471-496. Print.

Substance Abuse Mental Health Services Agency (SAMHSA). "Maternal Depression: Making a Difference Through Community Action: A Planning Guide" Mental Health America, 2008. Web. October 2014.

Szymanski, Dawn M. "Racist Events and Individual Coping Styles as Predictors of African American Activism." *Journal of Black*

Psychology 38.3 (2012): 342-367. Print

Thomas, Trudelle. "'You'll Become a Lioness': African-American Women Talk About Mothering." *Journal of the Motherhood Initiative for Research and Community Involvement* 2.2 (2000).

Walker, Alice. *In Search of Our Mothers' Gardens: Womanist Prose*. Boston: Houghton Mifflin Harcourt, 2004. Print.

Walker, Maureen, and Wendy B. Rosen, eds. *How connections heal: Stories from relational-cultural therapy*. New York: Guilford Press, 2004. Print.

Ward, Janie Victoria. *The Skin We're In: Teaching Our Children to Be Emotionally Strong, Socially Smart, Spiritually Connected*. New York: Simon and Schuster, 2000. Print.

Watt, Sherry Kay. "Racial Identity Attitudes, Womanist Identity Attitudes, and Self-Esteem in African American college Women Attending Historically Black Single-Sex and Coeducational Institutions." *Journal of College Student Development* 47.3 (2006): 319-334. Print.

Watt, Sherry K., Tracy L. Robinson, and Helen Lupton-Smith. "Building Ego and Racial Identity: Preliminary Perspectives on Counselors-in-Training." *Journal of Counseling and Development* 80.1 (2002): 94-100. Print.

West, Lindsey M., Roxanne A. Donovan, and Lizabeth Roemer. "Coping With Racism: What Works and Doesn't Work for Black Women?" *Journal of Black Psychology* 36. 3 (2009): 331-349. Print.

Motherland Mothers:
Experiencing African Motherhood
Home and Abroad

3.
Transnational Mothering

The Meaning of African Immigrant Lives

FLORENCE KYOMUGISHA

O
N A DAILY BASIS women negotiate their priorities to be able to improve the conditions of their lives and often these negotiations require women to redefine their needs and the needs of their children against society's expectations. The effort to achieve a better life often leaves many women with no choice but to change space and relocate to places where they can find economic opportunities and freedom from oppression. The liberalization of world markets offered women from African countries new opportunities to improve the conditions of their lives. Many African immigrant women in the United States come from social and economic systems that are characterized by extreme levels of the marginalization of women in the social and economic sector, the sexual division of labor, the subordination of women and often poverty. Furthermore, many African immigrant women are mothers who are largely responsible for the maintenance of their families, the wellbeing of their children and therefore, fully understand that the future of their children (and families) will largely depend on their personal capabilities and the choices they make. Globally mothering is understood as a practice that involves the caring, preservation, nurturance, and training of children for adult life. However, the type of mothering a woman provides to her children is determined by her location in the structures of society (Collins; Sudarkasa "Conceptions of Motherhood"; Walker). The mothering that immigrant women provide to their children transcends national borders and thus, lies outside the western model of mothering. This phenomenon of

women's experience has been referred to as transnational mothering (Hondagneu-Sotelo), and involves mothers actively creating alternative constructions of mothering to accommodate the spatial separation from their children; while sustaining the mother and child relationships and the survival of their families. In an effort to understand the experiences of transnational mothering interviews were conducted among twenty-one Sub-Saharan African immigrants who are living on the West Coast of the United States. In this paper I will simply refer to African immigrant mothers as transnational mothers.

Many African immigrant women, who come to the United States to seek opportunities to improve their lives and the lives of their children, often make the hard choice to leave their young children in Africa, knowing they will have to forge motherhood identities outside the conventional family structure. Therefore, this study explores a contemporary variation of mothering that is distinguished by race, class, culture and nationality. I start from the position that extended family and kin networks play a significant role in the mothering that African transnational mothers provide for the children they leave in their home countries. Scholars of African societies have found that despite the diversity in space and cultures in Sub-Saharan countries they are similarities in social organizations, familial institutions and extended family networks for raising children. In their research in West Africa, Aborampah and Sudarkasa highlight these institutions' and networks' role in "shared labor, socialization of children, education and placement of relatives, and support for the elderly..." (2). Kyomugisha and Rutayuga's experiences with families in East Africa reveal a common practice of children being sent to live with relatives or friends so as to help the biological mothers with the weaning, socialization or education of children (187-8). Other researchers of African society, such as Silverstein "have stressed the persistence of extended family networks as cultural bridges in modernization rather than impediments to development." (qtd. in Aborampah and Sudarkasa 2). Kilbride and Kilbride whose research focused on family life in Eastern Africa documents familial institutions and extended family and kin networks that are similar to those found in West and Central Africa.

AFRICAN VALUES OF THE INDIVIDUAL AND COMMUNITY
AND THE COMPLEXITY OF MOTHERING

The African model of raising children can be well understood only when we grasp the African concept of personhood, in other words, what it means to be a genuine human being. It is understood in Africa that "to be" is "to be with" as often heard in what John Mbiti identifies as a self-proposition: "I am because we are and because we are, therefore I am" (Akbar 407). The notion of being is extended to other human beings, nature and the supernatural world. Life comes to the individual through the ancestors and the parents, and it is protected and fostered in a community. More importantly, the primordial role that women play in the trans-mission of life is highly valued and is at the center of the life of a community. Kilbride and Kilbride explain that "East Africans, as we shall see do value their children.... The collectivity: family, clan, lineage, or ethnic group, takes precedence over the individual. The ideal typical person is one who is firmly rooted in the group with a commensurate orientation to social responsibilities. The parent, therefore, literally has children for the social group" (84-85). The African transnational mothering explored in this paper contradicts dominant Western, White and middle-class models of motherhood but not necessarily most African ideological notions of mothering. While some African women living in the United States have been socialized within the dominant mainstream western ideologies of mothering, many more African women have an extended and collective and contextual ideology of motherhood, where-by their mothering is validated by functioning in relationship with the collective whole. They understand interdependence and collective responsibility are central to the wellbeing of their future and the future of their children and community. Therefore, in order to understand the context of African transnational mothering we must recognize the role of the complex extended families in which mothers, fathers, grandparents, aunts and uncles and so many other people in the kinship group play in the raising children. (Collins; Blum and Deussen; Dill; Sudarkasa "Conceptions of Motherhood"). These complex extended family patterns often complicate mother and child relationships by the nature of the flexibility of these relationships. This is not to say however, that the relationships are weakened, but to emphasize the flexibility in the parenting role and the communal responsibility to ensure the wellbeing and maturing of a child into an adult and responsible citizen. (Aborampah; Kyomugisha and Rutayuga). Furthermore, this flexibility in parenting role does not minimize mothers' value in society, as Sudarkasa observed "motherhood enhances the status of wives in African family and community contexts" ("Reflections on Motherhood" 59-60). Sudarkasa explains that "[i]n indigenous African societies where adoption as known in the West was not common, women often assumed responsibility for the care and upbringing of one or more children of their relatives. Or, without asking for a child, they might have children 'given' or 'assigned to them'" ("Conceptions of Motherhood" 1). As this excerpt explains, the rearing of children within this communal network extends beyond the child's blood-parents; for instance, a child's earlier years may be spent with different members of the extended family so as to enable the child to receive the best rearing, education and training into adult life. Sudarkasa documents from her study in Nigeria:

> I saw many women who "had no issue," but had children they were rearing as their own. Sometimes one or more of these children might not even know that this was not his or her "birth mother" until they were well beyond school age. And even when they found out, they still addressed, and referred to, the woman with whom they were living as their "mother." ("Conceptions of Motherhood" 14)

THE ECONOMIC DYNAMICS OF MOTHERING
IN SUB-SAHARAN AFRICA

The diminishing economies of many Sub-Saharan African countries during the last three decades, and the daily struggle to make ends meet have forced many African women to find fundamental ways of reconciling their multiple roles of reproduction and production. While there are obviously numerous factors that have created this phenomenon in the lives of women, I concur with scholars who have argued that women and men's inequality in accessing economic resources in Sub-Saharan Africa was exacerbated by the International Monetary Fund (IMF) and the World Bank's Structural Adjustment Programs (SAPs) of the 1980s and 1990s. SAPs that mandated many Sub-Saharan countries to concentrate on trade and production, and cut expenditures on education, nutrition and health to boost their economies were not gender neutral, nor did they consider the various types of economic power imbalances in African society. As a result, women had limited access to economic resources and services to maintain their reproductive and productive roles in society (Gladwin; Earth). Ehrenreich and Hochschild also document that women in Sub-Saharan Africa like women from other Third World countries were adversely affected by SAPs that cut or reduced public services in areas of health, economy and education; and while Western countries have grown richer and Third World countries poorer, women in Third World countries have a strong incentive to seek economic opportunities in the richer parts of the world (8). In that vein, the recent globalization of the economy has enabled many African women to migrate to foreign countries, mainly in the West where they often get a chance to establish themselves economically and socially, and subsequently improve the conditions of their children and families.

Well before the transnational mothering of African immigrant women, there were two types of mothering: mothering in the urban setting; and mothering in the rural setting. The majority of women in the workforce in urban and industrial centers in Sub-Saharan Africa rarely have the economic security that permits a biological mother to be the only one exclusively involved with mothering during her children's early years (Collins; Sudarkasa). Historically and in contemporary times, women who work outside the home but lack the resources that allow for exclusive, full-time, round-the-clock mothering rely on various arrangements to care for their children. Sharing mothering responsibilities with female kin and friends (Collins) or hiring a "house girl" (usually a member of the kin network) are widely used alternatives (Kyomugisha and Rutayuga). In contrast, in rural Sub-Sahara Africa where women engage in subsistence farming or other petty income generating activities, women make arrangements that allow them to work while tending to their children. However, urbanization, weakening economies and the recent globalization have created a situation in which many women leave their homes in rural Africa and migrate to urban centers or other parts of the world to look for employment. Generally, the women who leave home in search of economic opportunities are expected to bring essential income to the families and households they leave behind. For instance, Abo-rampah explains that "[i]n contemporary Ghana, family members living abroad remit substantial sums of money to needy family members" (86). However, there are some situations where mothers (especially single mothers) who migrate to the cities or urban centers do not earn enough income to support their children and a house-girl in the city. These employed poor mothers are forced to create alternative strategies of mothering, which include entrusting their children to the grandmothers or other female kin in the rural areas, who are able to engage in agricultural work or other activities alongside the children they raise. The women who are entrusted with the children become the "other- mothers" (Collins 219) for the duration the biological mothers are away. In her research, Sudarkasa observed: "During my studies of Yoruba traders in Ghana, I found that many of them were rearing the children of their brothers and sisters back in Nigeria. These children were treated 'as if they were their own' because in fact, the principles of joint responsibility and reciprocity within the family, meant that those children were indeed 'like their own'" ("Conceptions of Motherhood" 10).

METHODS

African immigrant women and the researcher occasionally met at social and community events and had conversations which focused on issues related to work and the families they left in Africa. These conversations generated the researcher's interest in exploring the experiences of these mothers who left their young children in Africa and were engaged in transnational mothering. The researcher herself is an African immigrant who came to the United States in the mid-eighties but does not have the experience of transnational mothering because her children were born and raised in the United States. Nevertheless, the researcher was born and raised in Africa and is therefore familiar with kin networks, interdependence and the collective responsibility of raising children. The aim of the study is to understand African immigrant transnational mothering that is influenced by the women's location in the structures of class, race, culture and nationality (citizen/immigrant). The questions addressed are: How do African transnational mothers define the value of their lives in the United States? What is the meaning of African immigrant women's role of mothering that lies outside the western ideology of mothering? Interviews were conducted among twenty-one transnational African mothers who live on the West Coast of the United States but who have left their young children in Africa. All the transnational mothers came to the United States after 2000, and they came from Uganda, Kenya, Rwanda, Ethiopia, Tanzania, Zambia, Nigeria and Togo. Most of the mothers were recruited for the study at beauty salons; others were recruited through the churches, at community gatherings and friends who were participating in the study referred a few. The interviews, which were both face to face and over the telephone, were conducted at the transnational mothers' homes or the researcher's office. The interviews were tape-recorded and were conducted over a period of twelve months in 2010 and 2011. Transnational mothers' narratives explain: (1) their reasons for migrating to the United States; (2) child rearing arrangements that transnational mothers negotiated; (3) how transnational mothers define their mothering along African ideological norms of raising children; (4) the social and emotional challenges of being separated from young children and the strategies they employ to accommodate the spatial separation from their children; and (5) the meaning and value they attribute to their lives in the United States, that help them to deal with western societies' contradictions and expectations.

TRANSNATIONAL MOTHERS' NARRATIVES

Reasons for Migrating to the United States

The transnational mothers fell into four categories of reasons why they came to the United States including: those who came as students to pursue college education in the United States; those who came for some other form of professional training;

those who came on a visitors' or tourist visa; and those who are in the country under the political asylum program. The largest category is the transnational mothers who came to the United States on visitor's visa and decided to stay—they have either changed their visa status or they are staying in the United States "illegally." Most of the transnational mothers had been professionals in Africa and a few were small-scale traders. The transnational mothers in the study expressed how they felt lucky to get away from Africa because of economic crises in the home countries; and believed coming to the United States offered better opportunities for economic advancement and a better future for themselves and their children.

At the time they came to the United States, five transnational mothers were married, seven transnational mothers were single (never married) and the rest of the transnational mothers were separated, divorced or widowed. Nine of the transnational mothers who were not married (single, divorced, separated) when they arrived in the United States are now either married or cohabitating with a male partner. Their husbands have since joined three of the five transnational mothers who were married when they first came to the United States and one mother has since been divorced. All the transnational mothers were employed at the time of the interviews; however, most of them were employed in jobs that were not related to the training or work experience they had in Africa. The jobs that transnational mothers were engaged in range from domestic workers and live-in nurses—to bus drivers—to accountants and insurance brokers. While all the transnational mothers freely talked about their employment situations, daily experience and family, many of them were reluctant to talk about their immigration situation. It is reasonable to assume that some of these transnational mothers may have legal immigration situations that they want to protect with confidentiality. A few transnational mothers expressed that they felt ashamed because they have been in the United States for many years; making statements like "You do not want to know, it is embarrassing." Feelings of embarrassment are attributed to the transnational mothers' sense of failing to get established in the United States, especially if the woman has not been able to obtain a stable or good job. Furthermore, the few transnational mothers who did not have legal documents to live in the United States were subjected to very low paying jobs.

ALTERNATIVE CHILD REARING ARRANGEMENTS THAT TRANSNATIONAL MOTHERS NEGOTIATE

All the transnational mothers expressed that the decision to leave their young children behind as they worked "tirelessly to establish themselves in America" ensured that their children would have some stability in Africa until it was "time for them to come" to the United States. The number of children individual transnational mothers left behind in Africa ranges from one to three, and the transnational mothers selected a sister, mother (grandmother), or female kin to care for their children during their absence. All the transnational mothers had confidence in the "other-mothers" to care for their children and perceived this arrangement to be normal and necessary. To highlight the confidence the transnational mothers had in the "others mothers," some transnational mothers explained that they themselves were raised by "other-mothers," such as their step mothers, their aunts or grandmothers. In addition, some transnational mothers explained that they too had cared for other relatives' children before they came to the United States. All the transnational mothers were providing some form of help to relatives in Africa, including relatives who are not raising their children.

Eleven transnational mothers had children who are attending boarding school in Africa. Despite that the children spent more than three quarters of the year in boarding schools, transnational mothers negotiated or made arrangements with a family member or a friend (other-mother) who would be responsible for working with the school to ensure the safe keeping of the child during the school year. On a regular basis, the fathers or the "other-mothers" and their families visited the children in boarding schools, and the children stayed with the "other-mothers" or some other family when school was not in session. Fifteen transnational mothers left their young non-school age children with their mothers (grandmother) or sisters or sister-in-laws who had children of their own; and as these children grew older, most of them went to boarding school.

The transnational mothers expressed that they trusted and could fully depend on the "other-mothers" to provide physical, spiritual and emotional needs of their children, as one mother explained:

> *I had no concerns, because he was being cared for, by my mother, my father and sisters.... I was encouraged, because this was an opportunity for my family to spend time with Tim, particularly my parents, they were overjoyed.... He is their first grandchild. In Rwanda, grandparents play an important role in their grandchildren rearing—this was an opportunity of a lifetime for them....Our separation allowed me to concentrate on my studies.*

Financial arrangements the transnational mothers made to provide for their children in Africa varied, and the transnational mothers were constantly sending money home, through Western Union, United States bank accounts transfer of funds, or through friends who were visiting in the home country. Some transnational mothers made monthly remittances to the accounts of the "other-mothers" or family member raising the children. Some transnational mothers had negotiated a certain amount of cash that the "other-mothers" received on a monthly or quarterly basis. One transnational mother who has a house in her hometown negotiated to let the "other-mother" live in her house and in exchange she would raise two of the transnational mothers children along with her own. A few transnational mothers who left the children with their fathers expressed that the fathers had improved on their childrearing skills and housekeeping skills in the absence of the transnational mothers. One woman explained:

> *Their father is very involved in caring for our children much more than he did when I was there. He spends more time with the children and less with his friends or the bar. He attends all the teacher/parent meetings and makes sure the children are well fed, cleaned and well clothed, of course, with the help of his sisters and mother.*

Another mother reported:

The last time I visited I was impressed with what he is doing with our son. He is spending time reading to our son. It was beautiful to see the relationship they had with each other.... He supports what I am doing in the U.S. He appreciates the money I send home. We have been able to buy two taxis.

Most of the transnational mothers expressed that they felt that their children were in a better environment for their socialization at this early stage of their lives. One mother stated, "I somehow feel lucky that my children are being raised in my African culture and traditions." Some transnational mothers expressed that they hoped that their children in Africa would be socialized into learning and appreciating work, and good morals and ethics. One mother whose son stayed with the father in Rwanda stated: "My son was going to be exposed to our culture and would learn the value of education, responsibility, and respect for elders.... He was going to learn our different languages. He would be able to witness poverty in my country, which would help him appreciate what he has in America."

TRANSNATIONAL MOTHERS DEFINE THEIR ROLE AS TRANSNATIONAL MOTHERS

Six transitional transnational mothers have had other children since they came to the United States. There were two categories of transnational mothers' involvement in decisions regarding their children in Africa: Six of the transnational mothers reported that they aspired to have the maximum possible influence over what goes on in their children's life. These transnational mothers were involved in the decision making of almost everything that relates to the child including, the schools they attended, where they lived, the medical care they received, their diet, the vacations they went to, as well as the events or functions they attended. The rest of the transnational mothers expressed that they had confidence in the "other- mothers" and trusted their judgment and skills in making the right decisions about their children. This group that was less involved and left most decision making mainly to a husband, boyfriend, sister or a close female friend who had children of her own. Nevertheless, all the transnational mothers expressed that they required to be frequently informed by the "other- mothers" of any major incidents, situations or milestones related to the children. Some of the transnational mothers expressed that they were fully aware of the responsibility they had for the maintenance of the family or household that kept their children. These transnational mothers are invoking the reciprocity and sense of joint responsibility that is characteristic of the extended network system of caring for children and family, where everyone understands that no one is self-reliant (Aborampah; Kyomugisha and Rutayuga).

THE SOCIAL AND EMOTIONAL CHALLENGES OF
BEING SEPARATED FROM CHILDREN

The period of physical separation of mother from children ranged from sixteen months to seven years. Even though all the transnational mothers expressed that the separation from children was tolerable and necessary, they revealed a sense of longing to see their children. They talked about how they missed to "see them grow, to touch and feel them." One transnational mother explained her coping strategy as follows: "The way I get through each day is to work so hard that I don't have idle time to think about how I miss my children." Faith and religion also played a significant role in how some transnational mothers coped with the separation from their children. Most transnational mothers' experiences were captured in this mother's words, "Prayer was and is still important in my life. I have spent countless hours on my knees praying for her safety. I will see her soon. I am her mother, will always be, no one can take that away from me." A few transnational mothers talked about attending support group meeting or going to get-togethers for transnational mothers through their churches as a strategy for coping with the separation from family in Africa. All the transnational mothers made every effort to stay in touch with their children in Africa, and believed frequent communication with them was an integral part of a healthy relationship between a mother and her children. The transnational mothers expressed how emails and the cell phone have played a significant role in helping them to stay connected to their children. Most of the transnational mothers expressed that even though telephone bills "can add up" they "enjoyed and achieved gratification" from the long telephone conversation with their children, and phone conversation helped the transnational mothers to "maintain emotional ties" with their children. All the transnational mothers were encouraged that their children will join them in the near future because they had seen several of their friends who had brought their families to the United States. In addition, some of the transnational mothers were able to visit their children in Africa after they obtained a "green card"; however, other transnational mothers had not been able to see their children for years because they did not have "proper papers" that would allow them to travel back and forth to Africa.

THE MEANING AND VALUE OF
TRANSNATIONAL MOTHERS' LIVES

The transnational mothers had a very strong sense of community and despite that many of them worked many hours in mostly low paying jobs, they were able to keep in touch with other African women and men in the community, as well as supported each other in various ways. Common places and events where Africans frequently congregated include churches, beauty salons and African restaurants. Most of these transnational mothers were highly motivated to participate in gatherings at the community members' homes to celebrate milestones and during the gatherings they shared traditional African dishes as well as danced to African music. The occasional gatherings played an important role in building their community and helped the members to maintain the connection to their African culture and develop a sense of belonging. The transnational mothers described the "tough" times when they first arrived in the United States and how they depended on the generosity of friends or relatives who were already living in the United States; and who helped them to cope or who provided them with food and shelter until they were better situated to care for themselves. The transnational mothers expressed that they worked hard on their jobs—from working long hours—to keeping two full-time jobs—to "live in." All the transnational mothers reported that they

had better access to economic resources in the United States than they did in Africa and were now able to provide a better life for their children, including sending them to good schools, providing good healthcare, nutrition and general wellbeing. The transnational mothers were also able to provide for other members in their extended families and believed that the economic independence as well as the ability to provide for their families enhanced a sense of self-worth, and they perceived themselves role models for their children, especially their daughters.

CONCLUSION

African mothering occurs within kin networks for raising children that extend beyond blood parents; are rooted in the African world view that values the community over the individual; and emphases interdependence and collective responsibility. Thus, African transnational mothers in the United States develop coping mechanisms and redefine they role of mothering along African ideological notions of mothering that help them to deal with western society's contradictions, expectations, and stereotypes about mothering, and the stigma, guilt, and criticism from United States mainstream culture. The findings of this study inform the need for mainstream America to challenge monolithic notions of family and motherhood that rely on the ideological conflation of family, woman, reproduction, and nurturance. Scholars from various backgrounds suggest that we need to be inclusive and look at mothering from a different perspective taking into consideration the cultural, social and spatial location of the people instead of using western middle class definitions and concepts of family and mothering as the yard sticks for measuring mothering in a global context (Collins; Walker; Sudarkasa, "Conceptions of Motherhood"). While the globalization of the economy has magnified the feminization of poverty in the world, it has also created employment opportunities for many African women, enhanced their sense of value and enabled them to fulfill their role of mothering while feeling dignified and empowered within their families and their communities. Due to their earning potential and ability to be the main providers in their families, these transnational mothers acquire a greater degree of respect of their decision making from spouses and other family members. Societal beliefs in men as the primary bread-winners and women as the homemakers are challenged and often contradict the lived experience in the households of transnational mothers where these gendered roles are becoming increasingly fluid. This phenomenon has positive effects on African society when fathers become effectively involved and committed to the daily needs of their children. The transnational mothering experiences of these women inform the need to initiate serious public discourse and advocacy for United States immigration policies that will address the challenges and the effects of the global division of labor on families.

WORKS CITED

Aborampah, Osei-Mensah. "A Time of Transition: Contemporary Family Networks in Ghana." *Extended Families in Africa and the African Diaspora*. Ed. Osei-Mensah Aborampah and Niara Sudarkasa. Trenton: African World Press, 2011. 71-93. Print.

Aborampah, Osei-Mensah and Niara Sudarkasa, eds. *Extended Families in Africa and the African Diaspora*. Trenton: African World Press, 2011. Print.

Akbar, Na'Im. "Afrocentric Social Science for Human Liberation." *Journal of Black Studies* 14. 4 (1984): 395-414. Print.

Blum, Linda and Theresa Deuessen. "Negotiating Independent Motherhood: Working-Class African-American Women Talk About Marriage and Motherhood." *Gender & Society* 10 (1996): 199-211. Print.

Collins, Patricia. H. "Black Women and Motherhood." *Rethinking the Family: Some Feminist Questions*. Ed. Barrie Thorne and Marilyn Yalon. Boston: Northeastern University Press, 1992. 215-245. Print.

Dill, Bonnie. T. "Our Transnational Mothers' Grief: Racial-Ethnic Women and the Maintenance of Families." *Journal of Family History* 13 (1988): 415-31. Print.

Earth, Barbara. "Structural Adjustments and its Effects." *Canadian Woman Studies/les cahiers de la femme* 6.3 (1996): 122-28. Print.

Ehrenreich, Barbara and Arlie Hochschild, eds. *Global Women: Nannies, Maids, and Sex Workers in the New Economy.* New York: Henry Holt & Company, 2002. Print.

Gladwin, Christina H. "Women and Structural Adjustment in a Global Economy." *Food and Resource Economics Department.* Gainesville: University of Florida, 1992. 87-112. Print.

Hondagneu-Sotelo, Pierrette. *Domestica: Immigrant Workers Cleaning, Caring in the Shadow of Affluence.* Berkeley: University of California Press, 2001. Print.

Kilbride, Philip L., and Janet C. Kilbride. *Changing Family Life in East Africa: Women and Children at Risk.* University Park: The Pennsylvania State University Press, 1990. Print.

Kyomugisha, Florence and John Rutayuga. "Extended Family and Kinship Network Systems for Caring for Children." *Extended Families in Africa and the African Diaspora.* Ed. Osei-Mensah Aborampah and Niara Sudarkasa. Trenton: African World Press, 2011. 183-199. Print.

Sudarkasa, Niara. "Reflections on Motherhood in Nuclear and Extended Families in Africa and in the United States." *Extended Families in Africa and the African Diaspora.* Ed. Osei-Mensah Aborampah and Niara Sudarkasa. Trenton: African World Press, 2011. 45-69. Print.

Sudarkasa, Niara. "Conceptions of Motherhood in Nuclear and Extended Families, with Special Reference to Comparative Studies Involving African Societies." *JENDA: A Journal of Culture and African Women Studies* 5 (2004): 1-27. Print

Walker, Cherryl. "Conceptualizing Motherhood in Twentieth Century South Africa." *Journal of Southern African Studies* 21.3 (1995): 417-437. Print.

4.
Motherhood and Empowerment in West Africa

The Case of Buchi Emecheta

DELPHINE FONGANG

THE NOTION OF MOTHERHOOD and mothering find special resonance in the fundamental ways in which African women define their subjectivities. The preoccupation with motherhood is very central in most contemporary African women's writings, especially in the writings of West African writers such as Buchi Emecheta, Ama Ata Aidoo, Mariama, and Naffisatou Diallo, among others. These writers celebrate the joys of motherhood as well as the woes with the loss of a child. Motherhood underscores women's power as it is the conceptual space in which some West African women find solace and peace from stifling traditional and patriarchal constraints. Women's empowerment in Africa is intrinsically linked to their pro-natal ability that allows them to achieve agency and their self-definition is linked to pro-natal reproductivity, which defines their womanhood. Motherhood is a source of strength and a position of identity construction that allows African women not only to achieve status in society but also to establish their sense of fulfillment and happiness in life. Emecheta's *Head Above Water* reveals how motherhood is a socially sanctioned arena where she has control over her identity and the means of production.

Although motherhood is a source of strength and empowerment for African women, it can also be a site of vulnerability. Motherhood and mothering in relation to patriarchal ideals is a position of victimhood because motherhood as an institution under patriarchy oppresses mothers. Adrienne Rich in *Of Woman Born* clearly distinguishes between motherhood as an institution and motherhood as an experience, arguing that patriarchy controls the institution of motherhood whereas women experience motherhood (60). Rich therefore shifts the focus away from Western feminists' yoking of motherhood and victimhood that had preoccupied early feminist discourse on motherhood. Here I show that motherhood as an experience (mothering) is a position of power and agency for most West African women, whereas motherhood as an institution under patriarchy oppresses women. Under the institution of motherhood, most often, mothers are oppressed as wives through physical, sexual, and emotional abuses, which necessitates the distinction between wifehood and motherhood (Nnaemeka 17). Oyerónke Oyewumí states that "the importance of the wife/mother distinction is that 'female subordination' is embedded in the position as 'wife,' whereas the position as 'mother' is a position of power in African contexts, motherhood [being] the preferred and cherished self-identity of many African women" (qtd. in Arnfred 24). West African writers and fictional characters show this distinction. For example, Adaku in *Joys of Motherhood*, Aissatou in *So Long a Letter*, Emecheta in *Head Above Water*, and Esi in *Changes*, among others, reject wifehood but not motherhood. Phanuel Egejuru emphasizes this distinction as he alludes to Igbo (tribal group in eastern Nigeria) males placing importance on mothers over wives (15). Although the Igbo society does not tolerate wife abuse, literary characterizations such as the examples mentioned above, still show men abusing their wives. Emecheta, who is from the Igbo society, accepts the temporary hardships of marriage to ensure a more ennobling state of motherhood-a state that confers prestige and permanent power to her (Egejuru 16). Thus motherhood becomes the self-actualization process for West African women who define their womanhood in terms of reproduction.

Pro-natal ability confers on West African women social status and power in society. Having children does not only assert one's womanhood, but confers power and authority in most African societies. Florence Dolphyne asserts that the respect and status that motherhood confers on an African woman is greater than that conferred by marriage per se (16). In most West African societies, a childless woman cannot join certain secret societies and lacks the authority to speak out against patriarchal ideology. Although the subject of childlessness is not my central concern here, one cannot resist questioning existing models for womanhood. Many West African writers such as Flora Nwapa in *Efuru*, Emecheta in *Joys of Motherhood*, and Aidoo in *The Dilemma of the Ghost* have questioned certain extremes that women will go in order to have children. Although some women fail to have children like Anowa who commits suicide in *Anowa*, Aidoo is making the point that a woman can still reinvent herself in other ways and achieve empowerment. Although motherhood confers power that power must be used in positive ways towards self-definition. African feminists call on African women to engage in a balancing act by combining their pro-natal ability and power to conquer oppression and inequalities in society. Thus the struggle for African women's empowerment must always be linked to motherhood and mothering, which are intricate components to women's identity and self-definition.

African constructions of womanhood and motherhood differ radically from those of the industrialized Western world. Western feminists might question that African women take their reproductive roles seriously, celebrate their ability to give birth, and refuse to subordinate their biological role to other roles within society. African feminists see motherhood and childbearing as the strength of African women. Catherine Acholonu in *Motherism* radically rejects some white Western feminists' anti-mother, anti-child, and anti-nurturing rhetoric (85). Although there is a shift in theorizing motherhood, the attitude against motherhood has not quite changed in the West. In contrast, the pro-natal aspect of African feminism represents women's dignity and contribution to the cultural line as they ensure the family lineage. Still, African feminists insist that women should be able to define themselves beyond motherhood. Some African women are doing just that as their biological roles do not prevent them from taking on political and economic responsibilities that give them autonomy and independence from the imposed social constraints. In rural societies women who have the responsibility to feed their children go out to the fields and engage in farming, while their educated counterparts in the cities take jobs to help provide for their families. Some African women effectively balance their dual roles as mothers and breadwinners, but their mothering and nurturing roles still remain primary in defining their identity. West African women writers as mothers (such as Emecheta, Diallo, and Aidoo) combine motherhood and literary creativity, which is an inclusive process that shows the fluidity between private and public spheres; they navigate in empowering ways their dual roles as mothers and writers, which redefine their subjectivities beyond a narrow social role.

Motherhood is intrinsically and intimately linked to every aspect of African women's life and defines their worldview. No matter the economic standing or position a woman holds in West Africa, childbearing and rearing still play an important part in defining her identity. Just like the women writers mentioned above, most African women see the path to empowerment as an inclusive process that must involve their role as mothers in the struggle for socio-economic, cultural and political independence. In *Woman Cross-Culturally,* Filomena Steady reiterates the importance of motherhood to African women:

> The importance of motherhood and the valuation of the childbearing capacity by African women is probably the most fundamental difference between the African woman and her Western counterpart in their common struggle to end discrimination against women. For the African women, the role of mother is often central and has intrinsic value. (29)

This preoccupation with motherhood is very central in most contemporary African women's writings. African writers present, among other things, the joys and/or pains of motherhood; the anguish of women who have trouble conceiving; the ridicule of barrenness and the agony of being denied motherhood. Therefore any discussion on African women's empowerment and means to achieve agency must be related to their pro-natal ability. One cannot take away motherhood and expect African women to feel empowered. Their power comes from motherhood and mothering, and the issue at stake is how they use that power to achieve greater things for themselves; and resist patriarchal control. The agency and resistance of African women is still evolving, but the empowering actions of some African women like Emecheta are noteworthy.

MOTHERHOOD AS AGENCY

Motherhood is a source of pride to parents, and in the Ibo society in Nigeria, it brings blessings to the family. Motherhood is intrinsically linked to assuring the family lineage, which represent the status and power mothers have in society. Emecheta in *Head Above Water* celebrates motherhood and mothering by alluding to the extraordinary mothers in her life: her mother and aunt. It is important to recognize how she uses the collective term "mothers" to refer both to her natural mother and aunt in an attempt to show the indistinguishable labeling of the act of mothering and motherhood in African communities. In most African societies, one's aunts are most often referred to as "mothers" because of the social mothering role they play. Therefore Emecheta celebrates the mothers in her life as they both ensure cultural continuity and are custodians of the tradition. They have the power to pass down tradition through storytelling and morality tales. Emecheta recalls the stories of her birth told by her aunt, "Big Mother," which inspired her creativity as a writer; she uses the story telling pattern of her "mothers" to recreate her extraordinary journey from victimhood to empowerment. Although Emecheta's "mothers" were powerful figures in traditional Igbo society, they were still culturally enslaved by patriarchal ideologies. Emecheta transcends the position of vulnerability her "mothers" experienced by recreating herself in empowering ways. She breaks the vicious circle of women's enslavement in her family by resisting patriarchal order and imagining a better life for herself and her five children (239). The shifting boundaries within marginalized spaces points to the generational shift from circumscribed spaces of victimhood to positions of relative power and agency that define the lives of West African women like Emecheta.

The narrating subject's determination to live a life far removed from the culturally constrained environment of Igbo society in *Head Above Water*, demonstrates enormous courage and self-definition in the early 1960s—a time when many of her "mothers" were trapped by patriarchal order and colonial hierarchal distribution of power that favored males. Although Emecheta was well-off with a job at the American Embassy in Lagos, her dreams of making a better life for herself and two children in the metropolis was never thwarted: She writes, "I was almost eighteen in 1962, the mother of two babies, Chiedu and Ik, both still in their nappies, when my dream finally came true" (26). Despite her in-laws attempt to dissuade her from moving to the metropolis (26), Emecheta was resilient and optimistic about a brighter future in England. Her extraordinary courage as a teenage mother moving to a strange world shows that not even motherhood could slow her down from achieving her dreams in the metropolis. Emecheta's success in England reconfigures motherhood from the long held traditional gender role of exclusivity and nurturing to one of creativity and productivity.

Emecheta was determined to reinvent herself beyond the role of motherhood, but was dismayed that England was not as friendly as she thought. Expecting the serenity and warmth of a Georgian world, she finds instead coldness, dirt, greyness, and a sense of death:

> I came to England in a plush first-class suite with a nurse for the children. I booked the best I could afford because I thought everybody lived like that in England. I thought people in England lived like they did in Jane Austen's novels ... England gave me a cold welcome.... It felt like walking into the inside of a grave. I could see nothing but masses of grey, filth, and more grey, yet something was telling me that it was too late now. (26-27)

Emecheta is shocked, but knows she has to survive or perish in England. In a dilemma, she says, "'I must make it here or perish.' And I was not going to allow myself to perish because if I did, who was going to look after the babies I'd brought this far?" (27). It becomes clear that Emecheta's desire to survive was not only for herself, but intrinsically linked to the well-being of her children. The collective plight of both mother and children define and shape the fight for agency in a system that oppresses them.

Motherhood and mothering become intrinsically "linked to socio-cultural, economic and political issues that shape the mothering context" (Collins 58). Interconnected structural systems of oppression such as racism, classism, gender, ethnicity and nationality all work against Emecheta and her family in the metropolis. Emecheta's educational background does not guarantee a smooth transition into the new system, and being black and a mother does not help her case. She laments that:

> ...we faced rejection after rejection. No respectable landlord wanted a black family. We realized that however well-educated we were, our colour which had hitherto regarded as natural was repulsive to others and posed a great problem. Our hosts in our new country simply refused to see beyond the surface of our skin. (29)

Emecheta has to negotiate the shifting structural categories of oppression in order to find a space and place for herself and her children. The struggle to survive in the new country is far more complicated for an immigrant like Emecheta who has to continuously negotiate the borders of marginality as she fights for agency. The struggle is constant but the resilience to succeed is the driving force behind her fight for empowerment. Finding herself in a constraining environment does not deter Emecheta's determination to succeed in the metropolis, and her mothering role becomes the driving force behind her tenacity.

Motherhood and mothering gives a West African woman like Emecheta a new sense of purpose in life. As an immigrant, Emecheta looks for opportunities in England not for her individual aggrandizement, but for the survival of her children because the well-being of her children is as important as any dreams of hers. This, in turn, shapes the decisions she makes about her life. Instead of following the normal path taken by African immigrants who work in English factories, Emecheta rejects this and opts for a librarianship. Pregnant with her third child, Emecheta is determined to get a better job that can allow her to move up the economic ladder, a goal her education helps her to achieve:

> Things were tough. I think Jake was conceived the very night I arrived in Britain, but I was successful in hiding it from a doctor who examined me before I was taken on as a member of staff at the North Finchley Library.... Our

neigbours and landlord could not take it at all. All the Nigerian women in the house worked at a shirt factory in Candem Town and they had taken the trouble to reserve a position for me there, but I refused because I knew I could get something better.... People were surprised that I was called for interviews at all, but what they did not know was that even in those days I arrived with ten 'O' levels and four 'A'-and all our papers were marked here in England. (28-29)

Her educational background allows her to penetrate the system and opens up possibilities for a better life for herself and family. Working at the library is an important step towards the search for space and economic status in a socially structured society.

Between her job at the library and the demands at home, Emecheta struggles to balance the act of mothering and working in the public sphere. The duality of motherhood and work reveal how Emcheta recreates herself in multiple ways to meet the responsibilities she has to shoulder. She is able to juggle mothering and work, at times relying on the support of other women in the neighborhood to babysit while she works at the British Museum (32). In most African societies (like Cameroon) communal mothering is not uncommon as other women provide care for peers' children or grandchildren while the natural mothers work in the public sphere or engage in long hours in the fields farming. Communal mothering reveals women's sisterhood, which is an aspect of African feminism where women rely on the support of each other to carry on whatever life throws at them. Such solidarity empowers women like Emecheta to dare to imagine something better for herself and family, and opens up possibilities for recreating herself in the metropolis. As a subject in transit, Emecheta has the ability to shift the boundaries of her marginality by reinventing herself, moving from librarianship to museum employee. Emecheta's fluidity reveals her desire to achieve economic status and social stability that will allow her to move from the margins to the center of society.

Since mothering is still exclusively a woman's domain in Africa, the responsibility for the well-being of the children rests on the mother. Like some African women, Emecheta shoulders the burden of raising her children without any assistance from her husband. Emecheta complains that, "Sylvester refused to go to work! He had been used to staying at home for too long, and regarded each day that he went to work as purgatorial" (31). Emecheta cannot force her husband to work to support the family, which points to a patriarchal ideology of power and manipulation that constrains the economic productivity of the family. She has to take up the economic and social burden of maintaining the family, or else, she and her children will "perish." With the entire burden of running her family resting on her shoulders, Emecheta seeks a new way of providing for her family by becoming a writer, which was a childhood dream of hers.

Contrary to many people's view, Emecheta was determined to be a successful writer. Nothing would stop her as she affirmatively sought to achieve her goal as this statement reveals: "Sometimes it is very good to meet people like Carole, Miss Humble and Sylvester. Such people were particularly good for me and my Chi, because one way to set my mind on achieving something was for another person to tell me that I could not do it. I would then put all my thoughts into it. I would pray for it and go out for it, in search of the miracle" (46). The opposition to Emecheta's career is wide: Carole, the social worker, thinks that writing novels cannot make Emecheta rich enough to buy a house; Miss Humble, her literature teacher in high school, believes that being a writer is a sin; and Sylvester, her husband, strongly thinks it is unachievable. Although at the start Emecheta's writing career had a few hitches with publishers, she never gave up, and her determination paid off as she became an internationally acclaimed writer. Carole Boyce Davies in "Private Selves and Public Spaces" underlines the riches Emecheta's determination to write brought to her:

> The act of autobiographical writing itself fulfills a range of personal requirements. It allowed her to make sense of painful experience, to articulate herself, to write herself, to deliberate on the position of women, of the poor, of African people, to support her children and herself, and above all to create. (123)

Emecheta's story embodies the collective experience and plight of most African women, yearning for empowerment. Writing not only empowers Emecheta, but also allows her to be economically independent, which is a very important step towards African women's empowerment. Emecheta's life writing therefore gestures towards that economic freedom, which many African women need in order to achieve agency and be empowered to take a better control of their lives without patriarchal domination.

Creativity and motherhood become intricately linked as Emecheta balances raising her children and finding time to write. This might sound unattainable but as Emecheta says: "I have to write because of them [children]" (60). Her children give her the drive and inspiration to pursue writing, which some Western critics who know the demands of child rearing might doubt. That is why Alice Walker is struck by Emecheta's dedication of *Second Class Citizens*, "To my dear children ... without whose sweet background noises this book would not have been written." Walker observes: "The notion that this is remotely possible causes a rethinking of traditional Western ideas about how art is produced. Our culture separates the duties of raising children from those of creative work" (qtd. in Okunlola-Bryce 203). Although the act of child rearing and writing might be mutually exclusive in the West, it is an inclusive act for West African women as exemplified by Emecheta's ability to combine mothering and writing.

Emecheta strategically plans her writing opportunities:

> As soon as they woke, I would be in the kitchen, occupied for the next four hours until everyone was dressed and out to play. I found that even with the noise of children coming in and out and banging doors, I could type.... So I worked out a plan. While my family slept I wrote the ideas, and when they were awake I typed them out. (60)

Her determination to write even with the children's noises paid when she produced her first novel, *The Bride Price*. Attaining such creative productivity even with all the odds against her, symbolizes her unrelenting determination to succeed and attain economic stability. Emecheta considers her novel her "brainchild," thereby correlating creative productivity with pro-natal productivity. The inclusivity of motherhood and creativity is shared by other African women writers such as Flora Nwapa, Nafffisatou Diallo, Fadumo Korn, and Wirie Dirie. Jane Bryce-Okunlola emphasizes that for some writers motherhood "is a metaphor for the creative process itself, and points to the source of their creativity in the communal story-telling tradition of their foremothers" (Okunlola-Bryce 201). Through the act of writing, Emecheta, like other African women writers, challenges patriarchal power over the written word. Writing becomes the exclusive uncolonized space that defines her identity and agency.

Although Emecheta finds agency as a writer, she is marginalized from patriarchal power and authority by those who do not view writing as a woman's domain. Her success as a writer is met with contempt from her husband who thinks that she lacks the intellect to be a writer, doubting her ability to write. Her effort is ruthlessly shattered by her husband who burns the novel on the pretext that it depicts their failed marriage and is a betrayal of tradition that shames their family as he is portrayed as a failed husband and father. Destroying Emecheta's "brain child" is a terrible act and parallel to killing an offspring. Since creating a work of art is like producing a baby, destroying it can be considered murder. Writing meant everything to Emecheta and the destruction of her manuscript was the last straw on the camel's back; she left her husband and found accommodation at another flat with her children. The oppressive nature of the institution of marriage puts her in a vulnerable position, but Emecheta fights for her life by refusing to subscribe to patriarchal ideology and moves forward with her life by getting an education and embarking on a writing career. Writing allowed her to recreate her experiences in the borderlands, but above all, to develop her subjectivity and agency in migrancy. Emecheta's positioning is shared by other African immigrant women who "redefine their roles to assert a measure of autonomy and independence from their husbands. They avail themselves of the opportunities that the new world offers" (Arthur 112). Emecheta's positionality in the metropolis therefore allowed her to break from confined patriarchal spaces by establishing herself as a writer; this, in turn, gives her the economic stability to raise her children as a lone parent.

Her path to independence, free from patriarchal power, is not an easy ride. There is still the continuous presence of her husband in her life. Although living apart, Sylvester felt he still had authority and power over her body and sexuality. Emecheta attests: "Sylvester found out where we lived and came to demand what he called his 'sexual rights' as a husband. I was virtually raped for Alice to be conceived, though, looking at her now, I'm glad it happened" (33). Emecheta turns an otherwise abusive act, rape, into something positive, the birth of her daughter. She is glad about the experience of motherhood, but rejects the institution of motherhood that gives patriarchy the authority and power over a woman's body and sexuality. The institution of motherhood under patriarchy puts women in a vulnerable position because they are victims of unplanned motherhood that goes unchecked or censored. Marital rape is not something that many African women talk about and the actions of many husbands go unchecked. Some West African women writers, like Aidoo in her novel *Changes,* has written about marital rape, which apparently does not have an African appellation. This might be the result of patriarchal control of dominant discourses that prohibits expressions betraying men's power. Although Emecheta did not do anything about her rape, she, like other West African women writers, protests against sexual inequality and patriarchal control of women's bodies. Her story is a shared collective experience of patriarchal sexual domination that has for so long been a taboo subject of discussion in most African communities. Speaking out is the first step towards the eradication of patriarchal control of women's bodies and sexualities.

Emecheta eventually cuts Sylvester out of her life. Having endured so much pain and humiliation in marriage, Emecheta finds the courage to send Sylvester out of her house with the following strong words:

Sylvester Nduka Onwordi, you have lost your second chance to show the world that you could be a real father and husband. Please go out of my life forever. Don't you ever come back. If you have anything to pay for the chil-

dren, pay it through the court. Don't you ever come near
me again. (91)

This is the only instance in *Head Above Water* where Emecheta
overtly confronts Sylvester so harshly. Emecheta, like many other
African women, does not challenge patriarchy overtly, and to take
such action against her husband proves the extent of Emecheta's desire for autonomy. Many African women, like Emecheta,
are oppressed in their status as wives. Their ability to mother is
constrained by patriarchal control, which makes a woman like
Emecheta to give up marriage because she considers it the source
of her anguish. Emecheta's separation from her husband is not
welcome news to her in-laws and other Nigerians in England who
believe in the traditional family structure with the man at the head.
Emecheta's action challenges established traditional and cultural
norms that are shunned by most Africans. Despite societal rejection
of her separation from her husband, Emecheta moves on in life by
building on the love of her children.

Emecheta sees her children as the source of strength and happiness that kept her grounded. Emecheta laments that although
society never prepares children for single parenthood (67), she
was determined to raise her children in the best way possible. In
court, Sylvester denied paternity in order to escape responsibility,
but that did not stop Emecheta from providing for her children to
the best of her ability. Emecheta has to negotiate her positionality
as a single parent by taking full responsibility of her life and those
of her children. Her children are the reason for her survival and
they give her the power to cope with adverse situations beyond
her control.

Motherhood becomes synonymous with power as it is the conceptual space in which African women find solace and peace from
stifling environments, characterized by traditional and patriarchal
constraints. Oyerónke Oyewumí (*African Women*) reiterates that
African women's role as mothers is a source of power and strength.
Motherhood therefore becomes the preferred and cherished form
of self-identification for many African women ("Family Bonds"
1096). African women define their subjectivity in relation to
their pro-natal ability; and West African women in particular,

celebrate motherhood and mothering, which is evident in most of the scholarship and literatures about West Africa (Newell, 2006 and Kolawole, 1997). For instance, Emecheta uses her pro-natal ability to live a fulfilled life despite societal misconceptions about single mothers. Although Emecheta faces difficulties as a single mother (like landlords refusing to sell a house to a single mother), she integrates her new role as immigrant and mother with her minority status in complex ways as a multi-dimensional subject resisting marginality. Emecheta's determination to assert herself in a constraining environment is remarkable and this attests to the narrating subject's ability to turn adverse situations into strength. Single motherhood does not deter Emecheta from accomplishing whatever she sets her mind to do in life. Contrary to popular belief, motherhood can allow a woman to reinvent herself in multiple ways, and to have a purposeful life knowing that the well-being of her children rests on her shoulders. Despite being negatively stigmatized as a single mother, Emecheta worked hard (she earned a degree in sociology, became a writer and bought a house) to become a successful single mother in London.

Combining motherhood and education, with a career might seem unattainable for an expatriated African woman. Emecheta's life was hectic, but she was able to balance her life successfully by maintaining a structured schedule: "I would be at home in the mornings to send the kids to school and then get myself ready and go down to college. I did not have lectures every day, thank the Lord, but on my free days I would not stay at home. I went to the college anyway and spent my time at the Senate House Library" (53). Studying and raising children simultaneously challenges traditional Igbo gender roles expectations that limit most women to the private sphere. Traditional gender roles for women are not only peculiar to Nigeria, but are also commonly experienced by African women in other regions on the continent. In most African societies, women do not stray far from their gender roles of nurturing and care-giving. Emecheta comes from an Igbo society that values a woman's worth most when she becomes a mother, so for Emecheta to try to balance that role by attending the University of London is clearly breaking traditional gender roles. As a mother of five children, Emecheta would normally be confined to the domestic sphere, but she recreates herself as someone who can balance her dual role of raising her children and getting an education. Juggling school and taking care of children is not an easy task, but Emecheta is up to the challenge. Emecheta successfully completes her sociology degree, but her achievement is not readily welcomed by some Nigerians in London who feel she has become westernized and does not represent their way of life. Emecheta is even rejected and physically abused by black youths in a Youth Club in London where she worked as a social worker (149). She becomes an outsider among her own community of blacks, doubly marginalized by the system and her own people, never fully belonging neither with the black community nor with the British society. She describes her disillusionment and her social limbo:

> I was not aware then that I stood for the very type of black image they felt emphasized their failures. They knew that blacks like me who could claim to have made it were a pain to the masses of blacks who could never make it. They also knew that my type of black suffered from a kind of false consciousness. We think that we have been successful in achieving equality with white middle-class intellectuals because we say to ourselves, have we not been to their universities, have we not gone through the same degree of socialization via the educational system? (133)

Emecheta soon realizes that although her education has brought her self-fulfillment, it nevertheless strained her relationship with other Africans and blacks in general. Emecheta is also conscious that gaining an education does not guarantee inclusion in the white middle class. She moves upward socially, but to a black middle class. This means that she is still oppressed under the British system, although she has moved beyond the poverty line in the black community. The hierarchal structure of society limits Emecheta's economic mobility, which affects the kind of life she wants to build for herself and family. Motherhood in this instance is constrained by structural inequalities in society that thwart the economic empowerment of a diasporan subject like Emecheta. Being pushed to the margins, Emecheta fights back by reconstructing her subjectivity not in fixed, but multiple ways. She shapes her subjectivity by focusing on the things that matter in her life: motherhood, family values, education, career, and economic stability. Emecheta manages to create a space for self and her family within the constraining environment.

Surmounting structural inequalities shows the ways in which Emecheta complicates the margin-center boundaries by positioning herself as a fluid and transitional subject, manipulating the borders in empowering ways. She moves from getting a sociology degree, when it was thought difficult by others, to writing novels, even though some thought this was unattainable, to buying a house when blacks faced racial discrimination in the housing sector. Buying a house in North London marks the peak of Emecheta's accomplishments and the house represents a sanctuary free from patriarchal culture, as well as a way for her to briefly escape the constraining borderlands characterized by race, class, gender, ethnicity, and nationality. She recreates her own space within societal boundaries, which allows her to achieve agency and self-definition. It is a space and place she can call "home," where her children and she could escape the scrutiny and marginalization of the outside world. This accomplishment did not please other Nigerian married women who thought that buying a house was not meant for single women. Emecheta therefore shies away from married Nigerian women in her community who believed that owning a home is the preserve of married couples. Emecheta rejects this traditional ideology that many African women have been socialized to believe: "As a child, I was brought up thinking that a happy home must be headed by a man , that we all had to make a home for him, not for ourselves, the women. A home without him…at the top is incomplete" (228). Emecheta reverses this patriarchal order by not only buying a home, but also becoming the head of the household. She acknowledges that marriage is lovely and sharing a home with a man is good as well, but if marriage does not work, one "should not condemn oneself" (228). Emecheta's accomplishments show that African mothers can accomplish whatever they want to without worrying about breaking traditional norms or customs. Her accomplishments exemplify how other African women, and mothers in particular, can live happier and more fulfilled lives if they were ready to defy tradition and work towards empowering themselves in various walks of life.

It might sound idealistic to suggest that Emecheta's upward economic mobility and stability in the metropolis means empowerment and a good life; even though she faces constant daily struggles to adjust to the ever hostile environment as an immigrant subject. But her tenacity to belong in the new community attests to her determination as a migrant mother. Although confronted by structural inequalities and patriarchal control, she never gives up her dream of creating a better life for herself and her family. Emecheta attests: "Living entirely off writing is a precarious existence and money is always short, but with careful management and planning I found I could keep my head and those of my family, through God's grace, above water" (229). For a West African woman writer like Emecheta, finding and expressing a sense of empowerment and location in the metropolis changes the dialogue of the diaspora from one of loss to a new configuration of hybridity that affects individual migratory subjects.

Emecheta's path to empowerment is inspiring and shows the possibilities for other African women to transform their lives beyond tradition and patriarchal culture. Her achievement of empowerment strategically progresses by moving from victimhood to subjecthood and power. Emecheta overcomes societal inequalities and patriarchal domination by recreating motherhood as a powerful source of strength and inspiration that drives her desire for self-definition and agency. Motherhood is still paramount in defining African women's subjectivity as it represents a comfort zone by which African women find power and the strength to carry on with what life throws at them. Becoming a mother is an achievement equated with attaining the full development of a complete person to which many African women aspire, and Emecheta pushes that feat further by connecting motherhood to other aspects of her life such as gaining an education, and becoming a writer. Seeing motherhood beyond the boundaries of the home is an important step towards African women's empowerment and agency.

Although motherhood can be empowering as exemplified by Emecheta's experience, it can also be a position of vulnerability for some African women. Emecheta's story exemplifies both sides of motherhood, but the experience of motherhood triumphs as she lives a fulfilling life with her children. Unlike Emecheta, not all women experience motherhood in empowering ways; women in diverse African communities still need to break free from the grip of patriarchy and the control of their bodies and sexualities that often leads to unplanned motherhood, forced marriages and marital abuse. Since many African women still value motherhood and mothering, they must resist repression and take control of their bodies and sexuality. Although children are not the only route to African women's happiness, having children remains an essential part of their complete fulfillment and agency. Valuing and controlling the path to that fulfillment and agency must be fashioned by women.

WORKS CITED

Acholonu, Catherine O. "Motherism: Afrocentric Alternative to Feminism." *Women in Environmental Development Series* 3. In Collaboration with the Nigerian Institute of International Affairs, 1995. Print

Aidoo, Ata Ama. *Changes: A Love Story.* New York: The Feminist Press, 1993. Print.

Aidoo, Ata Ama. *Dilemma of a Ghost and Anowa.* London: Longman, 1970. Print.

Arnfred, Signe ed. *Re-Thinking Sexualities in Africa.* Sweden: Almqvist and Wiksell Tryckeri, 2005.Print.

Bâ. Mariama. *So Long a Letter.* London: Heinemann, 1983. Print.

Collins Hill Patricia. " Shifting the Center." *Representations of Motherhood.* Eds. Donna Bassin, Margaret Honey, and Meryle Maher Kaplan. New Haven: Yale University Press, 1994. 56-74. Print.

Davies, Boyce Carole. "Private Selves and Public Spaces: Autobiography and the African Woman Writer." *Crisscrossing Boundaries in African Literature.* Eds. Kenneth Harrow et al. Washington, DC: Three Continent Press, 1991. 109-27. Print.

Davies, Boyce Carole. "Motherhood in the Works of Male and

Female Igbo Writers." *Ngambika: Studies of Women in African Literature*. Eds. Carole Boyce Davies and Anne Adams Graves. Trenton: African World Press, 1986. 241-56. Print.

Diallo, Nafissatou. *A Dakar Childhood*. Trans. Dorothy Blair. London: Longman, 1982. Print.

Dirie, Waris. *Desert Flower: The Extraordinary Journey of a Desert Nomad*. New York: Perennial, 2001. Print.

Dolphyne, Florence. *The Emancipation of Women: An African Perspective*. Accra: Ghana University Press, 1991. Print.

Egejuru, Phanuel. "The Paradox of Womenbeing and the Female Principle of Igbo Cosmology." *Nwanyibu: Womanbeing and African Literature*. Eds. Egejuru, Phanuel and Ketu Katrak. Trenton: African World Press, 1997. 11-20. Print.

Emecheta, Buchi. *Head Above Water*. Oxford: Heinemann, 1994. Print.

Emecheta, Buchi. *The Joys of Motherhood*. New York: George Braziller, 1979. Print.

Newell, Stephanie. *West African Literatures: Ways of Reading*. Oxford: Oxford University Press, 2006. Print.

Kolawole, Modupe. *Womanism and African Consciousness*. Trenton: Africa World Press, 1997. Print.

Korn, Fadumo. *Born In The Big Rains: A Memoir of Somalia and Survival*. New York: The Feminist Press, 2006. Print.

Nnaemeka, Obioma. "Imag(in)ing Knowledge, Power, and Subversion in the Margins." *The Politics of M(O)thering*. Ed. Obioma Nnaemeka. New York: Routledge, 1997. 1-25. Print.

Nwapa Flora. *Efuru*. London: Heinemann, 1979. Print.

Okunlola-Bryce Jane. "Motherhood as a Metaphor for Creativity in Three African Women's Novels." *Motherlands: Black Women's Writing From Africa, the Caribbean and South Asia*. Ed. Susheila Nasta. New Jersey: Rutgers University Press, 1992. 200-218. Print.

Oyerónke Oyewumí, ed. *African Women and Feminism: Reflecting on the Politics of Sisterhood*. Trenton: African World Press, 2003. Print.

Oyerónke Oyewumí. "Family Bonds / Conceptual Binds: African Notes on Feminist Epistemologies" *Signs* 25.4 (Summer 2000): 1093-1098. Print.

Rich, Adrienne. *Of Woman Born: Motherhood as Experience and Institution*. New York: Norton, 1986. Print.

Steady, Filomina, ed. *The Black Woman Cross-Culturally*. Cambridge: Schenkman, 1981. Print.

Musing Black Mothers:
Reflecting Black Mothers in Poetics and Literature

5.
Everybody's Mama Now

Gloria Naylor's *Mama Day* as Discourse on the Black Mother's Identity

RASHELLE SMITH SPEARS

IN 1903, W. E .B. DU BOIS explained in *The Souls of Black Folk* that black people in America had to face a sense of twoness because they were black in America. "One ever feels his twoness—an American a Negro; two souls, two thoughts, two unreconciled strivings; two warring ideals in one dark body, whose dogged strength alone keeps it from being torn asunder" (215). This double consciousness, as he named it, resulted in blacks being prevented in some way from clearly viewing themselves as they were, but instead seeing themselves through the eyes of someone else, namely through the eyes of white people in America. Because such a perspective was often inadequate, black people had to create separate identities, the self among their own people and the self among the public.

In Gloria Naylor's *Mama Day*, the "self" among the public has become the permanent identity for her lovers, George Andrews and Cocoa Day. Like so many black people in America, they have worn the mask so long that it has become their permanent features. As New Yorkers, George and Cocoa live their lives in a white world, aping white standards of behavior and experiencing a disconnect from their cultural heritage. For Naylor, however, it is important that these characters, which represent all African Americans, recognize that they must maintain their African identity while performing within a world that demands they assume an American (read: white) identity to be functional. The novel itself is a testament to this philosophy, claiming that African Americans must find a way to be just that—African and American. They must find a way to balance the demands of one identity that calls for an allegiance to community and heritage with the demands of the other which advocates for one's individuality. While her characters George and Cocoa are ideal illustrations of this philosophy, in fact, the ones scholars most often fail to consider, Miranda Day, the title character, is also an effective example of Naylor's argument. So often, critics overlook Miranda, or Mama Day, in their discussions of cultural identity and connection. I submit, however, that as the title character, she should be the prime character examined. Her struggle in creating a balance between the self created by the community and the self created by the individual stands as a mirror not only for the characters in the novel, but also African American women and African Americans as a whole.

In "'The Whole Picture' in Gloria Naylor's *Mama Day*," Susan Meisenhelder, writes that Naylor presents a love story that "deals with the issue of maintaining black cultural identity in the face of attempts by the white world to order, control, and define black people" (405). Meisenhelder, like Nagueyalti Warren, who claims that the story centers around George and Cocoa in its focus on the individual versus the community, is right in that Naylor is presenting an argument for the maintenance of the African cultural heritage in the face of assimilation efforts by the American mainstream. They are both also correct in their assertion of the primacy of George and Cocoa's relationship in the novel. These two individuals serve as effective illustrations of Naylor's point that African Americans need to find the balance between the world from which they came and the world in which they live. George, orphaned by his mother who was a prostitute and his father, her john, grows up in a state-run home for boys, insuring that he will have the values and beliefs of the system. His philosophies and behaviors are Western in focus and nature. For example, he is a serious football fan and his favorite football team is the Patriots, illustrating both a love of sports and a love of country; he is an engineer (which is a logic-based profession); and he dates a white woman, which is meant to further indicate his disconnect from his own heritage and culture.

Cocoa, on the other hand, is almost completely antithetical to George. Although she, too, is orphaned by a deceased mother, and a wayward father, she grows up in a female-centered environment, acknowledges the spirit world, and marginally understands the importance of familial connection.

Their marriage, then, represents the joining of these two worlds. During their courtship, George helps Cocoa navigate more successfully in American society. He helps her gain employment, and he shows her the network of communities within New York City, for instance. He also helps her reconnect with herself. He says to Cocoa, "But it was a fact that when you said my name, you became yourself" (33). By bringing George to Willow Springs, the African-esque hometown of Cocoa, she introduces him to a part of himself and his African heritage that he was never able to know. Through marriage, these two individuals, who represent two different worlds, become one and illustrate what should happen when the African American successfully blends the two halves of his/her identity.

George and Cocoa are not the only ones to exemplify this point, however. Mama Day functions as an illustration of the psychological tightrope that black people must walk in the creation of their identity. Although she presents a confident and wise face to the people of her community, as readers we are made privy to her moments of vulnerability and indecision. These moments function to reveal her as more than a pillar of strength—which can be distancing and dehumanizing—but as a woman full of humanity. Readers are allowed to witness the sacrifices and hardships that go in to creating not just Mama Day, but Miranda as well.

Naylor presents to us the pull of the individual in the character of Miranda. We see her as a child, a young woman, and even as an older woman who is not always sure of her path. Each of these periods in her life shapes her into the woman whom George comments as seeing as "just a little old lady." She is a little black woman who is neither powerful nor formidable. Instead, she is a girl whose mother has emotionally abandoned her at a young age. Her mother suffers the death and loss of one of her babies (Peace) and thus has an emotional breakdown and loses her inner peace. Because of this tragedy, Miranda, as the oldest, is not afforded the opportunity to be mothered although as a young girl she still needs and yearns for her parent. She inwardly cries for her mother: "But

I was your child, too" (Naylor 88). When her mother makes the individual choice to withdraw from her family, she leaves Miranda alone to fend for herself and her sister, creating an emotional longing within the child.

This longing has the potential of being assuaged when as a young woman she falls in love with a young man whom she cannot choose. He wants her to run away with him, but ever aware of her responsibilities, she tells him no. "How can I go with you? She asked him. One foot before the other, he told her; a voice dancing on the fading night wind" (Naylor 89). Readers see throughout the novel in the relationships of George and Cocoa, and other community members such as Junior Lee and Ruby, that Miranda has a keen understanding of love relationships and what they can inspire in the individual for better or worse. But Naylor only presents this brief moment in Miranda's life for readers to see her in relation to a romantic and sexual equal. Considering Naylor's claim in "Love and Sex in the Afro-American Novel" that love causes one to be vulnerable, readers can acknowledge this moment as one that illustrates that Miranda was once willing to be vulnerable. The moment resurfacing as a memory reveals its significance to her and highlights the strength she had at such a young age to make the choice of community over the individual.

Finally, Miranda is revealed as an older woman who recognizes that she cannot do everything by herself. Described by Cocoa as stubborn, she still does not narrow-mindedly insist that she act singularly in crisis situations. While she is powerful, Miranda does not take self-congratulatory stands or seeks to stand alone in the limelight. Although she has reached near-goddess status in the community, she understands her need for help from George when her Cocoa is sick. She knows that "He's a part of her" and in order to heal her, he must fight along with Miranda (Naylor 267). She proves herself to be a woman who loves and who is willing to fight, but recognizes her own limitations.

Although Miranda is the woman that George sees and that the reading audience is allowed to see fully, she also has an identity from the community as Mama Day. For the people of Willow Springs, she becomes a leader, facing outside forces (white lawmen and land developers); she is a doctor, healing the sick and delivering the community's babies; and finally, for the community, she is the legacy bearer, carrying the memory of the first foremother, the one who gave them the land and their freedom. This identity given to her by the community is created because of her birthright and because of their very real need for someone to help maintain their sense of self.

In "Gloria Naylor's *Mama Day*: Bridging Roots and Routes" Daphne Lamoth claims that representatives of the mainland pose a threat to the continuation of cultural memory on Willow Springs island (156). This continuity is endangered by the white land developers who will literally overtake the land if afforded the opportunity as well as by the values and beliefs of western culture that will subtly erase the culture when imposed by islanders who go to the mainland and come home. To this end, Lamoth asserts that island women thus become important for the transmission of these memories (156). Mama Day is perhaps the most significant memory bearer in this instance because she is a direct descendant of Sapphira Wade, the ancestral matriarch of Willow Springs. Although she, like the other citizens, cannot remember Sapphira's name, she carries the memories of Sapphira's legacy in her body, affirming what Lamoth claims when she writes: "[C]ultural memory is grounded in a collective history that is encoded on bodies that bear the physical and psychic scars of trauma. This memory is carried by black bodies as well as on the tongue through orality" (160). Sapphira Wade is the slave woman who refuses to be enslaved, who rebels against her oppressor by manipulating him, killing him and procuring land from him for all the slaves on the island. She is a symbol of resistance for the people, and Mama Day, as the daughter of the seventh son of the seventh son of Sapphira Wade, carries that legacy of resistance in her being.

She also bears the memory of the community's history. Born in the early part of the twentieth century and living into the twenty-first century, she has a wealth of historical knowledge, which enables her to assist in maintaining the community's traditions as well as maintain some level of perspective about them. During one Candle Walk (the island's response to Christmas), she contemplates how the older generation laments the younger one's erosion of the traditions.

But Miranda, who is known to be far more wise than wicked, says there's nothing to worry about.... It'll take generations, she says, for Willow Springs to stop doing it at all. And more generations again to stop talking about the time "when there used to be some kinda 18 & 23 going-on near December twenty-second." By then, she figures, it won't be the world as we know it no way—and so no need for the memory (Naylor 111).

During her childhood, her father relayed the practices of Candle Walk as performed in his day, and she not only remembers what her father told her about Candle Walk and some of what *his* father said about Candle Walk in his day, but she also understands and demonstrates the significance of memory to the community. It shapes the community's traditions and thus identity, revealing it as a changing body that is still attached in many affirming ways to its past.

Because memory is so integral to the identity of the people, Mama Day's role becomes that much more necessary. Carrying the memory of the woman no one knows by name means that the community is dependent on Mama Day for their very identity. They look to her to be the leader in their community; she is the living matriarch. When white developers come to the island to offer to buy the land to develop tourist attractions, island inhabitants say "We knew to send 'em straight over there to her [Mama Day] and Miss Abigail" (Naylor 6). The developers must go through Mama Day to be successful with the members of the community. Similarly, when one of their own comes back from the mainland to study the community's history and identity, they say if he really wanted to know who they were, he would have gone to talk to Mama Day.

It is clear that the community of Willow Springs sees her as a mother-figure, but her role as mother is even more personal. She is called "mama" although she has no children, but she is needed as a mother for her sister Abigail. Because of their mother's breakdown, she is not emotionally capable of mothering her two remaining daughters. Miranda remembers her childhood: "No time to be young. Little Mama. The cooking, the cleaning, the mending, the gardening for the woman who sat in the porch rocker twisting, twisting on pieces of thread.... Being there for mama and child. For sister and child" (Naylor 88). She goes on to contemplate, "Why, even Abigail called me Little Mama till she knew what it was to be one in her own right. Abigail's had three and I've had—Lord, can't count 'em—into the hundreds. *Everybody's mama now"* (89, emphasis added). Because there is a need for her to be the mother, she becomes one to her community, to her sister and even to her own mother.

Cocoa also needs a mother and is consequentially regarded as her child as well. While she is actually the granddaughter of Abigail, she is mothered by Mama Day. Cocoa says that together, Abigail and Mama Day made the perfect mother. Her grandmother would serve as a space for nurturing and comfort, but Mama Day would maintain order in Cocoa's life. Cocoa's need for a mother goes beyond the need for boundaries and nurturing. Cocoa is the last surviving link of Sapphira's legacy and must become the memory bearer.

Lamoth argues that Cocoa is reluctant to accept this responsibility because she does not accept the traditional role of women as mother and wife that is intrinsic to the island's customs. Lamoth's argument is flawed, however, in that Willow Springs is representative of the feminine and does not actually advocate for patriarchy. David Cowart declares that Naylor's book implies "that humanity will achieve its redemption only by restoring the proper mythic/religious relations between the sexes. The larger vision here involves recognizing and re-embracing a mother-deity displaced, in remote antiquity, by a host of unhealthy patriarchal alternatives." His argument as well assumes that some hierarchy is being asserted, in this instance with the woman as leader. I argue, however, that while yes, women are wives and mothers, Mama Day, the community's leader who sets the tone for the group, believes in the equality of women and thus an equality between the sexes. She is most impressed by George's assertion that Cocoa has all that he has. Mama Day explains that this "means sharing. If he got a nickel, she's got a part in it" (Naylor 136). To Mama Day, relationships are designed to be equal; there must be a sharing of the minds, not a hierarchy. And so Cocoa, knowing the tenor of the island as set by Mama Day, would not assume that the island's traditions are patriarchal. I submit that Cocoa is reluctant to accept her position as memory bearer because she has spent too much time on the mainland in a sterile world that does not encourage her to nurture her second sight nor her African way of knowing/ seeing the world.

Ironically, it is this time spent in the Western world that makes Cocoa the best candidate to carry on Sapphira's legacy. Lamoth is correct in claiming that Cocoa is "best able to adapt to both environments" (163). Cocoa knows both worlds, the African and the Western and is a part of both. This position allows her to exemplify Naylor's underlying argument that the African American must learn to accept both parts of his/her identity. It is true, however, that Cocoa needs help in accepting this destiny. Mama Day is the one who has to help her.

Mama Day must become a bridge for Cocoa. When Cocoa is near death, she hopes to heal her with the help of Cocoa's connection to the Western world and her other half, George.

> He believes in himself … but she needs that belief buried in George. Of his own accord he has to *hand* it over to her. She needs his hand in hers … so she can connect it up with all the believing that had gone before. A single moment was all she asked, even a fingertip to touch hers here at the other place. So together they could be the bridge for Baby Girl to walk over. (Naylor 285)

Although George does not hand over his belief, he does enough that Mama Day is able to nurture Cocoa through her reluctance and come into her destiny as the memory bearer.

Cocoa's destiny and her reluctance in accepting it as well as Mama Day's role in shaping it are familiar ideas to black women in America. African American women must contend with the forces of double consciousness that require them to make choices between their individual identities and their communal selves. Western thought says that they must make choices that will benefit themselves: Should they disassociate with the controversial black person in the office or should they befriend and teach them? Should they sacrifice their careers to stay home and raise the children and nurture their husbands' aspirations or should they strive to become a star in their profession, sacrificing the needs of their family or even family at all? Margaret Walker, scholar and author of neo-slave narrative *Jubilee*, relays her experience of being a working wife and mother in "Black Women in Academia." She states that she suffered ignominies, humiliations and devaluation of her work. On several occasions she is publicly humiliated. After being "openly attacked" in one faculty meeting, she exclaims, "Had I been single, I would have quit that day, but I had three children and a husband, and I had just moved" (458). She illustrates the choice women must make between their own needs and those of their families, sometimes choosing to sacrifice and suffer indignities for the sake of the family. These choices are not limited to manifestations within the mainstream only; even within and from the black woman's community, the dilemma is posed for them. Frances Beale, in the 1970's argued that it was erroneous to believe that the black woman's role as wife and mother was just as sufficient as a more active role in the workforce. She claims in "Double Jeopardy: To be Black and Female" that those women "who feel that the most important thing that they can contribute to the black nation is children are doing themselves a great injustice" (149). She calls for women to join the workforce as scientists, teachers, and political scientists and wage the war for black liberation in this manner rather than "sitting at home reading bedtime stories" (149). In this instance, Beale is charging women to make a choice not only between family and self, but also between self and the community. While Beale was writing over thirty years ago, the pressure from all sides remains the same. The expectations are perhaps even greater now. Just as it does for Miranda, history makes certain demands and the needs of the community are great. Anna Julia Cooper writes that "Only the BLACK WOMAN can say when and where I enter in the quiet undisputed dignity of my womanhood, without violence or special patronage; then and there the whole Negro race enters with me" (31). Considering this claim, the black woman is compelled to acknowledge the need of the community in shaping her own identity. I am not arguing that she must choose the community to the exclusion of her own desires as Miranda does; rather, I am arguing that she must find a way to blend the demands of the individual with those of the community so that she can serve as a bridge for the next generation.

WORKS CITED

Beale, Frances. "Double Jeopardy: Being Black and Female." *Words of Fire: An Anthology of African-American Feminist Thought*. Ed. Beverly Guy-Sheftall. New York: The New Press, 1995. 146-155. Print.

Cooper, Anna Julia. *A Voice from the South*. Xenia, OH: The Aldine Printing House, 1892. Print.

Cowart, David. "Matriarchal Mythopoesis: Naylor's Mama Day." *Philological Quarterly* 77 (1998): 439-459. Web. November 30, 2012.

DuBois, W. E. B. *The Souls of Black Folk*. 1903. *Three Negro Classics*. New York: Avon Books, 1965. Print.

Lamoth, Daphne. Gloria Naylor's *Mama Day*: Bridging Roots and Routes." *African American Review* 39 (2005): 155-169. Print.

Meisenhelder, Susan. "'Whole Picture' in Gloria Naylor's *Mama Day*." *African American Review* 27 (1993): 405-419. Print.

Naylor, Gloria. *Mama Day*. New York: Vintage Contemporaries, 1988.

Naylor, Gloria. "Love and Sex in Afro-American Novel." The Yale Review 78 (1988): 19-31. Print.

Walker, Margaret. "Black Women in the Academy." *Words of Fire: An Anthology of African-American Feminist Thought*. Ed. Beverly Guy-Sheftall. New York: The New Press, 1995. 454-460. Print.

Warren, Nagueyalti. "Cocoa and George: A Love Dialectic." *Sage* 7 (Fall 1990): 19-24. Print.

6.
Re-Envisioning Black Motherhood

The Performance Poetics of
Gwendolyn Brooks and Lucille Clifton

CELESTE DOAKS

WHILE NOT ALL AMERICANS may share my sentiments, most black females are ecstatic to be living in the era of the First Lady of "black motherhood," Michelle Obama. While Mrs. Obama's entrance into the White house has positively affected America's perceptions of black motherhood, many negatively constructed, regurgitated images of black mothers and black women in general still exist. Crack whores, prostitutes, and overweight "mammies" have proliferated television screens, movie theaters—and thus the imaginations of Americans—for decades. While this essay does not have the time or space to list them all, some cinematic examples include Hattie McDaniel's famous mammy role in *Gone With the Wind*, Halle Berry's appearance as a crack whore in *Jungle Fever*, and Queen Latifah's seductive mammy role in *Bringin' Down the House*. These unfortunate visual images were all too frequently attached to black mothers and women in the past. These images elicited reactions of disgust, skepticism and curiosity. Americans have had few positive examples of black motherhood provided by the media, and until now, have never seen a black mother as the First Lady of the United States. With this new presidential family in the White House, Americans are being required to contemplate the black family, and more specifically, black motherhood more often. Likely at the forefront of Americans' dialogue, whether consciously or unconsciously, is a reexamination of these prevailing negative notions of black motherhood. Therefore, this is an ideal time to examine black motherhood, and especially how it performs in literary texts. Two of the best examples of progressive black motherhood represented in poetry hail from two equally iconic literary figures: Gwendolyn Brooks and Lucille Clifton.

These two black female writers share a number of intersections. Both writers wrote out of major American literary and socio-political movements. Clifton wrote out of the ever popular women's feminist/confessional movement of the 1970s and Brooks was heavily influenced by the end of the Harlem Renaissance, and on the periphery of the Black Arts movement. They each became Poet Laureate of their respective states and garnered numerous major literary awards, the most notable being Brooks's Pulitzer Prize in 1950 for *Annie Allen*. Perhaps two of the most pervasive commonalities they share include a love of poetry and also motherhood. Although Brooks had two children and Clifton bore six, the depth of their understanding of black motherhood is equally powerful. Both poets, in their performance of black motherhood, consistently found ways to challenge its ordinary constrictions, and continued to tackle daring and politically resistant territory for black mothers of the 1950s and '60s and forward. It is the aim of this essay to show how poems from both *Blessing of the Boats* by Lucille Clifton and *The Selected Poems of Gwendolyn Brooks* perform black motherhood in a progressive feminist way that constructs new paradigms challenging ordinary notions of what a black mother is and does.

But before delving into the specifics of black motherhood in these poets' work, the idea of performance must be examined. Performance, a term generally reserved for theater, film, opera, and musicals, can also be applied to texts. Texts are often read out loud, and poetry's beginnings as an oral tradition also hearken to this idea of performance. Therefore, if a poem is brought to life by the reader's delivery of the text, then the body of that text performs just like any other physical body can/would/does. While some critics may argue with the idea that a poetic performance text even exists, performance studies scholar Judith Butler says in *Bodies That Matter* that because terms such as race, gender, and sex have been defined and confined within oppressive structures of power "they ought to be repeated in directions that reverse and displace their originating aims" (123). Butler is speaking directly of how the subjugated have been narrowly categorized within the dominant system. She advocates that in order to face these -isms head on, the oppressed must confront these ideologies in ways that challenge and debunk the original intent. Both Clifton and Brooks reinforce this by the way they perform their ideas of black motherhood. Critics may say that if the ideas expressed in the poems' content could be factual, or based in autobiographical details, it could negate the fictionalized effect of the performance. However, whether a poem is truth or fiction does not mitigate its operation as a performance text. Therefore, I believe that Clifton and Brooks perform black motherhood in their texts *Blessing of the Boats* and *The Selected Poems of Gwendolyn Brooks*. This performance is one that struggles against restrictive and degrading notions of black motherhood and attempts to present new feminist and progressive ideologies.

Motherhood, and particularly black motherhood, is assuredly not an easy topic to address. Raising children is a joyous, painful, fulfilling and often nebulous undertaking. However, mothering while under the oppressive double layers of race and gender is another task in itself. But Clifton can still recognize and acknowledge all of the aforementioned, while pushing the ordinary boundaries of black motherhood. The challenges that race and gender bring to motherhood do not stop her from investigating, with un-flinching honesty, the hard truths of black motherhood. She does so in "what did she know, when did she know it." Here, Clifton tackles the issue of child abuse, and although she omits the question mark as punctuation here, readers know that the question is implied regarding what the mother knew, and when.

> why the little girl never smiled
> they are supposed to know everything
> our mothers what did she know
> when did she know it (Clifton 125)

Clifton has "written about the molestation in several of her poems and spoken of it in interviews" (Holladay 10). This may be the reason the performance of black motherhood here wants to attribute guilt to the mother, but has difficulty doing so. Finger-pointing is useless here. However, the "hard clench," "cold air," and "cold edges" at least connote some sense of disappointment in and lack of love for the father, and in the mother's response, or lack thereof. And while some readers may find the sentiment of this poem to be negative, I would disagree. The tone is rather curious about the mother's knowledge or ignorance of the abuse. This performance is non-traditional, especially considering it does not attribute guilt, or even address it, directly.

This performance of black motherhood may not be comfortable for many female (or male for that matter) readers, but Clifton does not evade hard-hitting issues that face black mothers. She always presents them from a feminist perspective that can be seen in her content and diction choices. One poem that is a prime example of her progressive black motherhood politics is "donor." Abortion is the topic of this poem, and the harsh realities of the situation are examined with an unflinching eye.

> i think of thirty years ago
> and the hangers I shoved inside
> hard trying not to have you.
> i think of the pills, the everything
> i gathered against your
> inconvenient bulge; and you (Clifton 17)

These two stanzas show the mother's desperation, her disappointment to bring another life into the world. The use of hangers can also be an indicator of the black mother's economic status. If the narrator of this poem were rich, she could simply head to the abortion clinic (if the actual pregnancy happened after 1973), or perhaps have a private doctor perform the procedure, but that isn't a choice here. Class clearly determines her options. Writer, poet, and feminist Audre Lorde says in *Words of Fire* that "poetry has been the major voice of poor, working-class, and coloured women" (286). And here we see the performance of black motherhood in this poem to be precisely an expression of this very statement. While readers have seen black mothers saddled with multiple children— one example being the character of Florida from the television sitcom *Good Times*—often they have not witnessed a black mother trying to get rid of a child. Feminist scholar Frances Beale feels that "Black women have the right and the responsibility to determine when it is in the interest of the struggle to have children or not to have them, and this right must not be relinquished to anyone" (152). Obviously Clifton's performance of black motherhood in this poem is in agreement with this statement. The second stanza exacerbates the despair by mentioning drugs and "the everything" the mother does to avoid this pregnancy. Even at the end of the poem, Clifton refuses to recline back into the traditional notions of black motherhood. The performance of motherhood here is not elated to be "with child" but rather disappointed that the child is still coming: "again I feel you/buckled in despite me" (Clifton 17). Clifton's black mother rejects typical notions of happiness ascribed to pregnancy and describes the seedling child like a "frown on an angel's brow" (17).

While the content of these poems is important, so is their diction. Diction is a craft choice that readers can examine to understand how these two poets perform black motherhood in a resistant, feminist way. Choosing to utilize the words "suppose" and "supposed" in "donor" and "what did she know, when did she know it," is daring because of their pseudo-conditional nature. The wording almost implies ambivalence or the weighing of both possibilities. In both of these poems the *what is*, or *what isn't*, isn't important, but rather the implication of such things makes them of interest. This word choice by Clifton shows her contemplating what "could" be, or what "could not" be. Clifton is resisting a simplistic assertion or affirmation. She is simply weighing her options, and by looking at both possibilities, readers are faced with a challenge—to avoid placing blame. This in itself is a new construction for black motherhood. Clifton is attempting not to reify typical reductive notions of black motherhood in her poetic performance. While linguists may disagree with my argument here about these two words, I still believe they were used deliberately at crucial turning points in both of these poems, used as a way to traverse new black motherhood feminist territory.

Of course, when the discussion of abortions arises, Brooks's "the mother" must also be considered. "the mother" is similar to Clifton's "donor" because it also does not necessarily paint a pleasant picture of black motherhood, but performs a truthful, challenging, and ultimately feminist perspective that must be addressed. This dramatic monologue poem gets at the heart of a black mother who, despite her decision, feels compassion for the children she never let live.

> It is just that you never giggled or planned or cried.
> Believe me, I loved you all.
> Believe me, I knew you, though faintly, and I loved, I
>   loved you
> All. (Brooks 5)

Some contemporary constructions of black motherhood may depict mothers who abort babies, then continue through life without any repercussions. However, Brooks starts off at the beginning of the poem telling us "Abortions will not let you forget" (4). And, as if this line isn't haunting enough, Brooks continues later in the poem stating how she heard her children's voices in the wind. Here the black mother recognizes the children in nature as a spiritual presence. This poem is a classic Brooks poem that illustrates, through razor sharp description, compassion for the mother and the children without the use of overtly sentimental language. It is yet another bold, mold-breaking poem from Brooks that overturns the typical constructions of black motherhood.

Brooks also is constantly covering new ground in her performance of black motherhood in her poems. In Brooks' *Selected Poems*, the ballad "Sadie and Maud" tells the story of two sisters who live completely different lives. However, the message about black motherhood is clear: Sadie is the wild girl who lives life to the fullest. Living life to the fullest includes her production of two babies out of wedlock. The other sister in the poem is Maud. This name is derived from the old German, meaning "powerful battler." This name may also conjure thoughts of Alfred Tennyson's poem "Maud," in which intellectual concerns and modernity are conflicting issues. While the focal point of this poem is about how to extract the most out of life, readers must also notice the performance of black motherhood in this compact, terse poem. Despite Sadie being an unwed mother of two, she has still managed to have "scraped life/With a fine-tooth comb" (Brooks 8). This line metaphorically represents Sadie extracting the most out of life—squeezing the sponge of life drip-dry. Later in the poem, her daughters mimic their mother and leave home, destined for a full life. Meanwhile, Maud does not fare so well.

> Maud, who went to college,
> Is a thin brown mouse.
> She is living all alone
> In this old house. (Brooks 9)

It is clear that Sadie, the mother, is the one who triumphed in life. She lived it to capacity and reaped the benefits. Meanwhile, her sister became a malnourished house pest. While this dichotomy exists, how does it forge new feminist territory for black motherhood?

"Sadie and Maud" refuses to hold Maud in higher esteem than Sadie, and thus makes a positive statement about unwed mothers. Here they are not villainized or denigrated, but actually shown in a positive, affirming manner. Feminist and scholar Frances Beale states in *Words of Fire*, "a woman who stays at home caring for children and the house often leads an extremely sterile existence" (147). And her opinion is characteristic of early feminism, it is too constraining. Brooks paints a more well-rounded feminist vision of a black mother. In this poem Brooks asserts that one can have children and still indulge in all the benefits life has to offer. In fact, by using Sadie with Maud as contrasting characters, it might be assumed that Brooks favors Sadie's lifestyle.

Among the examinations of these poetic characters, the black motherhood performance in "Big Bessie throws her son into the street" may not be a comfortable one for many black mothers, but it does show Brooks' commitment to creating a progressive feminist construction of black motherhood. Bessie is a mother who kicks her son out of her house, hoping he will find his own way. While children mature and eventually must move out of their parents' houses, Bessie is rushing hers out the door. Readers with traditional notions of black motherhood may find this act heartless or selfish, but Brooks paints it in a positive light:

At the root of the will, a wild inflammable stuff
New pioneer of days and ways, be gone.
Hunt out your own or make your own alone.
Go down the street. (Brooks 127)

Brooks' character Bessie is only interested in her son's independence. This is a progressive stance considering traditional black mothers are constructed as coddling or babying their children. That is not the case here. This is a prime example of how Brooks' characters, and perhaps Brooks herself, see motherhood differently. In *Gwendolyn Brooks: Poetry and the Heroic Voice*, Brooks scholar D.H. Melhem comments on Bessie's character, stating "in trying to be a good mother, ... she bravely faces her deficiencies" (151).

Also in Brooks' "Big Bessie" poem, yet again reinforcing a progressive performance of black motherhood, is the way in which the character refers to pregnancy. The line "Bright lameness from my beautiful disease" is directly referring to the carrying and birthing of her son. While the two contrasting terms of "lameness," and "bright" are presented on the same line, the idea of pregnancy and black motherhood here still has a positive tenor. Even if the son is lame, he also represents brightness, light, truth or hope for the future. When *Selected* was published in the 1960s, some women and men may have felt that pregnancy was a disease, but Brooks' character envisions it as a beautiful one.

The social-political climate during certain time periods is important, but so is the cultural climate. That said, when Clifton published "white lady" in 1991, cocaine was proliferating American streets of many urban areas. Through repetition and stark word usage, the performance of black motherhood in this poem is confrontational, blunt, and determined to find an answer. Clifton asks "what do we have to pay" and "what do we have to owe/to own our own at last" (61). And while this poem may not seem as overtly feminist as the others, it has those intentions, considering this performance mentions male children twice, and female children three times. This performance of black motherhood is concerned with the male children, but even more worried with the outcome of the female children. At the time when this was published few black female poets were examining the issues of drugs controlling the inner city. Therefore, this poem and its performance of black motherhood is resistant, political and ultimately feminist in that nature.

Both Brooks and Clifton show on-going concern for the state of black mothers through their writing and in their poetic careers. Specifically in *Selected Poems* and *Blessing the Boats*, both poets produce a performance of black motherhood that supersedes most one-dimensional, reductive constructions. These two acclaimed poets push forward progressive feminist epistemologies and expand the boundaries of what a black mother is, does, and wishes. Whether it's exposing the feelings of a black mother who had an abortion but still feels and hears her unborn children, or one who is worried that cocaine will devour her children, these two poets approach black motherhood head on without fear of past or modern day constructions. The yoke of race and gender do not stop either writer from delving into exciting, murky, woman-centered and ultimately ground-breaking territory.

This author has often seen Clifton speak of her children directly before a reading, while Brooks reveres her children so much that she dedicated all thirty-four poems in *Bronzeville Boys and Girls* to her two children, Henry Jr. and Nora. It is obvious that these two renowned poets care about the state of black mothers, including themselves, everywhere.

WORKS CITED OR CONSULTED

Beale, Frances. "Double Jeopardy: To Be Black and Female." *Words of Fires: An Anthology of African-American Feminist Thought*. Ed. Beverly Guy-Sheftall. NewYork: The New Press, 1995: 146-155. Print.

Brooks, Gwendolyn. *Selected Poems*. New York, Evanston, and London: Harper & Row, 1963. Print.

Butler, Judith. *Bodies That Matter: On the Discursive Limits of Sex*. New York: Routledge, 1993. Print.

Clifton, Lucille. *Blessing the Boats: New and Selected*. Rochester, NY: BOA Editions, 2000. Print.

Davis, Angela Y. *Blues Legacies and Black Feminism: Gertrude*

"Ma" Rainey, Bessie Smith, and Billie Holiday. New York: Vintage, 1998. Print.

Hilary, Holladay. *Wild Blessings: The Poetry of Lucille Clifton.* Baton Rouge: Louisiana State University Press, 2004. Print.

Lorde, Audre. *Sister Outsider: Essays and Speeches.* New York: Crossing Press, 1984. Print.

Melhem, D. H. *Gwendolyn Brooks: Poetry and the Heroic Voice.* Lexington: University Press of Kentucky, 1987. Print.

Mootry, Maria K., and Gary Smith, eds. *A Life Distilled: Gwendolyn Brooks, Her Poetry and Fiction.* Urbana and Chicago: University of Illinois Press, 1989. Print.

7.
Mothering, Mothers and the Historic Representations of Black Motherhood in Fiction

Barbara Chase-Riboud's *Sally Hemings*

LISA ELWOOD

S HE IS A PREGNANT sixteen-year-old, living in France, and, for the first time in her life, free. Knowing her position in life if she returns as a slave to the United States of America, she demands her freedom from her master in a most triumphant way; however, when the conversation ends, she is his forever. She, and the growing baby inside her, follow him back to his plantation in Virginia in a mixed state of love and fear. Her role as mother, even at this tender age, is what defines her legacy as presented in Barbara Chase-Riboud's novel, *Sally Hemings*. According to Chase-Riboud's fictional account of part our American legacy, Sally Hemings' reason for returning to a life of slavery is due to her role as mother to the children of one of our founding fathers, Thomas Jefferson.

In revisiting many alternate forms of documenting history, many writers have laid claim to narration by way of fiction as a legitimate form of expressing and critiquing historical representations of cultural attitudes. These more recent forms of understanding historical places have become much more valuable to feminist critics and historiographers regarding the notion of motherhood. The novel, *Sally Hemings*, can be used as a tool to deconstruct the history of motherhood in regards to slave women with their master lover. In that same moment, we can see how race is also constructed in 19th century Paris, France and Virginia. The ability of the writer to use historic facts and documents to write a story that can also represent cultural attitudes is extremely valuable. According to Jane Tompkins' *Sensational Designs: The Cultural*

Work of American Fiction 1790-1860, examples of fiction are "attempts to redefine the social order...novels and stories should be studied not because they manage to escape the limitations of their particular time and place, but because they offer powerful examples of the way a culture thinks about itself articulating and proposing solutions for the problems that shape a particular historical moment" (Tomkins, Intro, 1). Since there is a debate surrounding the truth of this famous relationship, examining how an African American woman writer chooses to represent the story in fictional form is important in the study of maternity and motherhood in history, specifically within black culture.

According to Adrienne Rich and Audre Lorde, universal categories like "womanhood" and "motherhood" lose their universality when focused on the lives and circumstances of women of color living under systems of oppression: ie, slavery. In Patricia Hill Collins' *Black Feminist Thought,* she argues that "Feminist work on motherhood from the 1970s and 1980s produced a limited critique of these views. Reflecting White, middle-class women's angles of vision, feminist analyses typically lacked an adequate race and class analysis" (174). She continues to show the lack of good, solid critiques regarding black motherhood from this emerging research on universal motherhood. Research for black motherhood is extremely limited in the sense of documentation, but available through other means: oral storytelling, family history, and anthropology. In this paper, I argue that using fiction to tell a story that is still debated today, Chase-Riboud has the opportunity to present the story in such a way that she can celebrate the history of Sally Hemings and the sacrifices she made for her children. Historically, many women subscribed to the ideals of motherhood and engaged in a privileged lifestyle with little or no thought of the other woman. According to African Feminist critic, Filomina Chioma Steady, the subordination of poor, black women is "vital to world order" since those same women hold up our "unequal and unjust planet" (4). Even today, this continues when we review history and lay claim to those who count in historical texts and ignore those who do not count. In this novel, what we know about historical events and people are challenged; the black female characters are agents of their own lives, which contradicts assumptions of race and gender. Barbara Chase-Riboud does not just represent one woman's story, but she offers surrounding circumstances that help to explore Heming's means of survival as an agent of her own life and what that entails for her children and her children's children.

Motherhood becomes Sally Hemings means of survival within the institution of slavery as presented in this novel. This analysis offers up a positive perspective on a long awaited woman's issue. With an African Feminist lens, this paper will seek to analyze the literary representation of one of the oldest American families in our nation's short history. For so long, the Hemings have been ignored and almost forgotten in American political history. Barbara Chase-Riboud uses the fictional form to offer her version of an extremely controversial relationship in our American History. In this narrative, we learn about a real-life slave and how she may have used her position to not only survive but become empowered. I connect the African roots of this historical woman as represented in Chase-Riboud's novel. I also point out how the protagonist's story and the novel, in general, "draws on features in traditional tribal societies" (Steady 5). These features include power in female reproductive lives, executive positions within the tribe (Queen Mother), and a different view of women's status within the community. African women served in these powerful roles for centuries as tribal women (Steady 6-7). This novel places Hemings in that position as the mistress of Monticello. These characteristics play out in this novel by way of Elizabeth Hemings, Sally Hemings, and Thomas Jefferson among others. In the end, the Hemings character is self-reliant and believes she does own herself and her children as she expresses when "given" her freedom:

> Martha, I have no thanks to give. You cannot free me. Even he could not free me. He couldn't free me living, he couldn't free me dying, and he can't free me dead. He did what he had to do, as have you and I. I am an old woman, Martha, worth fifty dollars, and you are as worthless. Our lives havn't been all that much different, and death has us both by the hair. Can we not at least explain ourselves to the other before it's too late? (Chase-Riboud 350)

Sally Hemings' view of her status as woman is equal to Martha Jefferson, Thomas Jefferson's oldest daughter. They have both been mothers, they have both lost husbands, and they have both been devoted to the same man for over 35 years. Her status on the plantation that was being sold from under them was the same as the slave woman standing next to her. Martha and Sally remain enslaved in their own ways: Martha is forced to auction most of her father's possessions to pay the debt he left behind, and Sally becomes part of the slave auction at a mere $50 value. Chase-Riboud empowers a woman without power during a time when that power could have killed her or even worse, her children and all future generations (Gordon-Reed).

In the novel, Chase-Riboud begins her story with Sally's mother, Elizabeth Hemings. Elizabeth Hemings blames herself as the mother of Sally and the example she set with her master, John Wayles. Her own love story a tragedy: the Hemings name was a white man's name, but a white man who loved and wanted to buy Elizabeth and her African mother, whom he loved. Thus, begins Chase-Riboud's fictional legacy of the Hemings' women loving white men. Unfortunately, Master Wayles refuses to sell. Capt. Hemings tries to plead and threaten, and then steal them both, but Wayles wins in the end as the "ship sailed" without mother and child. Elizabeth's mother keeps trying to runaway to her white lover, but upon her return would be beaten for her attempt until finally Master Wayles brands her with the letter 'R' for runaway on her breast. She never tries to run away again. She is branded for life. Thus, her daughter's fate as mistress/concubine to a white master, is sealed as is her daughter's daughter. Elizabeth Hemings soon becomes the concubine to Master Wayles, raising her own children with that same storyline. The character, Elizabeth, even tries to explain it:

> They had all lived their lives according to the rules: The rules of master and slave, man and woman, husband and wife, lover and mistress.... She knew these two would mourn him [Thomas Jefferson] when his time came, more than they would ever mourn her, and could she blame them? They had been birth'd and trained for that. She herself had

trained her own daughter, her favorite child, to the triple bondage of slave, woman, and concubine, as one trains a blooded horse to its rider, never questioning the rights of the rider. If she hadn't done that, her daughter would never have come home from Paris. (36)

This tradition between master and slave begins long before Sally is ever born, and continues long after the end of slavery. Chase-Riboud reminds us through her characters that people, regardless of the institution of slavery, are still human and that interaction and closeness does not get erased simply because of race and the law. Her fictional portrayal changes the way we view femaleness and blackness. In her book, *Thomas Jefferson and Sally Hemings: An American Controversy,* Annettte Gordon-Reed contends that the major tragedy of slavery is that it "ran counter to human nature and demanded that people try to suppress and deny the existence of feelings that are completely natural to human beings" (166). With this American story, the black woman becomes one who is desired and wanted rather than the black jezebel/mammy images we have in our history books. Looking at historical interpretations of women's lives helps us to understand how we are and what we stand for as women today. In her article "Re-framing the National Family: Race Mixing and Re-telling American History," Catherine Squires argues that "Acknowledging hidden Black relatives can open the door to integrating and re-examining competing discourses of race, history, and American identity" (44). It is important for writers like Chase-Riboud to use fictional narrative to help assert that identity.

In changing one small piece of the story as Gordon-Reed presents it in her historical documentation, Chase-Riboud, in her fictional account, makes Elizabeth Hemings a Queen Mother. She makes the momentous decision to send Sally, "a child" (Chase-Riboud 68) to France. She is chosen to accompany 9-year-old Polly on the trip to Paris to see her father, Thomas Jefferson, the Minister to France. In fact, "there were some three hundred and sixty-four slaves she could pick from, at least half were female and grown" (68), so why send this "child"? Readers get a glimpse of the inner monologue of Sally's which revealed the sheer surprise and delight of the fourteen-year old, Sally, in joining little Polly on this particular adventure. At the time, Elizabeth Hemings takes over and announces that "Sally will go. She'll have James to look out for her" (67). Elizabeth saw this as her way of mothering her children to freedom. Her mother knew James Hemings was there, and since slavery was illegal on French soil, they would have each other to walk way to freedom. This assertion makes Elizabeth Hemings the Queen Mother. Knowing her own history, Elizabeth Hemings tries to alter the fate of her two children. In this depiction of how Sally Hemings ends up in Paris, France, Chase-Riboud offers readers a version of the Queen Mother deciding the fate of her children, which is historically empowering.

Barabara Chase-Riboud takes on Annette Gordon-Reed's argument about Sally being with Thomas Jefferson to "secure a future for her children" when she begins her love story between these two people in Paris, which is where Thomas Jefferson was residing as a minister to France. Immediately, the shocking attraction Jefferson has for his young slave is portrayed. She is the half sister of his beloved Martha and looked so much like her that Chase-Riboud even has him call Sally by his wife's name in their first moments together (106). At times, the language that Barbara Chase-Riboud uses suggests a few things: Sally is another possession or even a creation of Jefferson's (which in the beginning is all he may have wanted), but, for Sally, it was wanted, desired, and welcomed when he finally came to her. In chapter 15, readers glimpse the perspective of Thomas Jefferson's: he uses phrases like "the girl," "his slave," "the sleeping slave" (116-117). This type of language used to describe her is about ownership. Chase-Riboud reinforces this concept in her character, James, who tells Sally, repeatedly that she is just another one of his possessions. She further intimates the difference in their life stations by her physical descriptions of them both: "His huge body" and "Her smallness" (123). He is a powerful white man in a patriarchal world that buys and sells human chattel; ironically, their relationship starts in a country where a revolution is starting. Yet, their physical positions are clear with Chase-Riboud's use of language. Earlier in the narrative, Sally refers to Jefferson as a "demigod" (113), and later on she writes, "He had formed and shaped her himself" (123). Now, he is God.

Not only does he own her physical body as a slave, but he owns her soul: "He possessed something he had created from beginning to end, without interference or objections or corrections. In a way, he had birthed her. As much as he had his daughter. He had created her in his own image of womanly perfection, this speck of dust, this handful of clay from Monticello" (123). This couldn't be clearer: Sally is a new item in his world, something new for him to collect and admire.

Barbara Chase-Riboud offers a glimpse at the patriarchal ideology instilled in Jefferson's actions. She romanticizes this moment, but gently reminds her readers that there is a power dynamic here: she is young, and he is older; she is his slave, and he is her master. On the other hand, Sally's inner dialogue describes their beginning like a love affair. Riboud's use of language in Sally's inner dialogue is important here because she is more aware of her situation than many would believe of a young slave girl. Sally, is not a slave in Paris, but she knows that Jefferson "will claim" her (103). She exclaims: "I felt around me an exploding flower, not just of passion, but of long deprivation, a hunger for things forbidden, for darkness and unreason, the passion of race against the death of the other I so resembled" (106). Yet, in that same moment, she also knows that "Nothing would have free [d]" her from him (107). This is the beginning of Sally's means of survival. Her notions of self, especially from living in Paris, have changed who she is. She knows she is his slave, but she believes he needs her, which becomes a source of power for her later in the text. Setting up the relationship like this gives Chase-Riboud a space to illustrate the power Sally attains throughout the narrative discourse.

In France, Hemings is treated like a "lady," not like the slave she is in Virginia. According to Ashraf H. A. Rushdy in "'I Write in Tongues': the Supplement of Voice in Barbara Chase-Riboud's *Sally Hemings*" the letters written to her from Jefferson take on a magical appeal that did not allow her to think logically as her brother, James, was begging her to do. How does one, at fifteen, refuse a man, who is Thomas Jefferson and her master, and one who addresses his letter to a slave as "Mademoiselle Sally Hemings?" As a slave girl at fifteen, what are Sally Hemings choices, but to acquiesce? Young Hemings is flattered by his referral of her as a true lady. There is a power dynamic that she does not recognize. She sees "her name had stood independent of herself or her will on the thick white paper" which renders her powerless to his will (Rushdy 123). In the novel, Riboud explores notions of love through the eyes of Sally, but always reminds them that it is different for Jefferson. In her book, *Reconstructing Womanhood*, Hazel Carby purports that womanhood ideologies do not permit black women to have privileges, even love. Marriage between the races is against the law, so even if they wanted to be together under God and law, they could not. According to Barbara Chase-Riboud's fictional account, Sally engages in a privilege she is not supposed to have. Later, in the novel, Elizabeth Hemings is discussing France with Sally (one of the rare times she is able to discuss her children's surprising return) when Sally admits that she "didn't remember who [she] was" (220). Finally, Sally understands that she may have had some illusions about her relationship with Jefferson since they were in a different place. But Chase-Riboud shows the complexity of the human condition when enslaved and in love with the "enemy."

The themes presented in this novel exude strength, hope, and power in the black woman: first as a young girl chosen for a major role, next as a lover of a very powerful man, and, finally, as the mother of one of our founding father's children. The thematic representation of this notion of motherhood is profound in this text. Her first pregnancy occurs in France. Chase-Riboud shows how her fear and adamant refusal to give birth to a "slave bastard" becomes her battle cry as she approaches her master to demand her freedom: "I will not give birth to a slave! I am free now. I will never birth slaves!" (142). Only in her present state as soon-to-be mother does she finally demand her freedom. Thomas Jefferson acknowledges that when he responds: "you are free, as free as your heart permits" (149). Immediately, her inner dialogue recounts her own feelings: "I was lost. My heart was his, and he knew it. I faltered, cornered and weak" (149). Chase-Riboud illustrates this fictional promise between our founding father and his slave, despite the fact that there is no written documentation in any letter, nor does he actually free any of his children while alive. In Chase-Riboud's representation, Sally is convinced her relationship is different and her angry mother just does not understand. Perhaps it is. Chase-Riboud uses the most romantic city in the world to consummate their love, which also happened to be far away from the slave state of Virginia. Chase-Riboud's methodology here lays bare the foundation of an interesting relationship between a very powerful man and an equally determined black woman. Chase-Riboud illustrates how Sally believes the father of her children will treat her and their children differently. He even promises Sally the same thing he promised his late wife: no white mistress. She will always have Monticello as her safe haven for her and her children.

In the novel, another theme that pervades the literary circle in black women's literature is the true womanhood ideal. Barbara Chase-Riboud plays on this ideal in her fiction as well. The most specific scene is when Sally Hemings refuses to nurse her daughter, Harriet, and Elizabeth Hemings is furious. Instead, she uses a wet nurse while she binds her breasts like the French women she knew and admired while in Paris. Sally is acting like a white woman who use the slave woman as wet nurse. As Claudia Tate explains, the true womanhood ideal consisted of "a formidable social construction of absolute purity, piety, domesticity, and gentle submissiveness that matrimony and subsequent motherhood enhanced" (25). Hemings is not privy to this lifestyle, especially the privilege of motherhood, even as the mistress to one of our founding fathers. Yet, Chase-Riboud mimics this ideal by allowing Sally Hemings the privilege of white motherhood, for a little while at least. Later in the novel, she is reminded of who she is. Martha Jefferson has a baby too and Sally, as the slave, is required to nurse Martha's baby. This single act reveals the true mistress on Monticello. Elizabeth and Sally try to dissuade Martha, but to no avail. She is required to nurse the child, and she does as she is told with tears. This is a way to remind readers that her role as Thomas Jefferson's intimate partner did not come without the shadows of slavery. Sally Hemings lived a life of constant double consciousness. She had power, unless a white woman was near her. Then that power was in question. However, the underlying strength that Sally and many slave women exerted is now believed to have been from their African Heritage. It is best described by Nicole

Willy in her essay on motherhood as seen in Harriet Wilson's and Harriet Jacobs' texts:

In order to understand Wilson and Jacobs's ability to survive and nurture through such traumatic conditions, we must first understand the source of their strength, which lies in their 'collective ancestral knowledge' and philosophies. Andrea Benton Rushing notes the strength of African American women should be appreciated despite slavery, not because of it, due to their African heritage: "our mothers were strong: families sold apart; men unable to discipline their children or protect their wives from brutal beatings and routine rape; women working cotton, rice and sugar cane" (122). These extremely inhuman circumstances called for a philosophy of life and reserves of strength that came from a foreign soil, and gender ideals that did not replicate the European notions of women who fared best within the comforts of home. (Willy 194)

Survival in her role as a mother is ironic here since Sally refuses that role to emulate the white woman ideal, and, yet, Chase-Riboud chose a white woman to take it from her. The strength that Willy mentions above is profound for so many black women who suffered under the oppression of their white lover's families. Despite their ability to move about the big house as they please and make grand decisions regarding the slave population and so on, these slave mistresses have limited power in the presence of a white woman. Barbara Chase-Riboud uses this scene to gently transition her readers to Sally's evolving sense of self.

While the white woman is not supportive of Sally Hemings choices in motherhood, neither is her own family. According to the novel's portrayal, James Hemings' notion of motherhood for the slave woman expresses his disdain for his sister's decision: "Women! Somebody cover you with dung and you wipe it off, wrap it up and stat crooning a lullaby over it" (244). Chase-Riboud reflects on the historical representation of reactions by black people who chose this lifestyle. According to Gordon-Reed, "His [James] character represents the clear-minded black person living in a time when an educated mind or, at least, an enlightened mind would have viewed her relationship with Jefferson" (Gordon-Reed 165). Gordon-Reed continues to explain how Sally is a traitor, "giving ultimate aid and comfort to the enemy" (165). Free blacks and most slaves would frown on this activity since so many viewed the master as the enemy. The only slaves who understand are the ones who have done the same in similar situations. Chase-Riboud uses James to represent this population of African American slaves and freed people because she is demonstrating her protagonist's world of resistance to many decisions she makes. This, too, leads up to the final evolving self that Sally becomes by the end of the novel.

Chase-Riboud shows Sally's troubles as she raises her white children, but her true source of power and ancestral strength comes at Jefferson's most troubled hour. Thomas Jefferson's reputation is at stake when James Callender publishes his findings in *The Recorder*. Even Thomas Jefferson is not immune to the media's attempt to oust a politician they do not like, nor agree with. Once the word is out, publically, about Sally Hemings, Sally's true power on the plantation begins. Chase-Riboud does not have her run away and hide from white scrutiny, rather Sally decides to "stand, when [she] ... had never stood before" (264). The novel stands strong as a love-struck Sally gives Jefferson her all. Chase-Riboud offers a space for her protagonist to show fortitude and faith in her choices in life. Next, she declares her name "forbidden" for any person to speak, black or white. She does "not exist anymore" (265). Her reaction to the article by James Callender shows the power this woman yields in our history. According to this novel's version of the story, she becomes non-existent—she disappears. Chase-Riboud is brilliant here. She shows how it is not history who has forgotten, but Sally who removes herself. Thus, the power remains hers!

The novel takes a serious turn when Chase-Riboud offers another true test of character in her version of Sally's life when her beloved turns on her. Thomas Jefferson denies his paternity toward her boys, and Sally Hemings realizes that he does not view *their* children as *his* children. Chase-Riboud exposes Sally's vulnerability here when he breaks her heart, but it quickly turns around and only makes her stand taller and become even more determined. She recalls "the explosion of insulted motherhood" that she felt at the time of this particular conversation (295). Motherhood changes women; we know that. This is no different for the character, Sally Hemings, nor the woman, Sally Hemings when pushed by outside forces, even the supposed love of her life. She realizes her status as a woman in antebellum America, despite her privileged status as slave mistress. Barbara Chase-Riboud, uses that sense of motherly desire to show her strength as a fighter, one who will assure her children's freedom, something Hemings' mother could never do. Sally assists her eldest, Thomas, in his "stroll" which was the supposed, agreed upon terms with Jefferson. His denial pushes her into action. While the novel still purports love between the two of them, Chase-Riboud seems to come full circle in who operates the relationship: "She owned him just as surely as he owned her, the only difference being that her possession of him was a gift while his was a theft" (319). Chase-Riboud offers insight on the changing face of love over time. While a slave, Sally has limited options. As his mistress she begins to see her power as a mother to slaves.

As a father to slaves, Chase-Riboud exposes Jefferson's privileged whiteness. He has the option of claiming them or watching them "stroll" right out of history. What does this say about white fatherhood, or parental acknowledgement when those children are the product of a master/slave relationship? Even more, later in the book, there is a story about a slave father, Fennel, who loses Ely, his four-year old son, and then his newborn daughter. He fights back! "Fennel had howled his grief into the night, within hearing distance of the Big House, howled like an animal, like the wild wolves that sometimes came to the slave cabin doors" (329). While Thomas Jefferson watches both Thomas and Beverley leave, there is very little reaction from the master on the losses of both of these children, yet the black, slave father endures a severe flogging because of his reaction in losing his two children. Sally Hemings knows this slave family and hears this terrible story. At this point in the novel, her attitude about Thomas Jefferson as the father of her children begins to change. Chase-Riboud insists on Sally's witnessing the reality of her situation, and she begins to take action to free her children. Her strength as a mother means she cannot stand by and watch as her children are kept in slavery. Instead, she pushes for their freedom. Chase-Riboud takes reader full circle as she weaves a tale about two historical people. Her presentation of Sally as protagonist illustrates the dichotomy of women enslaved and women empowered.

While fictional, the ability of novels to portray truth through their characters' actions brings readers to a broader understanding of women's place in history and how, re-evaluated, it could change woman's status, specifically black women. In her essay, "Breaking Canonical Chains: Gloria Naylor's *Linden Hills*," Tracey Thornton discusses "the difficulties for African Americans in carving out identities that do not rely on the Eurocentric paradigms ..." (113). Barbara Chase-Riboud illustrates this by writing her fictional account of the Hemings story. She takes the idea of black motherhood to position of authority: "This time I could not keep the pride out of my voice. Was I not the legatee of my half sister? I had love. Did I not have a room of my own? I had privacy. Did I have a white mistress? No, I did run this place. Had I not saved ten black men from certain death? I had power. How could my brother speak of saving myself. I had no need to" (245). Sally Hemings, near the end of her story, is the Queen Mother. She runs the plantation, she takes care of Jefferson, and she has the keys to the main house. She does sees herself as more than a slave. She is a mother.

So, does ancestry reflect personal achievement and drive or ambition? "I think that if you grow up with the belief that you are a descendant of whomever you admire, then that will have shaped your cultural heritage, your attitudes, and many other things about your life..." (Foster qtd in Lanier 51-52). Novels like this one can slowly start to change the way we think of Hemings as a slave mother and all slave mothers. Barbara Chase-Riboud uses this idea in writing the novel the way that she does. Honoring the black slave woman by making her an agent of her own life is the author's way of showing others that life does not happen, you do have some say, even as a slave woman from the 1800's. Not only did she have a say in her own fate, but the fate of her children as well. Black motherhood is re-invented in this fictional account: it is honored, empowered, and remembered. Sally Hemings and her children are extremely important in understanding American history because they are a part of our authentic American story.

Another way Chase-Riboud honors her memory is by not making Hemings a mere victim or even a continuous survivor, but a woman who saw what she wanted. As a mother to the Jefferson family line, the story of Sally Hemings reinvents the history of black motherhood. According to Gwendolyn Mae Henderson, author of "Speaking in Tongues: Dialogics, Dialectrics, and the Black Woman Writer's Literary Tradition," "The absence of female voices has allowed others to inscribe, or write, and ascribe to, or read, them." This can be undone by way of novels like *Sally Hemings* where a black woman writer is celebrating the life of a woman whom we know very little because *she* wanted it that way, not because documents were destroyed or because politicians were ashamed. Instead, this one black woman and mother in our history chose for it to be that way. This may be the part so many Jeffersonian experts have a problem with—Sally chose not to have her story about her life with Thomas Jefferson made public.

WORKS CITED

Arndt, Susan. *The Dynamics of African Feminism: Defining and Classifying African-Feminist Literatures*. Trans. Isabel Cole. Trenton, NJ: African World Press, 2002. Print.

Brodie, Fawn. *Thomas Jefferson: An Intimate History*. New York: W.W. Norton and Company, Inc., 1974. Print.

Carby, Hazel. *Reconstructing Womanhood: The Emergence of the Afro-American Woman Novelist*. New York: Oxford University Press, 1987. Print.

Chase-Riboud, Barbara. *Sally Hemings*. NewYork: St. Martin's Griffin, 1999. Print.

Collins, Patricia Hill. *Black Feminist Thought*. New York: Routledge, 2000. Print.

Gordon-Reed, Annette. *Thomas Jefferson and Sally Hemings: An American Controversy*. Charlottesville, VA: University Press of Virginia, 1997. Print.

Henderson, Mae Gwendolyn. "Speaking in Tongues: Dialogics, Dialectrics, and the Black Woman Writer's Literary Tradition." *Changing Our Own Words: Essays on Criticism, Theory, and Writing by Black Women*. Ed. Cheryl A. Wall. New Brunswick: Rutgers University Press, 1989. 16-37. Print.

Lanier, Shannon, and Jane Feldman. *Jefferson's Children: The*

Story of One American Family. New York: Random House, 2000. Print.

Lorde, Audre. "Age, Race, Class, and Sex: Women Redefining Difference." *Literary Theory: An Anthology.* Eds. Julie Rivkin and Michael Ryan. Malden, MA: Blackwell Publishers, 1998. 630-636. Print.

Rich, Adrianne. "Notes Toward a Politics of Location." *Literary Theory: An Anthology.* Eds Julie Rivkin and Michael. Malden, MA: Blackwell Publishers, 1998. 637-649. Print.

Rushdy, Ashraf, H.A. "'I write in tongue': the supplement of voice in Barbara Chase-Riboud's Sally Hemings." *Contemporary Literature* 35.1 (Spring 1994): 100-135. Web. 10 Aug. 2011.

Steady, Filomina Chioma. "African Feminism: A Worldwide Perspective." *Women in Africa and the African Diaspora.* Eds. Rosalyn Terborg-Penn, Sharon Harley, and Andrea Benton Rushing. Washington, DC: Howard University Press, 1987. 3-22. Print.

Squires, Catherine. "Re-framing the National Family: Race Mixing and Re-telling American History." *The Black Scholar* 39.3-4 (Sept. 2009): 41-50. Web. 10 Aug. 2011.

Tate, Claudia. "Allegories of Black Female Desire; or, Rereading Nineteenth-Century Sentimental Narratives of Black Female Authority." *Changing Our Own Words: Essays on Criticism, Theory, and Writing by Black Women.* Ed. Cheryl Wall. New Brunswick: Rutgers University Press, 1989. 98-126. Print.

Thornton, Tracey. "Breaking Canonical Chains: Gloria Naylor's Linden Hills." *Postcolonial Perspectives on Women Writers from Africa, the Caribbean, and the U.S.* New Jersey: Africa World Press, Inc., 2003. 113-130. Print.

Tompkins, Jane. *Sensational Designs: The Cultural Work of American Fiction 1790-1860.* New York: Oxford University Press, 1985. Print.

Willey, Nicole L. "Mothering in Slavery: A Revision of African Feminist Principles." *Journal of the Association of Research on Mothering* 9.2 (2007): 191-207. Print.

Body and Soul:
Interpreting Black Motherhood in Reproduction and Religion

8.
Birthing Black Mothers

A Short History on How Race
Shapes Childbirth as a Rite of Passage

TYRALYNN FRAZIER

S HE WAS ON MEDICAID, and had not received prenatal care
before the birth of her daughter. Dim light surrounded us as
she spoke softly about what she considered important for
a healthy pregnancy. "Good morning. I notice that you did not
have prenatal care. You know this is dangerous for both you and
the baby." He then abruptly turned to address the intern who had
followed him into the room about tests that needed to be performed
on the baby. After about ten minutes, the doctor turned to me,
asking, "Oh, are you the social worker?" "No," I replied, "I am
just interviewing her for a study. Do you think maybe I should
step out of the room to give you both some privacy?" "Oh, yes,
of course," he replied, "This will only take a minute."

Birth is dangerous. Pregnancy is one of the leading causes of
death among women in the United States. According to the Division of Reproductive Health at the Centers for Disease Control
and Prevention, pregnancy-related mortality has increased from
7.2 maternal deaths per 100,000 live births, in 1987, to the current 17.3 maternal deaths per 100,000 live births, a statistic that
includes women of all races. Among Black women, pregnancy
related deaths are closer to 43 deaths per 100,000 live births.
Black women also have an increased risk of pre-term birth, still
birth, and neonatal morbidity when compared with White counterparts, even in the absence of other known risk factors such as
smoking, drinking, poverty etc. (Bryant et al.). What causes this
disparity? Current studies have found that increases in chronic
health conditions contributed significantly to this trend—condi-

tions such as Type 2 diabetes (Albrecht), chronic heart disease (Kuklina et al. "Hypertensive"), hypertension (Kuklina et al. "Hypertensive"), obesity and increased numbers of women entering pregnancy with morbidities and co-morbidities (Creanga) are over-represented in some Black communities. Compounding these disease factors are other reproductive health trends affecting all women in this country: increases in giving birth at an older age, fertility treatments resulting in twin births, and increase rates of C-sections. All of these statistical observations lead us to the understanding that conditions of reproductive health are situated within, and reflect, conditions of society. Regardless of race, these racial inequities in reproductive health necessarily reflect broader social inequities beyond the reproductive health trends impacting all women. Obstetricians are now calling for a greater inclusion and understanding of social factors contributing to such trends. It has taken the obstetrics community a long time to get to this point.

We have come a long way from the 600 maternal deaths per 100,000 observed a century ago (Loudon). This progression in reproductive health is spurred by a shift from a "business of being born," driven by what Irvin Loudon has described as unsafe "technologies" that often killed more women than they saved, to a medical practice overseen by more stringent medical standards that included advances in medical training, the advent of antibiotic usage, and more rigorous regulation on the technologies used on women. This shift of ethos in reproductive health practices coincided with growing tension between doctors and lay caretakers over who had the most authority in the domain of birth. This prioritization of safety led to very important improvements in reproductive health care, but it also elevated the authority of doctors above community-based workers. Rather than the historic definition of birth as an integrated part of a social context, this shifted the focus towards the technocratic orientation of the birth of a child at the expense of the mother. This new style of care was divested of many claims Black mothers professed as important. We will discuss the historical evolution of this process and, in doing so, try to better understand how to improve conditions of racial inequity within reproductive health.

One of the casualties of obstetrics care divestment from community was the *Granny Midwife* who provided a "spirit of recovery," detailed in Valerie Lee's book, *Granny Midwives and Black Women Writers*. Black women relied on Granny Midwives, during slavery and into the post-slavery era, as pillars of wisdom through the birthing process. They were "wise women who [stood] tall in their communities." Birth is not just the "re/production" of a child, but also the act of "re/producing" a mother, and in so doing transitioning a woman, physically and emotionally, into motherhood. These lay practitioners acted as guardian attendants who guided Black women through a pivotal transition. Entrenched in the philosophy of birth-attending as a spiritual gift, these "grand" (a positive meaning imposed on the negative connotations associated with "granny") women were honored by their communities, but, according to Lee, were deemed "manly," "dirty," "ignorant," and "superstitious" by the health care profession that preferred to disinfect the birthing process (Lee). Attendants, entrenched in the community fabric of Black lives, were supplanted in the name of technological advancement, a process with deep and intricate historical roots.

Hargraves effectively argues that by the 1930s, the American Medical Association (AMA) had successfully institutionalized and medicalized reproductive health care. This perspective emphasized treatment of the disease, not the treatment of the person, prioritizing physiology over life circumstances. In this work, Hargraves evaluated the claim-making process from the perspective of the medical profession, child welfare reformers consisting of charity and "benevolent" organizations, and neighborhood reform movements consisting of African-American women. The medical profession defined infant mortality as as a problem caused by physiological abnormalities of the mother. Child welfare reformers defined the cause of the problem as unhealthy social environments including unsanitary living conditions among America's immigrant population. Neighborhood reformers defined the cause of the problem as societal discrimination. "Indifference to their race's perceptions of what was needed in their communities, left them few choices but to save their own communities and care for the needs of people within the community. Emphasis was placed on developing and empowering the community to address their needs" (Hargraves 5). Black women's health has a long history of resistance to a more established system that does not value their concerns.

Two issues emerge within this discussion, one examines the context of a women's life in trying to understand both maternal and childbirth outcomes, while the other uses the context of the birthing process to understand the ritual transition into mother-hood. In the latter, birthing choices (such as using a midwife, and/ or having a doula present to advocate on behalf of the birthing mother) are not just about what women choose, but how women embody the knowledge that they have the freedom and agency of choice. The trajectory of women's reproductive health, from birth control to sterilization to abortion rights, has political resonance in the distribution of power through choice (Browner; Nelson). Browner has argued that structural factors "shape the climates and contexts within which women's reproductive activities are situated and take place" (773). Choice becomes interpreted as selfish rebellion. Even for women who feel ignored or uncared for by the obstetrics system, the message that resonates is one of restriction from freedom of choice within the very body the birthing mother inhabits.

Both the social context of birth and the ritual construction of birthing imply a community context in which the product of birth is much more than just a new baby. Throughout human history, this contextually engaged understanding of human birth has been essential to human survival. There is a biological relevance for this understanding within medical care because when an individual is most at risk for death or injury, and it is this social reality that can prove most protective against morbidity and mortality during reproduction for a number of different reasons (Trevathan). The events of human encephalization, or the increase in the complex-ity and relative size of the human brain, relative to the pelvic constraints of bipedalism, have resulted in a prolonged birth process for humans that requires help (Trevathan). Humans also have a prolonged juvenile period of development, compared with non-human primates, that also benefits from community help. In Sarah Blaffer Hrdy's *Mothers and Others*, she discusses the role of social context and "alloparenting" within human evolution.

Human social cooperation, a fundamental part of being human, is grounded in cooperative breeding where parenting responsibilities were spread throughout networks of friends and relatives. The classic model of the nuclear family was not, according to Hrdy, how our ancestors experienced parenthood. How did this transitional period into motherhood change from something that is inherently community-based and mother-centered to a process in which the mother disappears? The issue of choice is at the center of this evolution.

A BRIEF HISTORY OF CHOICE AND DISCOURSE

[D]iscourse is not simply that which translates struggles or systems of domination, but is the thing for which and by which there is struggle, discourse is the power which is to be seized. (Foucault 216)

Over the course of history, the centrality of the Black woman as a complex mix of influences integrating sexual decision-making with sexual freedom, reproductive responsibilities with reproductive rights, reproductive abilities with moral responsibility, and individual agency with federal control (Rosen) was devalued by those who controlled the discourse. The claim-makers who had the most sustained and influential voice in women's health were men in the medical community. The success of medical professionals in staking an early claim on defining the problems of reproductive health meant that other claims were either abdicated or marginalized.

This marginalization of ideas has a deep history tied to the evolution of the women's movement, women's health, and reproductive rights. Because of the America's racial history, Black women's bodies were seen as different whether through 1) the residual impact of the racist science of eugenics, 2) the sexist reproductive restrictions called for by men in the Black nationalist movements, 3) marginalization of their own claims on reproductive health, or 4) the White feminist criticisms of the sexist orientations of the civil rights movement. The complexities of reproductive health took on this "Black body" dimension where sex and reproduction in the context of Blackness were used to support other's claims without addressing the claims Black women themselves were calling for (Overbeck).

Early feminism focused on gender equity in legal contracts by promoting equality in property rights, and on political power through women's suffrage and the right to vote. After the passage of the Nineteenth Amendment to the United States Constitution (1919), which granted women the right to vote, feminism moved into the work place, and amidst the burgeoning post-WWII image of Rosie the Riveter, a new feminist voice emerged that some refer to as second wave feminism (Dicker).

Second-wave feminism brought the issues of sexuality, family, the workplace, reproductive rights, and gender inequities to the forefront. Between the 1960s and the 1980s several events marked the significance of this era in feminist evolution and women's health. The Administration's approval of oral contraception made "the pill" available in 1961 (hooks) and enabled women to have careers uninterrupted by unexpected pregnancy. Kennedy's Presidential Commission on the Status of Women, chaired by Eleanor Roosevelt (Goldstein), reflected women's broadening social engagement, and the more central organization of women in political action. Betty Friedan's *The Feminine Mystique* dispelled the media image of women depicted and marketed in popular media (*Father Knows Best, Leave it to Beaver*) (Cornell), stating that these portrayals were not a reflection of women's happiness but were rather degrading to women (Walters).

Around this time, women of color pushed for inclusion in the claim-making process of defining women's reproductive health. By the 1940s, the social processes of mobilization had changed, and the organizational base of African-American women shifted from decentralized neighborhood reform movements to more centralized and politically engaged organizations (Mathews-Gardner). As organizations such as the National Council of Negro Women (NCNW) moved towards centralized control (having a main office in Washington as opposed to only local representations), there was a shift in who engagement among Black women (Mathews-Gardner). It is possible that more middle-class and fewer lower-middle-class women were involved in the problem-framing process due to the times and money needed to be in or travel to a central location, but this is difficult to verify because these early records were not detailed.

At the same time, working-class Black women had declining membership in neighborhood clubs, becoming more engaged in Union activities that provided them with a space to get support for their demands of equality in the work place. This offered them a way of engaging in politics (Fehn). The general shift during this period is towards more centralization, more politically defined goals, and a decrease in the locally maintained organizational base. Class likely played a role in this shift because Union-based working women's organizations continued to be very locally driven, while organizations such as NCNW saw the need to be positioned in Washington to act on political opportunities to improve Black women's conditions quickly. By the 1960s, Black feminists, heavily involved in community-based "people's movements" such as the Black Nationalists and Black Panther movements, criticized the sexism embedded within claims that contraceptive control was a threat to the Black Power movement (Nelson).

All women benefited from the push for reproductive control, but the voice of Black women as claim-makers within the reproductive rights discourse was often lost, or went unrecognized by White feminists of the time (African American Women and Abortion). Frances Beal, organizer for the Student Nonviolence Coordinating Committee's (SNCC) Black Women's Liberation Committee (BWLC), called for a denouncement of "the sexism of Black Nationalist men and argued that Black women required voluntary fertility control" (Nelson 62), while also acknowledging that their experience with fertility control were dissimilar from that of White women. Women of color had to contend with the uncomfortable resonance of the relationship between the eugenic assertions of the early 1920s and its application to race, which defined sterilization not as a choice but, in some cases, an implicit obligation.

Eugenics were heavily criticized by many in the scientific community after World War II, but notable figures persisted in their defence of eugenics. In 1963, biologists and Nobel laureates Hermann Muller, Joshua Lederberg, and Francis Crick all spoke at a national conference strongly in favor of eugenics (Bashford and Levine). The association between eugenics and the racism that fueled racial violence (lynching and grave injustices enacted on Black men and women that were left unaddressed) created fear of efforts that promoted racial cleansing (Waldrep). This relationship between eugenic fears and reproductive control was not being addressed by White feminists. For example, sterilization was an important fertility control option for many advocates of feminism.

> In a letter appearing in the Boston Female Liberation Newsletter, a woman discussed her campaign to make sterilization available on demand. She declared that, as with abortion, 'Sterilization is a right that must not be denied to anyone desiring it, whether that person has ten children or none at all.' While her assertion made sense to women who wanted to end their capacity to reproduce, the letter-writer did not acknowledge the complexities of such a demand in the context in which some women were sterilized without their consent. (Nelson 74-75).

Black feminists argued that White feminists, while addressing working-class women's claim to birth control (Emma Goldmen and Margaret Sanger, for example), did not address the uncomfortable perception that feminists were not actively distancing, and distinguishing the call for reproductive freedoms from eugenics and population control rhetoric of the time (Nelson). Diversification and the inclusion of women and minorities into the medical establishment caused a distinct shift in the claim-making process, through the mid to late twentieth century. For example, Dr. Maritza Trias Rodriguez was sensitive to the concerns of minority women because of the health discrimination she witnessed firsthand in Puerto Rico (Wilcox). She was a pediatrician and an activist for the protection of women against forced sterilization. In the early 1970s, she organized a group of New York health care workers called the Committee to End Sterilization Abuse (CESA). CESA's continued pressure on the Department of Health and Human Services in New York pushed the department of health to establish a moratorium on sterilization for women under 21 years of age, or those unable to provide legal consent, and a 72-hour waiting period between the signing of consent and the procedure (Kluchin).

For poor women of color, reproductive health, choice, autonomy, and power were constrained by the reality that Medicaid paid 90 percent of the cost of sterilization procedures (Nelson); the medical community encouraged and supported these procedures (Solinger). A written statement that women would not lose benefits if they refused sterilization was mandated to address this in New York. Studies monitoring the compliance with this mandate by the American Civil Liberties Union (ACLU) and the Centers for Disease Control and Prevention in 1975 exposed widespread non-compliance with the guidelines (Solinger).

In response to this exposé, Dr. Rodriquez-Trias and the members of CESA were called to serve as an advisory committee to establish a new set of guidelines for public hospitals. In 1975, the committee required a 30-day wait period from signing a contract to having the procedure, along with a requirement to offer counseling services provided in the language the women spoke. And, the counseling could not be given by the doctors themselves (Nelson).

Even with these many successes, less fortunate and poorly educated women are still being denied the reproductive freedoms available to other women, and entitled to all. Dr. Rodriguez-Trias believes that although the organization of local groups has been effective in the sharing of information as well as in applying pressure to policy makers, only with raised consciousness, informed consent, and the existence and accessibility to real alternatives, can freedom of choice become a reality for all women.

Organizations fighting to amplify the voices of women of color did argue for the inclusion of sterilization issues into Roe versus Wade in 1973, but their voices got lost in the pro-life backlash. The broader reproductive health needs of minority and poor women were actually criticized as a distraction from the fight to maintain abortion rights. In 1977, Dr. Rodrigues-Trias became active with the Committee for Abortion Rights and Against Sterilization Abuse (CARASA). Many feminists within this group saw sterilization abuse as less urgent in the face of the Hyde Amendment (Nelson) that banned Medicaid coverage of abortion. Internal criticisms voiced by members of CARASA that focused on a "laundry-list" of demands, from safe work places to quality child-care, diluted the resources needed to protect contraceptive control (Nelson).

Such persistent pressure against contraceptive control has been damaging to the concerns of minority women because it created a battlefield mentality where issues of "pregnancy disability payments, control of the birthing process, a safe workplace, free, quality child-care, free medical care, and income equality" became secondary concerns due to persistent assault on the very basic issue of reproductive control.

Today, the concerns of minority women are still marginalized by continued threats against abortion rights and contraceptive control as well as the tensions produced by the forced allocation of resources. Because these claims originate from disparities that minority women experience with their local environments, sidelining such claims limits the choices minority (particularly poor minority) women have to find solutions to such problems as pregnancy disability payments, control of the birthing process, a safe workplace, free, quality child-care, free medical care, and income equality. This does not mean that these concerns have gone completely unaddressed. The Black Women's Health Imperative, Sistersong; Women of Color Reproductive Justice Collective, and those within the public health community (Hogue, Buehler, Strauss, and Smith; Schoenorf, Hogue, Kleinman, and Rowley; Liburd and Vinicor) have made declarations on racial bias and the unmet need to focus on social experiences within health care in general, and reproductive health care in particular. But, like rolling a boulder up hill, limitations in funding and marginalized interest have, until very recently, continued to threaten the inclusion of the claims that minority women have been pushing for within the reproductive health discourse. Black feminists have argued that:

> Part of the problem is that Black women have been and still are treated as 'invited guests' in the reproductive rights movement ... issues of access to abortion services, forced and coercive sterilization, reproductive tract infections (RTI's) and infant and maternal mortality and morbidity impact women of color, especially Black women, most severely. When Black women do come to the meeting, it is always a constant challenge to keep other reproductive health concerns on the table with the issue of abortion.

The majority of Black women support the right to choose but have difficulty with abortion always front and center. (Bond 2)

The seed planted in the early part of the twentieth century that marginalized the concerns of Black women, created a public/private split in which the private debates and concerns negotiated by Black women differed from the public conversations that seemed most accepted. The public/private interactions that women in general, and Black women in particular, have regarding their reproductive health, creates a public space within a private body, in which obstetrics care, policies, procedures, and regulations, take agency of choice away from Black bodies by focusing not on the claims they are professing as central to their health, but on the discourse that has risen in power.

We lack a contextualized application of our understanding of race at the level of obstetrics care. It has been observed for a while now that neighborhood levels of racial segregation are associated with giving birth to lower birth-weight children (Buka, Brennan, Rich-Edwards, Raudenbush, and Earls). Minority populations are more likely to live in environments that contribute to greater risk of being overweight or obese, and obesity increases the risk of pre-term birth, fetal death, gestational diabetes, Cesarean de-livery, and fetal growth restriction (Bryant, Worjoloh, Caughey, and Washington). Feelings of racial prejudice in a mother are as-sociated with low birth-weight babies (Collins), and these feelings influence a woman's trust in health care providers, which will in turn influence her future health care seeking behaviors (Dale et al.). Blackness as an object of inheritance, in this context, is not just defined by genes but also by the environments in which those genes are being expressed.

Saadde argues, in a commentary in *Obstetrics and Gynogology,* that obstetrics care has been highly focused on the outcomes of the baby by integrating well equipped NICUs into obstetrics facilities while giving little resources to the mothers whose own ill health likely contributed to the poor outcomes of the child. Furthermore, if many of these causal illnesses are chronic, then they are products of a lifetime of social influences that have gotten the body to that state (Link and Phelan). Void of the applied management of these contextual realities, poor Black women become distorted spaces defined by problems and not by experiences that can be addressed.

The doctor I witnessed, while conducting my research on pregnancy health experiences by race, turned to me after addressing the intern. Even more telling, he did so only to ask if I was with social services, implying that this poor Black mother's ability as a mother was in question before he even spoke to her. What was missing from this doctor/patient interaction began when the doctor immediately changed the atmosphere in the room by turning on the lights, disregarding his patient's comfort and preferences. He did not take the time to introduce himself to his patient, ask her name, or introduce her to the intern and explain the intern's role in the examination. Most importantly, rather than asking the mother why she had not received prenatal care, he immediately placed a judgment on the fact that she had not received such care. When I came back into the exam room, I took the time to ask this mother why she did not have prenatal care:

> *It was difficult in the beginning because I have three other kids, and I had to take the bus. I could not find anyone close who took Medicaid, and by the time I was able to go to someone, they said I was high risk so they would not take me as a patient.*

Turning the dim lighting up to full brightness, standing over the woman without addressing her on her level, and not waiting for the woman to respond to him after he had spoken to her, affectively removed the mother as human participant of the examination. Anthropologist Davis-Floyd has argued that American society has designed an obstetrical ritual where the medical system, defined by obstetricians, hospitals, and neonatal care providers, "symbolically demonstrates ownership of its product"—the healthy baby, and the mother is the machine through which that product is produced (Davis-Floyd and Sargent). Such orientations in the ritual production of a child takes agency away from the birthing mother, and makes the medical system the guardian of the birthing practice. I wondered, while talking with this mother, how did we get here?

Divergent agendas around the claim-making process were not always fueled by absolute disagreement among Black and White feminists. They were fueled by an urgency to defend against this ever constant presence of contestation, and the need to fight against forces threatening the reproductive freedoms of women through restrictions on abortion rights and contraceptive freedoms. This urgency has historically overshadowed the reproductive health needs that many women of color have had and continue to have. This coupled with a lack of access to community-based reproductive support for poor women of color (and really for all women) has left a void within obstetrics care.

Sitting in the hospital, watching how this mother was being treated by the obstetrician made me wonder how we might resolve the needs of women transitioning into motherhood, with the limitations that exist in our reproductive health care system. Community engagement and a broad spectrum of support have always been an essential part of being human, and pregnancy, birth and early child development have always been times when that need was heightened (Konner). Today, infant survival is markedly higher than any other time in history. Obstetrics care has played a key role in this, but this discussion is not about disregarding the gains that the medical community has made regarding women's reproductive health. It is about what has been lost or ignored in the process. In "Birth as a Rite of Passage," Davis-Floyd shows that many women have to go through a recovery process when they are treated dispassionately by the medical community.

Decentralizing women's private choices in pregnancy and birth are shaped by responses to public health experiences. Where to have a baby, how to approach prenatal care, and when and how major interventions are decided upon (such as C-sections) frame the contemporary dimensions of the reproductive rights discourse.

Detrimentally, Black women who are in the re/productive process of becoming mothers respond by teetering on a fulcrum between deference and rebellion. This is a fulcrum defined by agency. Deference and rebellion balance on the fulcrum of agency. When agency in motherhood is defined by the obstetrical care provider, and the pregnancy event becomes, as Davis-Floyd says, a "demonstration of ownership" of the process of producing a baby (Davis-Floyd and Sargent), then mothers in general, and Black mothers in particular, must either defer to this domineering culture or rebel against it. Rebellion can consist of preparing a defensive strategy when going into the hospital, delaying interactions with the hospital, or avoiding the prenatal obstetrics care altogether.

Significantly, 17.8 percent fewer Black women receive prenatal care in the first trimester of pregnancy than White women (58.4 percent compared with 76.2 percent), with reasons that include lack of education, lack of insurance coverage, ambivalence about pregnancy, and negative perceptions of health care providers (Bryant et al.). Black women who do not have prenatal care are more likely to have adverse pregnancy outcomes, and even with prenatal care, Black women dealing with asthma, connective tissue diseases, human immunodeficiency virus, genitourinary infections, and periodontal disease have worse pregnancy outcomes then White women (Bryant et al.). Mullings et al. has argued that, for Black women, limiting demeaning experiences within obstetrical medicine becomes a challenge that can limit prenatal care, lead to unintended and unplanned homebirth, or lead to emergency care (Mullings et al.), resulting in the very deference many women are trying to avoid.

For some Black women, rebellion can come as a form of self-empowerment. In the face of their knowledge of race and racism, and mixed messages of Black motherhood, many Black women claim identities that counter public messages by going to the Internet, forming groups, and finding midwives to help them reach the birth solutions that are right for them. But reclaiming empowered identities may render these women more susceptible to stress-induced negative health consequences when the stereotypes they are countering persist (Steele). Among poor Black women, these limitations can be compounded. Finances, transportation, childcare, and time constraints further limit the type of care they have access to, and this can also result in stalling going to the hospital or stalling care.

The mother I talked with gave birth to a healthy baby, but reproduction is situated within contexts that are shaped by multiple dimensions that extend beyond birth outcome. I wondered how the residue of this experience would influence her motherhood. Like so many human rituals from marriages to graduations, from religious rites of passage to simply sharing a meal on a daily basis, these are processes that define the meaning of our experiences. They are also fundamental instigators of how we define ourselves and connect with the individuals around us. Individuals whose knowledge, practical help and emotional support we need in order to survive. The structural inequities that impact race and class are conditions that exacerbate the depth of disconnect between the private spaces in which many of these rituals occur and public forces that impact what is possible within those private spaces. The social forces supporting inequity within race and class contexts are powerful because they often directly disrupt the possibilities for constructing support within these spaces. In addressing race and class inequities in reproductive health outcomes we must put more resources into understanding and addressing this contextual disconnect.

Supporting all women, and particularly Black women, does not require complex interventions. Integrating multiple services, from parenting support to mental health and high risk behavior interventions, into places like WIC clinics, having reproductive health centers integrated into community centers and near schools, and even just thinking about reproduction as a multidimensional process would go a long way towards supporting all women in this country. Just as the absence of these dimensions have had a disproportionality negative impact on the reproductive experience of Black motherhood, particularly poor Black motherhood, their inclusion would likely have a synergistically positive effect, into the modern era.

WORKS CITED

African American Women and Abortion. *Abortion Wars: A Half Century of Struggle, 1950-2000*. Ed. R. Solinger. Berkeley: University of California Press, 2001. 161-207. Print

Albrecht S. S., E. V. Kuklina, P. Bansil, et al. "Diabetes Trends among Delivery Hospitalizations in the United States, 1994–2004."

Diabetes Care 33.4 (2010): 768–773.

Bashford, A. and P. Levine, eds. *The Oxford Handbook of the History of Eugenics.* London: Oxford University Press. 2012. Print

Bond, T. "Barriers between Black Women and the Reproductive Rights Movement." *Political Environments* 8 (2001): 1-5. Print.

Browner C. H. "Situating Women's Reproductive Activities." *American Anthropologists* (2000): 773-788. Print

Bryant, A. S., A. Worjoloh, et al. "Racial/Ethnic Disparities in Obstetric Outcomes and Care: Prevalence and Determinants." *American Journal of Obstetrics and Gynecology* 202.4 (2010): 335-343. Print.

Buka, S. L., R. T. Brennan, J. W. Rich-Edwards, S. W. Raudenbush and F. Earls. "Neighborhood Support and the Birth Weight of Urban Infants." *American Journal of Epidemiology 157.1* (2002): 1-8. Print.

Collins, P. Hill. *Black Feminist Thought: Knowledge, Consciousness, and the Politics of Empowerment.* New York: Routledge, 2008. Print.

Cornell, D. *At the Heart of Freedom: Feminism, Sex, and Equality.* Princeton: Princeton University Press, 1998. Print.

Creanga, Andreea A., et al. "Pregnancy-related Mortality in the United States, 2006–2010." *Obstetrics and Gynecology* 125.1 (2015): 5-12.

Dale, H. E., B. J. Polivka, et al. "What Young African American Women Want in a Health Care Provider." *Qualitative Health Research* 20.11 (2010): 1484-1490. Print.

Davis-Floyd R. *Birth as an American Rite of Passage.* 2nd ed. Berkeley: University of California Press, 1992. Print.

Davis-Floyd R, and Sargent C, editors. *Childbirth and Authoritative Knowledge: Cross-Cultural Perspectives.* Berkeley: University of California Press. 1997. Print.

Dicker, R. *A History of U.S. Feminisms.* Berkeley: Seal Press, 2008. Print.

Fehn, B. "African-American Women and the Struggle for Equality in the Meatpacking Industry, 1940-1960." *Journal of Women's History* 10 (1998): 45-69. Print.

Foucault, M. "The Discourse on Langauge." *The Archaeology of Knowledge.* New York: Pantheon Books, 1972. 315-335. Print.

Goldstein, Mark L. "Blue-Collar Women and American Labor Unions." *Industrial and Labor Relations* (1970): 1.Print

Hargraves, M. A. *The Social Construction of Infant Mortality: From Grassroots to Medicalization.* Houston: University of Texas at Houston, 1992. Print.

Hogue, C. J., J. W. Buehler, L. T. Strauss and J. C. Smith. "Overview of the National Infant Mortality Surveillance (NIMS) Project-Design, Methods, Results." *Public Health Reports 102* (1987): 126-137. Print.

hooks, b. *Feminism Is for Everybody: Passionate Politics.* New York: South End Press, 2000. Print.

Hrdy, S. B. *Mothers and Others: The Evolutionary Origins of Mutual Understanding.* New York: The Belknap Press, 2011. Print.

Kluchin, R. *Fit to Be Tied: Sterilization and Reproductive Rights in America, 1950-1980.* New York: Rutgers University Press, 2011. Print.

Konner, M. *The Evolution of Childhood: Relationships, Emotion, Mind.* Boston: Harvard University Press, 2010. Print.

Kuklina E. V., C. Ayala and W. M. Callaghan. "Hypertensive Disorders and Severe Obstetric Morbidity in the United States: 1998-2006." *Obstetrics and Gynecology* 113.6 (2009): 1299-1306. Print.

Kuklina, E. V., and W. M. Callaghan. "Chronic Heart Disease and Severe Obstetric Morbidity Among Hospitalizations for Pregnancy in the USA: 1995–2006." *British Journal of Obstetrics and Gynecology* 118.3 (2011): 345-352. Print.

Lee, Valarie. *Granny Midwives and Black Women Writers.* New York: Routledge. 1996. Print.

Liburd, L. C. and F. Vinicor. "Rethinking Diabetes Prevention and Control in Racial and Ethnic Communities." *Journal of Public Health Management and Practice* 9 Supplement (2003): Suppl: S74-9. Print.

Link, Bruce G. and Jo Phelan. "Social Conditions as Fundamental Causes of Disease." Journal of Health and Social Behavior (1995): 80-94. Print.

Loudon, Irvin. *Death in Childbirth: An International Study of Maternal Care and Maternal Mortality 1800-1950.* Oxford: Clarendon Press, 1993. Print.

Mathews-Gardner, A. "The Postwar Black Women's Club Movement: the Intersection of Gender, Race, and American Political Development, 1940-1960." *Journal of Women, Politics and Policy* 31 (2010): 260-285. Print.

Mullings, L., A. Wali, D. McLean, J. Mitchell, S. Prince, D. Thomas and P. Tovar. "Qualitative Methodologies and Community Participation in Examining Reproductive Experiences: The Harlem Birth Right Project." *Maternal and Child Health Journal* 5.2 (2001): 85-93. Print.

Nelson J. *Women of Color and the Reproductive Rights Movement.* New York New York University Press, 2003. Print.

Overbeck, A. "Eugenics and the Discourse on Reproductive Rights of African American Women in the Twentieth Century." *Gender Studies of Science*, 2011. Web. Accessed: December 13, 2013.

Rosen, R. *The World Split Open: How the Modern Women's Movement Changed America.* New York: Penguin Books, 2006. Print.

Schoenorf , K. C., C. J. Hogue, J. C. Kleinman and D. Rowley. "Mortality Among Infants of Black as Compared with White College-Educated Parents. *New England Journal of Medicine* 326 (1992): 1522-26.

Sistersong: Women of Color Reproductive Justice Collective. March 1, 2014. Web. July 18, 2010.

Solinger R. *Pregnancy and Power: A Short History of Reproductive Politics in America.* New York: University Press. 2005. Print.

Steele, C. *Whistling Vivaldi and Other Clues to How Stereotypes Affect Us.* New York: W.W. Norton and Company, 2010. Print.

The Black Women's Health Imperative. (March 1, 2014. Web. July 18, 2010.

Trevathan W. *Evolutionary Obstetrics. Evolutionary Medicine.* New York: Oxford University Press, 1999. Print.

Waldrep, C., ed. *Lynching in America: A History in Documents.* New York: NYU Press. 2006. Print

Walters, M. *Feminism: A Very Short Introduction.* London: Oxford University Press, 2005. Print.

Wilcox, J. "The Face of Women's Health: Helen Rodriguez-Trias." *American Journal of Public Health* 92 (2002): 566-569. Print.

9.
Black Motherhood as a Metaphor of Christianity in Missionary Photography

EMILIE GANGNAT

WESTERN CHRISTIAN MISSIONS had a major role in the training of women in Africa during the nineteenth and twentieth centuries. Women are also important subjects of the iconography developed by missionary organizations in their various media (books, postcards, conferences, etc.). Motherhood is a particularly salient. Working to develop a Christian way of life in Africa, missionaries provide guidance to mothers regarding the values and practice of Christianity. But motherhood was also symbolically used to show the development of Christianity amongst the non-Christian populations. Connecting to some female figures of the Bible, missionaries presented motherhood as one of the elements that must be supported in order to spread Christianity. The missions took a motherly role toward the African people. Making themselves responsible for their education and their evangelization, missionaries considered themselves as mothers to the Africans and portrayed them as children faced with Western societies as parents.

From the particular example of the *Société des missions* évangéliques *de Paris* (Paris Evangelical Missionary Society or SMEP) and the photographs used by this Christian organization, this article will attempt to describe how motherhood could be used by Christian missionaries in their visual communication to present their activities and their status amongst the African people.

MISSIONARY WORK IN THE SERVICE OF AFRICAN MOTHERS

The *Société des missions* évangéliques *de Paris* was a protestant missionary organization founded in France in 1822. It sent its first missionaries to Lesotho, before developing other mission fields in different parts of Africa between 1880 and 1920, including (but not limited to) Northern Rhodesia (Zambia), Gabon and Cameroon. The female figures are present in the pictures that the SMEP disseminate in the nineteenth century. During this period, women are shown with men in images intended to mark the archaic and savage nature of African populations. They are also presented through their daily activities. In the nineteenth century, domestic chores and porting were two main aspects of the "image setting" of African women. In 1890, when they conducted their exploration for the SMEP in Gabon, pastors Urbain Teisserès and Elie Allégret typically present women occupied with the housework or the porting of wood or food. Seen from an exotic point of view and as belonging to primitive and wild populations, women are not shown with children in the late nineteenth century. The maternal aspect of female figures is usually set aside.

During the first half of the twentieth century, the SMEP continue to use representations of the domestic activities of women, but mostly in the area of the missionary stations. In Gabon, as in the Northern Rhodesia, the photographs of the SMEP show young women and girls attending classes in domestic science or doing domestic chores [Figure 1]. Women are also often shown with their children and their husbands in family photographs, which take up the visual codes of Western portraits.

In the 1910s, photographs of single women with children also appear in the various media of the SMEP. These shots of motherhood often present non-Christian women. In 1916, the newspaper À l'œuvre, published by Swiss committees which support the SMEP, published a photograph titled "Black Baby and white Baby" [Figure 2]. It shows a black woman, topless, looking at her baby that she carries on her hip. On the right, a white woman with her back to the reader looks at her baby she holds in her arms. Visually, the contrast between the two women is very pronounced: one front and one back, one black and one white, one naked, one dressed. It is the children who connect the two groups. They look at each other, suggesting a contact beyond cultural differences. This parallel is shown through the two babies because Africans and

Figure 1. Mrs Cadier, sewing lesson, 1913/1928, unknown photographer, Samkita (Gabon). Photographic print. Source: DEFAP

Figure 2. Black baby and white baby. Photograph published in *À l'œuvre, messager suisse de la mission de Paris*, November 1916, n°7, p. 59.

Europeans are considered at an equivalent stage of development during childhood (Gullestad). Children however, are not placed at the same height. They are in a position that requires the African to look up at the European, to suggest that the White baby keeps an authority over the Black baby. The Western reading direction, from left to right, also allows the image to be read as a metaphor of the Christian missions' goal: allow the Africans on the left to move to the Europeans on the right. So if this photograph shows two mothers, it also suggests an unequal relationship between the two women. With the black and white tones and the poses, the picture shows a contrast between "the pagan archaism" and the "Christian modernity."

Motherhood was an element on which many Christian organizations relied to evangelize the regions in which they work. The SMEP supported the education of women. As in the West at the same time, education of girls was separate from the boys. Photographs show an organization of educational missionary work based on gender: men and women receive different educations designed to give them a particular place in society. Girls and boys are most often photographed separately. If this separation appears natural in this context and this time, the portraits of girls and boys still show differences in the iconographic treatment of the groups, suggesting a different perspective focused on the group photographed, whether they are male or female. Girls and women are regularly photographed with a missionary's wife or a female missionary who holds the position of teacher. Children of missionaries also appear sometimes on these portraits. The girls are shown in a more domestic way than boys.

These images reflect the type of education that girls receive in missionary schools: lessons of sewing, cleaning, domestic care, etc. In the early twentieth century, they are primarily prepared to become good wives and good Christian mothers:

> It is obvious that during the four years of boarding school, we do not seek to make our girls learned first and foremost. The goal we are pursuing from the beginning, through all the lessons, all the work, the goal we put constantly before the eyes of our children, is to make them Christian women

capable of becoming Christian wives and mothers worthy
of their responsibility. All our efforts are in this sense, all
our concerns boil down to this desire, because we know
that it is the mothers of tomorrow who are the future of a
people. (*Société des missions évangéliques* 3)

One of the main branches of missionary education was child
care, with a theoretical, but also practical aspect. Mothers who
lived near missionary schools were required to bring their young
children to be bathed by schoolgirls who could then put their
knowledge into practice. The internship of the SMEP in Mabumbu,
Northern Rhodesia, even adopted a little girl whose mother died
during the delivery so that students could take care of this baby
to learn how to care for and feed a child.

After the Second World War, African women still appear in a
domestic context, concerned about the well-being of the home and
responsible for household activities: carrying of water and wood,
food preparation, field work, etc.

Education programs dedicated to women continued after the
independence of African countries. In the 1960s, courses offered to
women included training in hygiene of pregnancy, care of infants,
feeding of young children and childhood diseases. To overcome
the lack of milk of some women or the premature death of nursing
mothers, the SMEP promoted animal milk.

According to the SMEP, these courses were a great success. But
in 1966, a report on a training program organized in Cameroon
points out that it would be necessary that the trainings will be provided by "Cameroonian [women] who know and live better than
anyone female problems and who will find the best ways to reach
their sisters" (Picheral 7). In Gabon, the SMEP opened a House
of Mother and Child in M'foul. It offered primarily a technical,
theoretical and practical training in infant care, but the medical
missionary staff was clearly insufficient to support a real medical
work. The choice was then made to train young African women in
childcare so they can move from village to village to help mothers.

Clinics funded and run by missionary organizations also proposed consultations for mothers and their children. In the 1950s,
the SMEP inaugurated several maternity hospitals. Because young

mothers could be subject to customs that the missionaries wanted to erase, African mothers were discouraged from giving birth in their villages. They were invited to move to missionary maternity hospitals by different ways: they received clothes for themselves and their babies; they get powdered milk to feed children considered too puny, etc.

In Cameroon, the SMEP attempted a training experience among single mothers. A centre was opened in Ntolo in 1974 to accommodate girls with their children. The missionaries aimed for the integration of young single mothers into the economy of the country. These training courses offered to women by the SMEP were obviously integrated into catechesis and evangelization carried out by missionaries. Bible studies were available, but the training was mainly a way for missionaries to reduce the influence of some traditional African customs related to pregnancy, which were judged negative by the missionary organizations. For example, in 1967, a missionary woman of the SMEP in Lesotho writes about her fight against the influence of grandmothers who advise young women to stop breastfeeding their children to feed them with a kind of porridge. Until the 1970s, the missionaries judged the traditional African way of life incompatible with Christianity. The SMEP wanted to see African people adopt a lifestyle integrating the contributions of Western culture. The various courses offered to mothers were aimed to accompany them through the major changes brought with the conversion to Christianity.

THE MOTHER AS A SYMBOL OF AFRICAN CHRISTIANITY

After being associated with a non-Christian environment in the early twentieth century, the theme of motherhood begins to be used to show Christian women in the years 1930-1940. Women, however, continue to display different signs that the Western viewer could associate with African culture. In October 1957, the *Journal des missions évangéliques* published by the SMEP proposed a photograph taken by the missionary nurse, Claire Bornand. This picture shows an African woman with her baby in her arms [Figure 3]. The link between the two figures is made through the look of the mother towards her child. The background shows

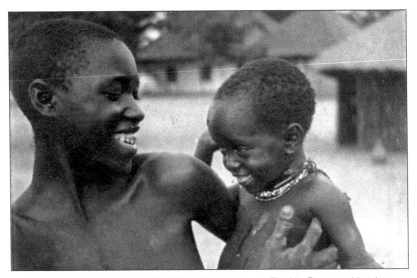

Figure 3. Zambezian smile, 1942/1971, Claire Bornand, Zambia. Photographic print.
Source: DEFAP

houses of Western architecture, which allow the observer to locate the scene in a missionary station. However, no clothes appear on the shoulders of the woman, leading the observer to think that she might be topless. The nudity is only suggested; the framing of the picture leaves the chest of the woman off-camera. But this appearance seems to point out the African culture of the young woman. Like her hair worn short and the collar of the child, her lack of clothes is a sign of "Africanism," a word used by the SMEP to characterize cultural elements that appear "purely" African. In this way, the SMEP shows African women as exotic figures to Europeans. But in the same time, despite these various elements used to link the model to African culture, the smile of the woman seems to imply her conversion to Christianity (Gullestad). The caption of the image, "Zambezian smile," stresses this particular aspect of the portrait and suggests the SMEP did not use this photograph to stigmatize African practices judged archaic, but to show that maternal love, value conveyed by Christianity, can be found in different nonwhite populations. By using this portrait, the SMEP intended to show that the Christian religion is universal.

Claire Bornand was particularly interested in the subject of women and motherhood in her photographs. Many of the portraits she

Figure 4. Northern Barotseland – Christian mother with her baby, postcard, s.d.
Source: DEFAP

made are quite similar. The photographer used the same framing, the same positions of the models and the same expressions of women. One of her images was published in December 1958 under the title "Do little smile..." [Figure 4]. This expression draws the viewer's attention to the model's smile, sign of her joy and her development in a context implicitly Christian.

In addition to these portraits, Claire Bornand also photographed African mothers with frames that depict the busts in order to show how women bear their children. Titled "Zambezian mummy" or "young mother," these images emphasize the maternal aspect of women's lives in Northern Rhodesia. Used as illustrations for different articles, Bornand's photographs do not maintain a link with the text and offer more a generic portrait of people whom the texts refer.

It is interesting to note that African women are mostly shown as mothers in a cultural environment identified as African. Men are totally absent in these images, in contrast to family portraits made in the mission stations. For missionaries, the men and women seem to have different roles in cultural transmission. According to photographs released by the SMEP, men appear to be major players in pagan religious practices which are cultural elements that SMEP tries to fight. Conversely, women seem more involved in domestic life and farming, activities that the mission intended to develop according to Christian morality. Men are often representatives of activities that must be removed; while women are related to the customs on which the SMEP tried to rely on to develop the evangelization in mission countries. The female figure is, therefore, used as a symbol of diversity possible among indigenous African tradition and Christianity. A photograph published in 1964 sums up the ambivalence of portraits of women. Captioned "Gabonese motherhood ... force of tradition," the image shows a topless woman wearing a loincloth around her waist, with three children. Clothing and partial nudity of the models put the portrait in an African "traditional" environment as outlined in the legend. But the caption also draws attention to the woman's motherhood, which is connected to values of Christianity.

The SMEP communicated extensively on actions amongst women and their children and it often used the portraits of women with their babies to illustrate articles on training for women in its media. In the missionary context, the portraits of women and children in Africa are highly symbolic. Most often used alone, their legends do not allow the observer to identify the individuals represented. Individualized by their physical features, undoubtedly related to the reality by their presence in front of the camera, the photographed models appear in representations for which the imagination of the viewer is particularly required. This ambivalence reinforces the symbolic value of the figures of motherhood in the missionary iconography: they are fixed in reality, while being invested with an universal value.

The presence of the child along with the woman in the missionary photographs is likely to be a way to evoke metaphorically the theme of the Madonna and Child. In the various publications of the SMEP, legends attached to mothers' portraits, however, indicate that such a sense of reading is never given to images. This corresponds to the position of Protestant theology in relation to images that

173

do not embody the religious figure, unlike the Catholic Church that focuses "on the effect of conviction provided by the display of religious mysteries" (Maresca, "Les images dans la société" 4). However, if African women are not portrayed by the SMEP as an incarnation of the Madonna and the Child, they are compared to other female figures of the Bible. In 1934, a text comments on a photograph of an African woman with her baby:

> Certainly it is an African woman; we first recognize the context in which she is located; her clothes or lack of clothing characteristic of the tropics; even the facial features of the young mother are very particular. She may be considered as a beauty amongst of her people, unless we are required to have the same opinion. But what is universal in this sight is the sense that we find everywhere, in every women, pride, tenderness, maternal love. When Eve, our first mother, gave birth to her first son, she proudly called him Cain because, she said, I have gave birth to a man and in the name ... there was all deep satisfaction, all the pride of a mother to her newborn. (O. P. 2)

The symbolic value of motherhood is clearly expressed here. The woman is seen as the origin of life and humanity. She is essential for the development of a new Christian world, as desired by the missionaries.

If the portraits of mothers with children gradually become symbolic representations of the development of Christianity in Africa, they also allow in the same time the so-called "humanization" of the figure of the African woman: "With its paradoxical combination of individuality and anonymity, it [the picture of motherhood] encourages identification with the African across racial boundaries"(Gullestad 191). Women are often shown in physical contact with their children: they hold them close as if it "wear" them, they are physically affectionate with them. If these gestures could be read as signs of Christianity, then the smile of women also evokes happiness of being a mother and to care for their children. In 1958 and 1960, the *Journal des missions* évangéliques used on the cover two portraits of women with children made in Northern Rhodesia [Figure 5]. The two images are not photographs taken by missionaries, but pictures purchased from the Northern Rhodesia Information Department. The first one [not shown in the Figure section] shows a "Toilet at the girls' School," a practical exercise in a domestic science course given to girls. If it is not the portrait of a mother, the reader can see this photograph as the image of a woman giving a bath to her child.

Figure 5. Mother with her child, 1950/1960, Nigel Watt (Northern Rhodesia Information department), Zambia. Photographic print. Source: DEFAP

The second picture shows on the other hand a "mother with her child." Both shots were made during sittings carefully prepared, probably in a studio as suggested by the background that appears in white. The first image gives an impression of energy and action with the woman leaning over the tub with a hand on the torso of the child. The second picture provides more a sense of sweetness in the gesture of the baby grabbing the hand of his mother. All are smiling and reflect the image of a happy life. Through this apparent domestic bliss and by the exposure of motherly symbolic gestures (to wash a child, to hold its hand), the SMEP offers visual signs, which could be immediately understood by Westerners. European people could then find cultural elements they know in these portraits of Black mothers and children and identify better with the models.

The female figures appear to be used to personify the synthesis that occurs between some indigenous African customs and Christianity. Shown in traditional domestic activities, the children who accompany women are used to mark their adoption of western Christian morality, while preserving the indigenous secular practices and customs. Presented as African and Christian in their daily activities or in portraits for which they pose, women are seen as the "fruits" of a peaceful missionary work.

During the second half of 1955, the SMEP used several portraits of women for the cover of the *Journal des missions évangéliques*. For the issue of September-October, the back cover shows a photograph of an African woman in profile carrying a baby on her back, her face turned towards the camera [Figure 6]. The hairstyle, the clothing, the way she holds her child are again elements traditionally associated with African culture. This tradition is not shown negatively. Instead, it is enhanced by the close-up frame. While most images of the magazine have a caption more or less descriptive, this photograph is not accompanied by any explanation. This absence of context and details tends to bring a symbolic value to the picture. The models appear beyond temporal and geographical context. In this way, the SMEP seems to offer a universal vision of the African woman who brings different qualities dear to the missionaries: the woman is at once Christian, mother, responsible of her home and heir of African cultural traditions.

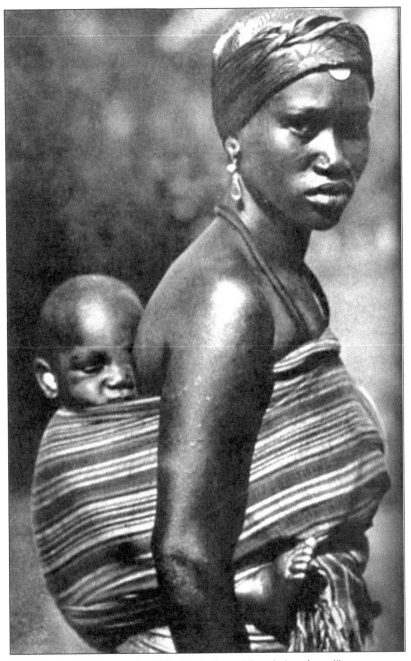

Figure 6. Photograph published in the Journal des missions évangéliques,
September-October 1955, n°8. Source: DEFAP

AFRICAN MOTHERHOOD AS A SYMBOL OF PROTECTION
PROVIDED BY THE MISSIONARY ORGANIZATIONS
TO THEIR "CHILDREN"

In a book on women in Cameroon, a missionary of the SMEP noted that many mothers die during childbirth. Traditional practices are accused of being primarily responsible for these deaths: hygiene and indigenous medicine are described as "odious manoeuvres." The missionaries see in these deaths the way to point out that medicine and Western practices would be beneficial to people, especially for women and children.

Moreover, portraits of African mothers only rarely show men. This separation of genders is due to the different activities of both sexes. However, it provides a way for the SMEP to present African women, and mothers in particular, as "victims" of traditional customs, including polygamy, for which men are explicitly denounced as responsible. In 1942, Ida Giugler, missionary of the SMEP, writes, "What about the African mother, often the victim of superstition and ignorance?" In presenting black mothers as victims who must be helped, Christian missionaries legitimize their actions amongst them.

Beyond the suffering they cause, the death of mothers is a subject used by the SMEP to present its work with orphans. From the 1940s, the SMEP built institutions called "nurseries" intended to collect very young orphans. Particularly concerned about the care provided to the lepers, the missionaries were sometimes called upon to collect children of mothers who die in hospitals run by the SMEP. Until the early 1960s, it seems that their fathers or their families eventually collected many children raised in missionary orphanages, but the SMEP did not approve return of these children to their villages. The missionaries expressed concern about the lack of protection and maternal affection, but also about the lack of hygiene. So in the late 1960s, in Cameroon, SMEP asked families to provide foster mothers to the orphans. These women were welcomed to the nursery where they were trained to care for a child.

Orphans are photographed extensively in all mission fields. Among children, they are indeed a particularly symbolic subject of missionary work: they are abandoned, with no family, no past.

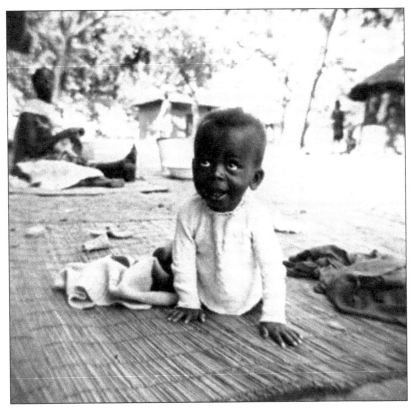

Figure 7. An orphan: Sepiso in silozi "promise" or more precisely "what is hope," 1956/1965, Marie-Claire Delahaye, Zambia. Photographic print. Source: DEFAP

They are people that Christian mission could raise and educate to become "Christian Africans of Tomorrow." In Northern Rhodesia, Marie-Claire Delahaye, nurse of the SMEP, produced portraits of many orphans. One of her photograph is captioned "An orphan: Sepiso in silozi "promise" or more precisely "what is hope" [Figure 7]. This title illuminates the look that the SMEP carries on African children. They are perceived as persons who will become "someone," people that are important to educate as Christians because they are the future of their country. They are the "seeds" planted by the Christian mission that wishes to develop Christian nations. They are a metaphor of "fertility" of the mission fields where the SMEP attempts to implant Christianity (Gullestad). Children are thus representations of the mission fields and of the hope placed in their future.

In this way, Christian missions positioned themselves as "mothers" towards the children. Innocent and fragile, the orphan is shown as a hope for the future where everything seems possible, but also as someone who needs care, protection and education. By treating and educating black children, the missionary is shown raising Africa of "tomorrow," that one day, will itself provide care to its own children.

The name given to the African churches born from the work of evangelization directed by the SMEP is significant and reveals the maternal aspect given by the missionary organization to its actions. They were called "Girls Churches" beside the French Protestant churches, known as "mothers."

Black motherhood is thus a major element of the iconography developed by missionary organizations such as the SMEP for its communication towards the Western Christians. Mothers and children are both symbolic and grounded in reality. They illustrate the missionary actions undertaken among them, but they are also used to be a visual metaphor of the development of a Christian Africa. "In the name of God and for their own good," missionaries believed that African people "needed" to be educated according to Christian values which are closely related to Western culture. Women and children are also especially perceived as people who need special care in Western imagination. The paternalistic look of the missionaries among them allows missionary organizations as the SMEP to legitimize their actions and encourage Westerners to support them.

WORK CITED

Gullestad, Marianne. *Picturing Pity*. New-York: Berghahn Books, 2007. Print

Jalla, Graziella. "Notes zambéziennes." *Journal des missions évangéliques* (October 1957): 216-218. Print.

Maresca, Sylvain. *La photographie. Un miroir des sciences sociales*. Paris: L'Harmattan, 1996. Print

Maresca, Sylvain. "Les images dans la société." *La vie sociale des images*. N.pub. 15 Dec. 2009: 4. Web. 8 Aug. 2011.

Nicod, Alice. *La femme au Cameroun*. Paris : Société des missions
évangéliques de Paris, 1927. Print

O. P. "Nos gravures." *Le petit Messager des missions* (November
1934): 1. Print

Picheral, Christiane. *Séjour au Cameroun du 9 juillet au 7 août
66*. Paris: Société des missions évangéliques de Paris, 1966. Print

Société des missions évangéliques. *Un internat de jeunes filles à
Mabumbu (Zambèze)*. Paris: Société des missions évangéliques
de Paris, s.d.. Print

What We Say, How We Do:
Interactions Between
Black Mothers and Daughters

10.
Black Mothers' Messages of
Pride to their Adolescent Daughters

TRACY NICHOLS AND REGINA MCCOY

FEW STUDIES HAVE DIRECTLY focused on the experiences of Black women as mothers of adolescent daughters and most studies on Black mother-daughter relationships center around issues of sexuality. Black parenting, which has been described as "precision parenting" (Mason et al. 2128) and "no nonsense parenting" (Brody and Flor 805), presents a unique interplay of warmth and control; an authoritarian approach combined with abundant affection and humor that is deemed necessary for successful navigation into adulthood. This unique parenting style is particularly evident in Black mother-daughter relationships. As Patricia Hill Collins ("Black Feminist Thought") notes, "Black mothers are often described as strong disciplinarians and overly protective; yet these same women manage to raise daughters who are self-reliant and assertive" (454).

Adolescence is a critical time in mother-daughter relationships (Nichols) and maternal strategies play a large role in socializing girls into womanhood. Equally important to understanding maternal influences on adolescent girls is understanding how Black women experience their relationships with their daughters. The study reported in this essay was designed to examine Black mother-daughter relationships and the messages Black women send their daughters regarding Black Womanhood. In this paper we attempt to represent the experiences of Black mothers through the voices of our participants and to express the complex and contradictory messages Black mothers send their daughters in order to help them successfully navigate into Strong Black Women (Harris-Perry).

185

METHODS

Taken from a larger study on mother-daughter relationships and health, the study reported in this essay pulls from ten semi-structured interviews conducted with working class, urban Black mothers of adolescent daughters in New York and North Carolina. All participants were Black working class women who had at least one daughter, aged eleven to seventeen, living at home. Six of the women resided in North Carolina and four in New York City. Seven of the women were single at the time of the interview and household composition varied considerably, with the number of children living within the home ranging from one to three with the exception of one mother reporting eight children in the home. Five of the mothers had at least one older child that was either away at college or lived on their own.

We created narrative profiles describing mother-daughter relationships from the original transcripts and then condensed the profiles into poems that crystallized the unique stories of each mother. We created the poems by using only the exact words of the participant. Words and phrases were kept in the order in which they appeared in the original transcripts within each poem. However, as is common to narrative analysis (Riessman), we created poems that expressed a specific story of the mother-daughter relationship for each participant. For some participants this resulted in multiple poems.

We then made multiple comparisons both within and across poems. We compared and contrasted poems for each mother as well as across mothers. From these comparisons we identified the following themes, which we will discuss in the remainder of the essay: Mother-Daughter Bond, Contradictory Messages, Fear of Desire, Controlling Sexuality, and Being A Lady. We examined these themes within the original narrative profiles to check for context that may have been missing from the poems, to expand our understanding of the themes, and to check for confirming and disconfirming examples. We wrote extensive memos throughout the analysis process and met regularly to review notes on the contrast and comparison analysis. Discrepancies were discussed and resolved within these meetings.

FINDINGS

Mother-Daughter Bond

Several of the poems spoke to the unique and powerful feelings that arise when mothering a teenage daughter. Collins ("Black Feminist Thought") reminds us that we may focus on the influences Black women have on their children, but we should not forget "how Black children affirm their mothers and how important that affirmation can be in a society that denigrates Blackness and womanhood" (459). The importance of that affirmation was expressed by the Black mothers in our study as they faced the realization that their daughters were growing up and would soon be leaving home. The poems that described the experience of mothering adolescent daughters were often bittersweet, as in Zahira's message to herself about her daughters.

> They can either stay home or go
> They're almost adults
> They're gonna have lives of their own
> I gotta get used to making it
> On my own
> They're not gonna be with me
> Everywhere that I go

Mothers spoke about changes that were occurring in their relationships with their daughters that depicted their daughters as growing more distant and more independent. There was evidence of concentrated efforts to maintain the mother-daughter bond, and for mothers with older daughters, acknowledgement that the relationship could and would continue once the daughter was on her own. The mother-daughter relationship was a strong and powerful bond for both parties and some mothers' poems, such as Felicia's, reflected the guilt they felt when they needed to separate from their daughters to meet their own needs.

> Your own alone time
> Be it if you're with someone else
> Whatever the case may be

It gives a little bit of
Sense of guilt,
It gives maybe
A little sense of neglect
On the daughter
Because they're so attached.
And my daughter is very attached.

One of the mothers in the study, Moesha, reflected upon the loss that occurs with everyday life. The demands of mothering, particularly as a single parent, often left little room for the more positive mother-daughter interactions. Moesha's poem brings forward an important context that lies beneath the mother-daughter relationship.

The stanza below reflects her awareness of the effects of her singular focus to provide for and raise her daughter.

Sometimes we get caught up in
Raising our child.
We forget about their happiness.
We just say okay,
I just wanna
Make sure she eats
I wanna make sure
She has a roof over her head
She gets her work done.
We forget about,
Wow, did I even ask her
If she wanted to go to the movies?
Or if she wanted
To do something together?

Black motherhood requires a heightened level of vigilance and care due to Black mothers' need to both buffer and prepare their daughters for living within the intersection of racism and sexism (Biederman, Nichols and Durham). To meet the demands of protecting and preparing their daughters, Black mothers' strategies may leave little time for fun or affection.

Contradictory Messages

The need to protect and prepare their daughters for living and succeeding in a world that denigrates both their race and their sex may cause some Black mothers to send seemingly contradictory messages. These contradictory messages may serve to empower their daughters while at the same time teaching them how to cope with the lack of power Black women have in society (Hinton-Johnson). Black mothers provide gendered-racial socialization (Thomas and King) of their daughters through a process of "armoring" (Edmondson, Ella and Nkomo).

To stand strong in the face of the invisible battle, or racial microaggressions, that disempower these mothers and their mothers before them, Black women cloak themselves with a "superwoman" armor that conveys strength and invulnerability, a determination to succeed, and the "by any means necessary" will-power to survive despite the uncertainties in life (Woods-Giscombe). Being strong and "armoring up" buttress Black women as they endure the pressures of racialized gender, an exhausting task that Beauboeuf-Lafontant refers to as "fighting strength with strength" (56).

The mothers in our study armored their daughters by delivering messages of pride, self-reliance, invulnerability, and confidence. Self-reliance was seen as a means for survival and often included distrust in men. At the same time, mothers' expressed a desire for their daughters to become both mothers and wives; to raise their children in loving, partnered relationships. Throughout all the interviews, mothers expressed education and delayed mothering as key to independence and success. Collins ("The Meaning of Motherhood") reports hearing young Black women state similar messages from their mothers.

> My students share stories of how their mothers encouraged them to cultivate satisfying relationships with Black men while anticipating disappointments, to desire marriage while planning viable alternatives, to become mothers only when fully prepared to do so. But above all, they stress their mothers' insistence on being self-reliant and resourceful. (42)

These messages are clearly expressed in one of Cynthia's poems, where harsh messages of independence were softened with warmth and humor.

> So you need to get an education
> Ok.
> And you've can't DEPEND on people.
> You can't depend on people.
> I'm not saying you don't trust,
> You don't love
> You don't do things like that
> But, husbands die,
> I'm sorry to say
> Husbands leave,
> I'm sorry to say.
> If you can not take care of yourself
> And your children,
> You will be calling me
> And I'll be on a boat,
> On a cruise.
> I will not be answering my phone.
> [laughter]
> There we have a problem.

We can also see contradictory messages in Celia's poem. Celia expressed her desire for her children to stand up for themselves; have strong opinions and voice these opinions. However this message of independence and self-reliance was tempered with knowing right from wrong action and accepting authority, especially maternal authority. Most of the mothers in our study delivered messages of strength and independence to their daughters but at the same time expected total compliance to their authority.

> I think kids need to know
> That we love you
> And we wanna hear what you say
> But we are the one that's in charge,
> We are the one

That is held responsible
So you need to listen until you're of age
Where you can make your own decision.

Equally as important as independence and self-reliance was educational achievement. The mothers in our study positioned education as the means to self-reliance, as can be seen in Cynthia's poem. Mothers put a lot of effort into promoting their expectations of educational achievement to their daughters. Expectations included attending college and/or graduate work, getting good grades, reading for pleasure, increasing reading comprehension skills, and having professional aspirations. Felicia expressed her expectations of leadership and education when she reminded her daughter "just graduating high school is not an option… the option is will you go to graduate school?"

Fear of Desire

Black mothers, who experience the affirmation of motherhood, raise their daughters with the expectation that they too will experience motherhood but at the same time fear their daughters becoming mothers too soon. The simultaneity of this juxtaposition of desire for and fear of their daughters' motherhood creates the need for contradictory messages. While motherhood is affirming for Black women and they both anticipate and want their daughters to experience mothering, they are highly concerned with their daughters' sexuality and the threat of teenage/young adult motherhood. This was true of all the Black women in our study but may have been especially salient for mothers who had been teen moms themselves. The mothers went to great lengths to communicate with their daughters on the dangers of teen (or young adult) pregnancy. Indeed there was scant maternal discussion on the joys of either sexuality or motherhood in this study. While we cannot confirm the reason for this absence, we suggest that mothers may have been concerned that discussing positive aspects would encourage their daughters' sexual behavior and lead to unintended and/or early pregnancy. Only one mother, Cynthia, mentioned sexuality as positive to her daughters and she acknowledged that she was criticized for doing so. However she told her daughters "there is a time and a place for everything" and explained to them the importance of delaying marriage and family.

> I tell them,
> You're supposed to have relationships.
> It's important.
> I don't want [them] to get so involved
> That they lose focus.
> When you're ready
> When you're done with college
> And you settle in life,
> You will be so taken up
> With the world
> Family and kids
> Then everything else,
> That all the things,
> You miss out on
> You may not be able to get them back

While Cynthia discussed the importance of relationships, she also cautioned about the loss that may accompany marriage and childrearing. This theme of loss or missing out often manifested itself in terms of education and career advancement. In Jewel's poem we see the message on the importance of education entwined with expectations of men's treachery.

> Don't date
> Until you are finished with your
> College education
> Then date physically
> But until then,
> Don't do it
> Because I'm sorry but
> Men will try to destroy you.
> [laughs]
>
> I that's what I told her
> I said

They'll try to trick you and
Tell you all kinds of stuff
That they think you wanna hear
And then you'll be pregnant,
And then,
You'll have to take care of the baby
And I'm not.

This explicit message of gendered relationships, which portrays men as deceiving women into sex and love only to strand them with the responsibility of children, was found woven throughout the poems. Cynthia described how she got this message across to her daughters.

I say
No mother is going to tell her son
To stay home and take care of the baby.
He's going to go to school
He's gonna finish school
You're going to have to deal with it.
There is only so much I can do.
I have no time.
I'm not going to be here forever
To look after you
So you have to look after yourself.

Moesha's poem takes men's treachery a step further when she described the words of warning she gave her daughter after having ended an unfaithful relationship.

I said one thing about a man.
I said you don't go backwards.
I said you don't ever do that.
I said you have to really be careful
In trusting a man.
They can make you think
They are the best thing on earth.
They can be

I just told her
They can be the scum of the earth.

Controlling Sexuality

Because of the dire consequences of early sexual behavior (which was most frequently discussed in terms of teen pregnancy but some mothers also mentioned HIV/AIDS as a concern) and the treachery of men, Black mothers in our study gave their daughters messages on the importance of controlling their sexuality. As previously mentioned, the theme of sexual communication has dominated the literature on Black mother-daughter relationships. This may stem, in part, from heightened concerns about sexuality among Black mothers of adolescent daughters.

Cynthia reinforced the importance of marriage and being marriageable to dissuade her daughters from pursuing their sexual impulses. In her poem we see strongly gendered messages about male and female behaviors in romantic relationships that underscore the themes of treacherous men and the need to control your sexuality.

I keep telling them
Boys would like to do that
But when the boys grow older
And they turn into men
And they want that woman
To settle down with
That's not the one they want.
That's not the one they're going to want.
Not the one that everybody feels up.
So I don't expect you to be,
To be that one.
Don't do that.

Babette, who was more concerned that her daughters would be exposed to the HIV virus, also offered gendered interpretations of heterosexual relationships by suggesting that it is men who want to have sex and that women will get used.

There's so much out here

Other than the fact that
You're going to get used,
Other than that fact,
There's a lot of diseases out here.
We know there's one
There's a killer.

Valerie took a more proactive stance when she planned to pur-
chase condoms and give her daughter a demonstration on how
to use them. While she still expected her daughter would remain
abstinent until marriage she was willing to entertain the need for
her to get an HPV vaccination.

She has a little friend.
They're going to wait until they get married.
Not just the baby thing but the sexually transmitted diseases
A lot of her girlfriends...got the HPV, that new shot
She wants it
"Well I don't want to get cervical cancer."
I was really impressed
REALLY impressed

Being A Lady

As previously mentioned, Black mothers "armor" their daughters
to help them thrive and survive in a world that is stacked against
them. But the women in our sample also felt it was important that
this armor not obscure femininity—a Black woman's armor needs
to be pink. Their expectations of their daughters included being a
lady along with being strong, resourceful and self-reliant. Just as
the mothers wanted to armor their daughters against sexism and
racism, they also wanted to empower their daughters with the
respectability that comes from being a lady. A lady demonstrates
refined behaviors associated with the comforts of a privileged
class. Just the mention of "act lady-like" from a mother conveys
images of feminine posture—legs-crossed, hands folded, and a shy,
wry smile. In a society where hegemonic white femininity is the
"normative yardstick for all femininities" (Collins "Black Sexual
Politics" 193) and Black women are depicted as hypersexual,

adhering to traditional images of hegemonic feminine behavior becomes essential. Babette spoke of these essential qualities in terms of being respectful and respected as she reminded her daughter of her "home training."

> This semester ... she's got attitude
> She has some type of rough
> Rough thing here going on.
> I don't like her like that.
> That's not a young lady
> You don't want to be acting like a
> A ghetto mama
> Ghetto ain't where you live
> You don't have to need to be acting
> Like you have no home training
> Because you do.
> I've been here—trained you.
> I know you've got home training.

Societal norms may support the double standard of promiscuity among men while women are virtuous in the face of sexual temptations, but Black mothers know it's not that easy for young Black women. Raising a daughter, especially in an urban disadvantaged neighborhood, heightens a mother's resolve to protect her daughters from real-life "boogey men" and societal "isms" that they encounter.

These mothers were skeptical of men because of their personal experiences with men in their lives—fathers, brothers, lovers, etc. Yet, they also wanted daughters to live their dream of one day being a strong wife with feminine touches; alluring, confident, and intelligent. We see Black women's desires for their daughters voiced in Amelia's poem.

> I want her to achieve all her dreams
> Just be a successful person
> She's on the right track
> She'll be 13 in July so
> I mean she'll be an adult soon

I just want her to be a successful young lady
I want her to do well in school

Being a lady means softer edges, a quiet strength powered by a tenacious core. Moesha, as with the other mothers, was proud of her daughter's independence but mindful of the preparation needed to "act like a lady." In this poem the Coach bag becomes a metaphor for femininity and class.

As a young lady
I even give her a Coach bag
To carry and she's like
[Smacks teeth].
She'd rather carry
One of those Nike backpacks.

I'm just like you're gonna have to
Carry something.
You can't pull pads
Out your pocket.
You got to carry a purse.
I think that's just one of my biggest
Expectation of her
Right now.
Being more responsible
As a young lady

Being a lady also means not being overtly sexual. Black women's sexuality has a history of being co-opted (Collins "Black Feminist Thought"), with images of the "Jezebel" morphing into the modern-day "Video Vixen." While the mothers in our study focused on fear of pregnancy and, to a lesser extent, STIs, their attempts to control their daughters' sexuality might equally have been influenced by the stigma of hypersexuality that is afforded Black women. "Being a lady" would protect their daughters from degradation by both men and society. We see this concern about sexual behavior and reputation in Cynthia's explanation of her expectations for her daughter.

You're going to see the boys,
You're going to like the boys,
The boys are going to like you,
But you have to know your limits.

I don't expect you
To be in a corner
In the school
And things.
I don't expect you
To have anybody touching up on you
I don't expect that of you.
And the day I hear that,
She has a problem
We have a problem.

DISCUSSION

The importance of mother-daughter relationships for Black women can be found in fiction, memoirs and womanist scholarship. Yet in the introduction to *Double-Stitch: Black Women Write about Mothers and Daughters* (Bell-Scott et al.) an anthology of essays, memoirs, stories, and poems on Black mother-daughter relationships, the authors write "this book represents the culmination of a dream to place a neglected relationship in the spotlight. Despite the heightened interest in the problems of Black families and the emergence of a feminist social science, the mother-daughter dyad has received scant attention from scholars of any persuasion" (3). In the twenty years since the book's publication there has been a growing literature of research studies, particularly public health research, on the importance of Black mothering for girls' health and well-being, with an emphasis on communication and pregnancy/HIV prevention (DiClemente et al.; Hutchinson et al.; Jaccard, Dodge and Dittus).

Far fewer studies have examined the experiences of mothering among Black women, especially mothers of adolescent daughters. In this study, we aimed to represent Black mothers' voices as they conveyed the complexity of their tasks as mothers. We also examined how Black women transmitted the meanings of Black Womanhood to their daughters at adolescence.

The mothers in our study conveyed a need to be clear to their daughters in an unclear world. Their messages were direct and to the point, reminiscent of the "no-nonsense" label attributed to Black parenting (Brody and Flor 805). They were concerned with being honest with their daughters but also wanted to instill hope. They wanted their daughters to dream big but to be prepared if the dream fails, as their own experiences have taught them failure is a very real possibility. They wanted their daughters to be independent but feared their daughters' sexual desires, as these desires may lead them off the very narrow path (i.e. education) to success. Preparing their daughters for the world outside of their homes; outside of their protection and support; required instilling contradictory messages.

These contradictory messages, of success and failure, of being strong and soft, were used to armor their daughters against the onslaught of racist and sexist arrows that life would throw at them. They feared having a tough exterior, an iron suit, without the softness of being a lady and all the privileges that come with it, was as dangerous as having no protection at all.

Black mothers know about the real dangers their daughters face and the invisible silent threats that lurk just ahead. Mothers, like Cynthia, know the pain and scars that are left from failed relationships and they find themselves in a contradictory position. These mothers know that sexual liberation was not and may not be granted to Black girls therefore they must tamp any part of their daughter's presence, clothing, mannerism, and even desires that could be perceived as sexual. These mothers know there is a chance the unnamed others will scrutinize their daughters through carnal lenses. Black girls and women are not afforded the chance to first be 'innocent until proven guilty' because even their adolescent budding and natural development is perceived as sexually dangerous and maliciously labeled (Tolman 256). Consequently, these Black mothers, who are proud of their daughters and who endeavor to be good mothers, must deliver unwelcome messages that have a hesitant tenor and suspicious tone. They must tamper their daughter's natural curiosities.

Felicia's poem tells us of her responsibility to shield her daughter through exposure.

If she's gonna be exposed
By me
It's better than her learning
From out there
In the world.
So, I'm honest with her.
I'm honest with her as far as what to do
And not to do.

The mothers in our study could have cared less about being perceived as dominate, over-burdening moms as long as their daughters were able to successfully achieve their goals and persevere. The collective goal among these mothers was the success of their daughters. They might not be about to change social mores but they could provide their daughters with strong protection that would help them navigate the intersection of racism and sexism that comes with being a Black woman. They knew the "several things against" their daughters and were trying to help them "wake up and smell the coffee." Their daughters would do more than just carry a purse instead of a bag, their purse would be a Coach bag that distinguished them from the rest. The unspoken sign that says "I am worthy."

We need to transform societal messages to give back the rights of daughters to just "be a girl growing up" without demonizing her sexuality. When we allow these messages to focus on the consequences of being a normal adolescent (that happens to be Black) with natural desires we are reinforcing the hypersexualization of Black women. Tolman articulates this point in her discussion of the myth of the sexualized "Urban Girl."

It is the social context, rather than the embodiment of The Urban Girl, that offers up meanings of adolescent sexuality and controls the material resources of education and contraception. It is the social context that must change to insure the safe integration of sexuality into a whole sense of an empowered self, enabling girls to have agency in their own lives. (268)

We also need to shift our focus in researching Black mother-daughter relationships to examine normative processes in both Black girls' development and family well-being. The voices of Black mothers and daughters in relationship need to be brought forward so we can see the full spectrum of their issues, not solely sexuality.

The messages of controlling Black girls' sexuality cause Black mothers continual stress and missed opportunities to connect with their daughters on multiple levels. Within the current zeitgeist of pathologizing Black girls' desire, Black mothers have found a way to balance their messages to their daughters. They are cleverly using 'being a lady' as a way to gain a win-win: my daughter is protected yet she is also attractive enough in her pink armor to bypass hypersexual stereotypes and aggressive suspicions and to be successful with options for the future (education, money, husband, mothering). If we can balance our own messages—by telling the whole story and not just the bad parts—the mothers may not have as many contradictory messages to send.

WORKS CITED

Beauboeuf-Lafontant, Tamara. *Behind the Mask of the Strong Black Woman: Voice and the Empodiment of a Costly Performance.* Philadelphia: Temple University Press, 2009, Print.

Bell-Scott, Patricia, Beverly Guy-Sheftall, Jacqueline Jones Royster, Janet Sims-Wood, Miriam DeCosta-Willia and Lucie Fultz, eds. *Double-Stitch: Black Women Write About Mothers and Daughters.* Boston: Beacon, 1991. Print.

Biederman, Donna J., Tracy R. Nichols, and Danielle D. Durham. "Maternal Navigational Strategies: Examining Mother-Daughter Dyads in Adolescent Families of Color." *Journal of Family Nursing* 16 (2010): 394-421. Print.

Brody, Gene H. and Douglas L. Flor. "Maternal Resources, Parenting Practices, and Child Competence in Rural Single Parent

African American Families." *Child Development* 69 (1998): 803-16. Print.

Collins, Patricia Hill. *Black Feminist Thought: Knowledge, Consciousness and the Politics of Empowerment.* Boston: Routledge, 2009. Print

Collins, Patricia Hill. *Black Sexual Politics: African Americans, Gender and the New Racism.* New York: Routledge, 2004. Print

Collins, Patricia Hill. "The Meaning of Motherhood in Black Culture and Black Mother-Daughter Relationships." *Double-Stitch: Black Women Write About Mothers and Daughters.* Eds. Patricia Bell-Scott, Beverly Guy-Sheftall, Jacqueline Jones Royster, Janet Sims-Wood, Miriam DeCosta-Willia, and Lucie Fultz. Boston: Beacon, 1991. 42-60. Print.

DiClemente, Ralph J., Gina M. Wingood, Richard, Crosby, et al. "Parent-Adolescent Communication and Sexual Risk Behaviors among African American Females." *Journal of Pediatrics* 139.3 (2001): 407-12. Print.

Edmondson Bell, L. J. Ella and Stella M. Nkomo. "Armoring: Learning to Withstand Racial Oppression." *Journal of Comparative Family Studies* 29 (1998): 285-95. Print.

Harris-Perry, Melissa V. *Sister Citizen: Shame, Stereotypes and Black Women in America.* New Haven: Yale University Press, 2011. Print.

Hinton-Johnson, KaaVonia. "African American Mothers and Daughters: Socialization, Distance, and Conflict." *The ALAN Review* Summer (2004): 45-9. Print.

Hutchinson, M. Katherine, John B. Jemmott, Loretta Sweet Jemmott, et al. "The Role of Mother-Daughter Sexual Risk Communication in Reducing Sexual Risk Behaviors Among Urban Adolescent Females: A Prospective Study." *Journal of Adolescent Health* 33.2 (2003): 98-107. Print.

Jaccard, James, Tonya Dodge, and Patricia Dittus. "Maternal Discussions About Pregnancy and Adolescents' Attitudes Toward Pregnancy." *Journal of Adolescent Health* 33.2 (2003): 84-7. Print.

Mason, Craig A, Ana Mari Cauce, Nancy Gonzales and Yumi Hiraga. "Neither Too Sweet Nor Too Sour: Problem Peers, Maternal Control, and Problem Behavior in African American

Adolescents." *Child Development* 67.5 (1996): 2115-30. Print.

Nichols, Tracy R. "Adolescent Children." *Encyclopedia of Motherhood*: Sage Publications, 2010. Web.

Riessman, Catherine Kohler. *Narrative Analysis.* Newbury Park: Sage Publications, 1993. Print.

Thomas, Anita Jones and Constance T. King. "Gendered Racial Socialization of African American Mothers and Daughters." *The Family Journal* 15.2 (2007): 137-42. Print.

Tolman, Deboral L. "Adolescent Girls' Sexuality: Debunking the Myth of the Urban Girl." *Urban Girls: Resisting Stereotypes, Creating Identities.* Eds. Bonnie Leadbetter and Niobe Way. New York: University Press, 1996. 255-71. Print.

Woods-Giscombe, Cheryl L. "Superwoman Schema: African American Women's Views on Stress, Strength, and Health." *Qualitative Health Research* 20 (2010): 668. Print.

11.
Getting the Parts Straight

The Psychology of Hair Combing Interaction between African-American Mothers and Daughters

MARVA L. LEWIS

ONE RAINY MORNING, after cleaning up the breakfast dishes, Regina begins her morning routine and ritual of combing her two-year old daughter's short, coarse hair. Known to her many family and friends as one who always speaks her mind ("that jus' Gina!"), she gently combs her daughter LaKeisha's soft mass of tight curls. As she carefully untangles her hair, she quietly smiles at La' Keisha's antics. She marvels at how adept her two-year old is at imitating her grandfather's gruff commands in a pretend conversation on her play phone. "Didn't I tell you to slow that car down or you gonna get in a' accident?" she asks her pretend caller in a singsong voice. As mother and daughter complete their hair-combing routine, Gina spontaneously begins to sing the Barney song, "I love you. You love me," from the popular PBS show. Admiring her work after she completes her task, Gina ends the task with a loving ritual where she looks her daughter directly in the eye, tenderly kisses and then hugs her. Later, she drops LaKeisha off at the same day care center that her neighbor Tonya's daughter, Ashley also attends.

On the same morning, in the apartment across the hall from Gina and LaKeisha, Tonya performs the same hair combing task but with a much different outcome for her two-year old daughter, Ashley. Jumping out of bed after oversleeping for the third time in a week, Tonya hurriedly begins combing through her daughter's hair. The fine-tooth plastic comb hits a tangle in the thick, tightly curled hair. Unable to form the words to explain to her Mama how tender headed she is, Ashley reflexively pulls away, recoiling from what feels like a sharp-toothed metal rake across her sensitive scalp. Glancing at the bright red numbers displayed on the microwave, Tonya angrily screams in a staccato voice, "Damn it. I-told-you-to-keep-your-stupid-butt-still. I'm trying to comb your nappy-ass hair!" With narrowed eyes and tightly pressed lips she repeatedly hits her daughter's legs and arms with the back of a nearby hard plastic hairbrush until a row of welts appear on her daughter's nut-brown legs.

Silently, Ashley repeats the same curse words to chastise her small body for flinching from the familiar pain of the touch of the comb to her sensitive scalp. She musters her entire lifetime of twenty-four months of resolve that she has available to command her body to STAY STILL! Like the well-worn, oily polyester scarf her mother ties around her hair on special occasions, the memory of the morning's painful hair event becomes tied up in her brain echoing the well-worn question that she can't figure out the answer: "Why my hair so bad and ugly?" Hot tears streaking down her face from the pain, she ends the perplexing routine with the only logical source of her problem, "I hate my hair!"

The next day the Day Care Center teacher makes a mandated call to Child Protective Services to report the bruising on the visible part of the Ashley's arms and legs.

Both of these African American mothers live alone with their daughters in low-income housing. Both experience the same environmental toxic stressors of poverty, urban community violence, and single parent status. Both of their daughters attend the same Day Care Center. Both mothers complete the same daily hair-combing task. Yet, each of these mother's distinct methods of responding to the stress of their environments reflects both their coping techniques and unrecognized modern legacies of the historical trauma of slavery. These two mothers' methods of performing this mundane task of hair combing have important outcomes for the quality of the psychological relationship that develops with her daughter. What will become associated in the area of their toddler's developing brain that stores long-term memories of this morning routine will be the intense positive or negative emotional experiences of having their hair combed by their mothers. These memories will be qualitatively different for each of the young daughters of these two mothers.

Unconditional love and acceptance by a primary caregiver form the earliest template for psychological growth and healthy socio-emotional development for all young children. Rohner (11) argues that in studies of children's perceptions of parenting practices across all cultures includes all the affects and emotions related to the child's feelings of acceptance and rejection by the person called mother or father, mama or daddy.

The primary time that LeKeisha and Ashley have alone with their mothers is during their hair combing time. Many single-mothers with children under the age of five, rear children in a context of crowded low-income apartment complex with a surrounding environment, like so many other urban neighborhoods, of high rates of violence. To pay the subsided rent and her portion of childcare, 25-year-old Tonya works two minimum wage jobs. The pragmatic reality of using public transportation to get to work on time chips away at all the reserves of patience she might have to her daughter's otherwise normal reactions during the hair combing task. She doesn't have the energy to notice the consistent responses of her daughter to any type of touch to her daughter's scalp and figure out that her daughter is tender headed.

For African American families the sociocultural context of child development includes the economic and psychological legacies of racism, discrimination, and minority status (Murray et al. 137; Rosser and Randolph 16). These emotionally toxic legacies may manifest in the everyday interactions of the most intimate relationships among members of Black families in the form of acceptance and rejection of children and each other based on stereotyped images of racial features. These traumatic legacies may set the stage for many psychological outcomes for young African American girls including her self-esteem, body image and future male-female relationships.

One legacy of the 400-year practice of slavery in the Americas is the practice of 'colorism.' This practice of valuing light skin over dark-skin, was intentionally created as a way to create divisions within communities of enslaved Africans (Blassingame 47; Eyerman 92). The practice of Colorism occurs among many oppressed indigenous, ethnic, racial and cultural groups around the world but was intentionally implemented as tool identification of enslaved humans as property and being a ready target of violence and terrorism (Lewis et al. 26; Russell et al. 33). The unconscious hierarchy and privilege associated with skin color may interact with other oppressions, and historical trauma resulting in within group acceptance or rejection of children by parents, family and the community. These legacies of slavery may be the unrecognized social mechanism for the intergenerational transmission of historical trauma in families with young children (Lewis, et al., 31). Further, the texture of hair and light or dark skin color may be important unconscious flashpoints in the daily interactions of Black mothers with their daughters and formation of attachment relationships.

There has been little exploration of the racial context that permeates the socio-emotional domains of relationships that develop between infants and young Black girls with their mothers (Lewis 33d; Rosser and Randolph 14). The racial context includes the historical trauma of racial stereotypes associated with African origin physical features of Black Americans. These variable features are skin color, hair texture, nose, and lip sizes. Each of these indelible phenotypic African features (dark skin, thick lips, broad nose and coarse kinky hair), and their more European origin counterparts (lighter skin tones, thin lips, narrow nose and wavy to straight hair), are associated with emotionally charged, negative racial stereotypes. The other legacy is the valuing of a European standard that distinguishes lighter skin tones, thin lips and nose and straighter, long hair as more beautiful and desirable. These volatile historical legacies carry with them unresolved issues of sexual stereotypes, exploitation of both female and male slaves, powerlessness and unresolved anger. In addition, there may be intergenerational legacies, family myths and secrets about the origins of skin color and hair texture that may unconsciously contribute to feelings of conditional acceptance based on the child's phenotypic racial characteristics. "She got that 'good' hair and light skin and think she somethin'!" Many adult women have not had the opportunity to reflect on the quality of their relationships with their mothers. They may be unaware how the intersection of stressors made up of everyday modern stress, like paying the rent on time, and may be coupled with the unacknowledged historical legacies of stereotypes about hair and skin color. The volatile mix of these stressors may impact their current relationships with their daughters.

There is universal symbolism and meaning of hair across cultures around the world (Lewis 64b). In the United States there are sociocultural legacies associated with hair. Though there is growing recognition in the politics of hair and symbolism of hair in African American women we have not yet looked at how these external political factors influence individual parenting styles observed while combing hair.

African American parents rear children in a racially stratified society in which Blacks are at the bottom on a multitude of social well-being and economic indicators (Murray and Brody, 43; Rosser and Randolph 28). Underlying the current challenging social disparities and realities of many Black families is the legacy of the history of enslavement of African Americans in the United States (Hill 66). Racial phenotype readily distinguishes Black Americans from other racial groups. This historical legacy includes a traumatic history of discrimination, stereotypes, and racism based solely on the indelible, genetically determined feature of race—skin color. Characterized as "the mark of oppression," skin color remains an emotional flash point within all social strata of African American communities. Phenotype racial features vary among individuals identified as Black as well as among children within the same family. These features are all associated with a complex, multi-layered legacy of racism and stereotypes about lack people (Davis et al. 19; Russell et al. 82; Rooks 21).

Many Black infants' hair texture may change during these early years range from straight or wavy and easy to manage, to a coarser and tightly curled texture that requires more attention, time and patience to style. Throughout their lifetime African American children may experience intense emotions associated with being accepted, rejected, or teased by family, friends, and others about their racial features. Similarly, the child's parents may have traumatic memories of acceptance or rejection by family members based on their African physical features.

From birth young children may be either highly prized or summarily rejected simply based on the lightness of their skin tone or straightness and length of their hair. In the past decade there has been an explosion of books (such as N. Rooks, 31; Harris and Johnson 15), movies such as comedian Chris Rock's movie on *Good Hair* and more recently Oprah Winfrey's showing of the movie, *Dark Girls*. This movie, released in 2013 by actor Bill Dukes, documents the experiences of dark-skinned African American women's emotional pain of racial rejection by members of their families and community. He has since released a follow-up documentary that a focuses on 'Light-skinned girls' and their emotional experiences of rejection within the African American community. Surprisingly, the social media in response to the airing of this video was intensely negative and unsympathetic. This response highlights the need for the African American community to address these unrecognized sources of psychological acceptance and rejection based on experiences of colorism. Further, understanding the impact of this internalized toxic stress may impact on the formation of secure attachment relationship of African American parent's and their young children. The daily ritual and routine of hair combing interaction may offer a window of understanding of how these external racial stressors may impact African American mother daughter relationships. The historical legacies of internalized oppression and modern stressors may permeate her everyday interactions with her young daughter and the quality of her talk, touch and listening while combing her hair.

HAIR COMBING INTERACTION AS A
CONTEXT FOR RESEARCH AND INTERVENTION

To understand what occurs during this everyday task, basic research was conducted with diverse African American women from a variety of cities in the United States. (See Lewis, Turnage, Taylor and Diaz for complete description of methods used in this study). A key finding was that during the interaction of combing hair there were discrete, stages of hair combing. There were individual differences in how long each mother and daughter remained in each stage during the task.

We also found individual differences in the perception of the task of combing hair based on qualitative analysis of their interviews. The findings suggest how a mother's childhood experiences related to racism, specifically around skin color and hair, and her internalized stereotypes; may contribute to the determination of her perception of the task of combing hair.

THE STAGES OF HAIR COMBING AND PERCEPTION OF THE TASK BY AFRICAN AMERICAN MOTHERS

African American mothers and daughters from different socio-economic groups were videotaped combing their daughters' hair. Based on analyses of multiple videotapes (over 65 dyads were recorded and analyzed), we found that many activities occur during hair combing interaction. These activities include verbal interaction, physical touch, and active listening to the cues of their daughter.

We discovered that there are discrete stages that African American mothers and daughters go through during the hair-combing task. We recorded the amount of time that it took for the mothers to comb their daughter's hair and found that the average amount of time spent was about 10.29 minutes. The shortest amount of time was about 31 seconds and the longest amount of time was about 49 minutes. From the start of the task until it was finished the mothers went through five distinct stages. These stages—preparation, negotiation, combing hair, play, and ending rituals—varied from mother to mother in terms of how much time each stage lasted. The quality of the relationship dynamics of verbal interaction, physical touch that occurred between the mother and daughter also varied. Some moms simply grabbed a comb, the child and started the process. Some mothers carefully laid out their combing utensils and then verbally invited their child to 'join them' in the task. Table 1 summarizes both the activities as well as the relationship dynamics that occur in each stage.

A TYPOLOGY OF MATERNAL PERCEPTION OF THE HAIR COMBING TASK

Interviews were conducted with a sub-sample of the total group of mothers who participated in the original African American

Table 1: *The Relationship–Based Stages of Hair Combing Interaction (HCI)*

STAGE	FOCUS and CHARACTERISTICS	RELATIONSHP DYNAMICS
PREPARATION	Prepares utensils, location and self to begin task. Prepares child verbally and/ or physically for task.	Mother or child dominant
NEGOTIATION	A variety of approaches are used to entice the child into the task. She may use voice commands, statements, verbal repetition, promises, play, or touch with child to engage child in the task. May state family rules and expectations of behavior.	Interactive – verbal interaction with mother and child participating in negotiation.
COMBING HAIR	The focus of this stage is to accomplish the task of combing the hair. The child is placed in a primary position of proximity to the mother at this time. This position may change periodically but mother returns the child to the primary position throughout the task.	Mother dominant in directing physical behavior of both.
PLAY	During the task playful talk or chatter between the mother and child may occur. Shared affect, loving touch, is directed at the mom toward the child or the child toward the mother.	Interactive – either the child or the mother may initiate the type of actual or symbolic play during this stage.
CLOSING RITUALS	Mother signals the end of the task. She may direct praise, reinforcement for behaviors, makes statements about gender or racial identity or sex-role training.	Mother dominant

Mother-Daughter Interaction Study (AMDIS-I) after they were videotaped combing their daughter's hair. They were asked a series of open-ended questions about that included the meaning of the hair-combing task to her and questions about her experiences getting her hair combed as a child. She was also asked questions about the relationship with her mother such as: "What memories do you have getting your hair combed?" A series of questions were then asked about their childhood experiences of racial acceptance and rejection by the mother, father, other members of their family and people in their neighborhood.

These interviews were transcribed and analyzed using qualitative methods of grounded theory and identification of emergent themes (See Lewis, Turnage, Taylor and Diaz for complete description of methodology). The mothers recounted experiences of being either prized or discounted based solely on their skin color and hair texture. They recounted negative and painful attributions made to their behavior by adults in their homes and communities that were tied to their skin color.

A typology of relationship-based themes emerged with four types of mother's emotional perception and approach to the hair-combing task. The four types were broadly labeled as Connected and Disconnected with three types of disconnection identified. These categories roughly parallel Mary Ainsworth's (77) four categories of parent-child attachment—Secure, Insecure Avoidant, Insecure Anxious, and Insecure disorganized. In addition the mothers were asked to rate themselves about their Adult Attachment style (Patterns A, B, or C). This is a statement about how they feel about close relationships with other people.

Connected – Type 1, A Time for Bonding

In this type the mother approaches the hair combing task as 'a time for bonding.' This behavioral style is one that includes a lot of warmth, talking, listening and responsiveness to the daughter during hair combing. An example of this type is a twenty-four year old, single mother of a 22 month-old daughter with an income of under $10,000. We will refer to her by the pseudonym of 'Elaine.' She was then a college student who had not yet completed her undergraduate degree. When asked, 'what does the activity of combing hair mean to you?' Elaine readily responded; 'I think of it as a time for like, um how can I phrase this, bonding, and we talk. Most of the time there's a conversation...." Later in the interview she was asked about the memories she had of getting her hair combed. Smiling she described in detail her hair combing experiences with her mother. "It was a long process, I remember that, it as a long process, and I used to like it because I used to like the way my mom combed my hair." This mother checked Pattern C as the adult attachment style that best describes her. The statement reads, "I am comfortable with closeness, and find it relatively easy to trust and depend on others. I don't worry about being hurt by those I'm close to."

Disconnected – Type 2: "It's My Duty."

This behavioral style is one of efficiency and lack of touch during the hair-combing task. There is little warmth shown to the child though the mother may be very responsive to the daughter during the hair-combing task.

To illustrate, a mother who will be referred to by the pseudonym of "Eleanor," age thirty, reported an income bracket of $31-40,000 in the working to middle-class income bracket. Her daughter, age 48 months at the time of the study, was an only child. Eleanor reported her marital status as 'living together' (unmarried) and for her education level she reported that she had received 'some college.' A practicing Catholic, she reported attending church weekly. Growing up as the oldest of five children, Eleanor checked the adult attachment style of Pattern A, 'very much like me.' This pattern was described as; 'It is important to me to be independent and self-reliant. I'd rather not depend on others or have others depend on me. I am comfortable without a lot of closeness."

During the interview at the end of the hair combing videotaped session Eleanor was asked about the meaning of the hair combing activity to her. Her response typifies the dutiful nature of this type of attitude about the task of combing hair. She reported, "Um, it's basically a method of preparedness for the day. It's just another activity. Um, not a lot of thought goes into it. It's routine. We just do it for grooming purposes."

She was then asked, 'What would it mean if you didn't comb your child's hair?" as a means to determine the cultural value each participant held about that task. Her response was "…With a girl, I always feel they should be neat in appearance at all times. So, that would be a big problem for me if her hair weren't combed."

Disconnected – Type 3, "Let Someone Else Do It."

This type of mother typically finds someone else to comb her daughter's hair. An example of one, 31-year-old mother's relationship we will call 'Crystal' with her own mother is illustrated in the following quote. Her mother had someone else comb her hair throughout her elementary school years until about fourth or fifth grade.

> The only memories I have of getting my hair combed is that I can remember one plait up here [she points to the top right side of her head], and down here [she points to the bottom left side of her head]. Because my mother never could get the parts straights." She never could part hair. She never could comb hair. And my aunt lived around the corner and I would get up early and run by my aunt house so she could comb my hair.

When asked in the interview how her experiences of getting her hair combed influences, if at all, how she combs her 24-month-old daughter's hair she responded:

> The only thing I thought was to make it better than what my mother did mine. More than anything I just practiced to make sure that it was always straight and even and that was it.

Another 30-year-old mother of a 29-month-old daughter and classified in this category describes her hair combing memories from her childhood with dispassion and forgetfulness. "I don't have any bad memories…. I don't have any vivid specific moments where I can say, I know we did this routine at home. I don't remember that." She then recalled that her aunt who lived with them (one of her mother's four sisters) was the primary person who combed her hair as a child. When asked how she felt about someone else combing her hair she stated, "I can't remember. I don't think I had a problem with it."

Disconnected – Type 4, "I Don't Know How to Do It."

This type of mother attempts to comb her daughter's hair but with generally poor results which characterizes this type of relationship. The mother often times gives up and the daughter's hair typically looks uncombed. This group of mothers typically experienced the early loss of their mother due to death or had an emotionally unavailable or substance abusing mother.

Additional findings suggest there were a variety of predictors of individual differences for women categorized according to their approach to the task. For example, one mother we refer to as 'Carol' was placed in this category provided what were concluded as rather 'incoherent' and disorganized responses to questions about her early experiences of getting her hair combed. Carol, a 24-year-old mother of a three-year old daughter reported her income as less than $10,000 per year. At the time of the study she had already given her three-year-old daughter a chemical permanent relaxer for her coarse, tightly kinky hair. When asked what memories she had of getting her hair combed, Carol's answer seemed inappropriate and disjointed. She stated:

> Oh, I can recall that one day, I didn't want to, um, go to church. Oh, I used to hate putting on them stockings, so my mom — as a matter of fact, it was Easter, I didn't want to go to church. When was I gonna go serve the lord? I just was mad at my momma because she bought me an ugly dress. I went into the bathroom, and my curls just fell. "You gonna have me late for church, but you going," and she just flicked my hair like once, and baby she said, "You gonna go the way you look because you messed it up." I didn't like the dress—with polka dots. A lot of people said I looked cute. I looked ugly. It was one of those sailor's polka-dot dress and I thought that was ugly.

Later in the interview when asked how she felt about the type of hair she had as a small child she reported, "I always wanted, like, you know, like Creole people? I always wanted to be light [skinned]." Her answers were charged with emotions but almost invariably not quite a direct answer to the question. She skipped the question of which adult attachment style best fit her.

CONCLUSION

These stories and findings from research illustrate the range intense emotions that occur during the daily routine and ritual of combing hair for African American mothers and their young daughters. These findings also suggest the potential psychological power of structured routines such as hair combing interaction (HCI) for strengthening mother-daughter relationships. HCI may also serve as an everyday context to help re-story the negative historical legacies of the trauma of slavery. Destructive legacies that have been part of families for generations may be un-done with support and awareness of shame, guilt, and anger associated with these childhood experiences of racial acceptance or rejection.

There are other issues that may underlie shame-based methods of control relate to stigmatization of racial physical features of the child (skin color, hair texture and nose and lip size) by either the mother or the Black community. In both group and individual therapy with Black women, anger and resentment over the discrimination practiced within the Black community about the issue of skin color frequently are presented (Boyd-Franklin 10). "Feelings of resentment and anger about the possibility that one is too dark or too unattractive to males are just as common as feelings of guilt and shame about the possibility that perhaps one has enjoyed unfair advantages because of lightness of skin color or straightness of features" (Neal and Wilson 330).

Other sources of family-related shame are "family secrets" (Boyd-Franklin 60). Such "secrets" concern informal adoption, true parentage, unwed pregnancy, and a parent who had "trouble" at an earlier age, White ancestors and skin color issues. These shame-inducing secrets may be passed down through the generations by some family members but not shared with other members, particularly the younger generations. These secrets may represent sensitive areas in the present family systems that are never discussed; yet generate varying degrees of stress and perhaps even shame. These secrets may provide a powerful psychological tool to be used by some mothers or other family members to achieve compliance in children.

Finally, the simple routine and ritual of combing hair can be used for building parent-child relationships. From ages 0-12, when mothers spend ten minutes per day for 365 days of the year, the everyday routine of combing hair provides 4,380 opportunities for interaction between mothers with their young daughters. When implemented in a caring way, the hair-combing ritual facilitates bonding between mother and daughter. It also contributes to the young girl's many dimensions of her developing sense of self. This sense of self as a daughter, and an African American female, may also include her self-acceptance, self-love, self-esteem, and self-confidence. The lessons she learns during this daily ritual with her mother may be the foundation that she needs to deal with a world where the image of little girls who look like her with dark skin and 'nappy' hair has been vilified with stereotypes and her beauty unrecognized by the larger society.

A daughter may learn affirming life-lessons from the verbal interaction that goes with her mother on while sitting between the safe legs of her mother who talks to her about her day. 'Get your homework done first honey before you play with your dolls.' Similarly, a daughter may experience the pleasurable, nurturing physical touch from her mother as she strokes and pats her hair in place at the end of their daily routine and ritual. Finally, and most importantly, a daughter learns the unconditional acceptance from her mother - something that every human being needs to not only live, but to survive. 'Does that barrette feel too tight Ashley?' 'How do you want to wear your hair today LaKeisha?' fundamentally are questions that communicate, 'Your opinion matters to me!' The quality of these verbal, physical and listening actions by the mother become stored in the daughter's brain for the rest of her life (Shore 23).

Consequently, their daughters have different emotional experiences and memories that shape the mother-daughter bond, their image as an African American woman, and their concept of self. Unexamined, little Ashley's underlying question, "Why my hair so bad and ugly?" may define the relationship with her mother for the rest of their lives. The everyday ritual and routine of combing hair can be used to create a new narrative that connects mothers not only to their daughters but also to their culture, communities and their selves.

WORKS CITED

Ainsworth, Mary D., M. C. Blehar, Everett Waters and S. Wall. *Patterns of Attachment: A Psychological Study of the Strange Situation.* Hillsdale, NJ: Lawrence Erlbaum Asssociates, 1978. Print.

The Association of Black Psychologists on 'Dark Girls.' Discussion guide by the National Association of Black Psychologists, 2013. Print.

Blassingame, John. *The Slave Community: Plantation Life in the Ante-Bellum South.* New York: Oxford University Press, 1972. Print.

Bowlby, John. *Attachment and Loss: Vol. 1.* New York: Basic Books, 1969. Print.

Boyd-Franklin, Nancy. *Black Families in Therapy: A Multisystems Approach.* New York: Guilford Press, 1989. Print

Byrd, Ayana, and Lori Tharps. *Untangling the Roots of Black Hair in America.* New York: St. Martin's, 2001. Print.

Collins, Patricia H. Black *Women and Motherhood Black Feminist Thought.* Boston: Hyman, 1990. Print.

Davis, Katheryn, Maurice Daniels and L. A. See. "The Psychological Effects of Skin Color On African American's Self-Esteem." *Journal of Human Behavior in the Social Environment* 2.3 (1998): 63-90. Print.

Dill, Bonnie T. "Our Mothers' Grief: Racial, Ethnic Women, and the Maintenance of Families." *Race, Class, and Gender: An Anthology.* Belmont: Wadsworth, 2013. 314-26. Print.

Eyerman, Ron, "Cultural Trauma: Slavery and Formation of African American Identity." *Cultural Trauma and Collective*

Identity. Eds. J. C. Alexander, R. Eyerman, B. Giesen, and N. J. Smelser. Berkeley: University of California, 2004. 60-111. Print.

Grier, William H., and Price M. Cobbs. *Black Rage.* New York: Basic Books 1968. Print.

Harris, Juliette, and Pamela Johnson. *Tenderheaded: A Comb-Bending Collection of Hair Stories.* New York: Pocket, 2001. Print.

Hill, Robert. *The Strengths of Black Families.* New York: Emerson Hall, 1972. Print.

Lewis, Marva L. "The Childhood Experiences of Racial Acceptance and Rejection Scale: Development, Reliability, and Validity." Biennial Meeting of the Society for Research in Child Development, Minneapolis, Minnesota, 2001. Print.

Lewis, Marva L. *Factors Influencing the Interpretation of Emotions in Infants by African American Mothers.* Boulder, CO: University of Colorado, 1993. Print.

Lewis, Marva L. "The Hair-Combing Task: A New Paradigm of Research with African American Mothers and Daughters." *American Journal of Orthopsychiatry* 69 (1999) 1-11: Print.

Lewis, Marva L. "The Historical Roots of African- American Mother-Daughter Relationships and the Psychology of Hair Combing Rituals." *Afrikan American Women: Living at the Crossroads of Race, Gender, Class, and Culture.* Ed. Huberta Jackson-Lowman: Congealer/ University Readers, 2013. Print.

Lewis, Marva L. "The Cultural Context of Infant Mental Health: The Developmental Niche of Infant-Caregiver Relationships." *Infant Mental Health.* Ed. Charles H. Zeanah. New York: Guilford, 2000. 91-107. Print.

Lewis, Marva L., Barbara Turnage, Shannah Taylor and Jillian Green. *Nappy Haired Ghosts in the Nursery: Intergenerational Legacies of Hair Texture and Skin Tone and African American Mother-Child Proximity During the Hair Combing Task.* New Orleans: Tulane University, 2008. Print.

Lewis, Marva L., Carmen R. Noroña, Nina McConnico, and Kandance Thomas. "A Legacy of Historical Trauma in Parent-Child Relationships: Clinical, Research, and Personal Perspectives." *Zero to Three Journal* 34.2 (2013): 11-23. Print.

McAdoo, Harriette P. and John L. McAdoo. "Racial Attitude and Self- Concept of Young Black Children Over Time." *Black*

Children. Ed. John L. McAdoo. Beverly Hills: Sage, 1985. 213-42. Print.

Murray, Velma M., Mia M. Bynum, Gene H. Brody, Amanda A. Willert, and Dionne D. Stephens. "African American Single Mothers and Children in Context: A Review of Studies on Risk and Resilience." *Clinical Child and Family Psychology Review* 4.2 (2001): 133-55. Print.

Pinderhughes, Elaine. *Understanding Race, Ethnicity, and Power. The Key to Efficacy in Clinical Practice.* New York: Free, 1989. Print.

Porter, Cornelia P. "Social Reasons for Skin Tone Preferences of Black School-Age Children." *American Journal of Orthopsychiatry* 61.1 (1991): 149-54. Print.

Rohner, Ronald P. *The Warmth Dimension: Foundations of Parental Acceptance-Rejection Theory.* Newbury Park: Sage, 1986. Print.

Rooks, Noliwe. "Wearing Your Race Wrong: Hair, Drama, and Politics of Representation for African American Women at Play on a Battlefield." *Recovering the Black Female Body: Self-Representations by African American Women.* Ed. M. Bennet and V. D. Dickerson. New Brunswick: Rutgers University Press, 2001. 279-83. Print.

Rosser, Pearl L., and Suzanne M. Randolph. "Black American Infants: The Howard University Normative Study." *The Cultural Context of Infancy. Vol. 1: Biology, Culture, and Infant Development.* Ed. J. Kevin Nugent, Barry M. Lester, and T. Berry Brazelton. Westport, CT: Ablex Publishing, 1989. 133-165. Print.

Russell, Kathy, Midge Wilson, and Ronald Hall. *Color Complex: The Politics of Skin Color Among African Americans.* New York: Anchor / Doubleday, 1992. Print.

Shore, Alan. "Attachment and the Regulation of the Right Brain." *Attachment and Human Development* 2 (2000): 23-47. Print.

Stern, Daniel N., and Robert N. Emde. "The Representation of Relational Patterns: Developmental Considerations." *Relationship Disturbances in Early Childhood: A Development Approach.* Ed. Arnold Sameroff. New York: Basic, 1985. 52-69. Print.

Closing Thoughts

Mothering the Girls We Were Then:
Prose and Promises

KAREN T. CRADDOCK WITH TRACY ROBINSON-WOOD

WITH HONOR TO and reflection of the mothers who came before us, who shepherded us into existence, guided our paths, released us to our own truths and to one another, we share whispered assurance, bold proclamation and a missive of realization, calling and self-love....

Windtouch (then and now)

I've uncovered rare jewels
Nestled within my being
They have been there waiting
Wanting me to see
The power I have in my own life
To love and to be free
To know the holiest gift of all time
Simplicity
                    —Tracy Robinson-Wood (1990)

Let us decide to excavate, you and me
Bearing witness to what we see
To honor the girls who journeyed here
Pushed forward by ancestors
Whose spirits beckon, go!
Transcend time and know
Truth chose me and you

Embrace our power, strong
Our purpose is now
—Tracy Robinson-Wood (2015)

Reflections: Mirrored Voices (then and now)

I saw my faces in the broken fragments of life's glass at my feet, and in my tears I felt hundreds of years of struggle, pain, and exhaustion roll down my cheeks.
My mothers are crying out from the depths of my soul for all the agony we face and have faced in efforts to be Whole.

See me? Here I am, all of me, can you see me?
All of the lonesome nights wondering and questioning your own self worth bombarded by a world that is frightened by your power and determined to hide it from you.
Then, prodding endurance from quiet hushes and palms of strength massage and heal your worn heart and mind.

Mothers call forth and demand that you stand up … stand up for you and for them.
Find the way to sing our song, the one that those out there think they know, but never really took the time to listen to—for fear their ears would ring in maddening truth.
Others cannot stand to stand in the light of our being which is full of all that we possess.
I am certain in these moments that they would shrink in disgrace, or explode with disbelief from that they have worked so hard to suppress.

Here I am … and I am still learning what that is.
All I know is that it is here … I am here … and I have to find a way to get it out and live it.
I will find a way to pick up these shards at my feet, knowing that the blood that will surely come from my fingers as I do…will only add to the colors of the kaleidoscope that I will make.

— Karen T. Craddock (1998)

I have found you in the cool blue Indigo and the warm red
clay of my ancestral soul
Here, the brilliance of light beyond time gathers me up
and into newness of life
Home and harvest to be and become
Happy, healthy and whole.

—Karen T. Craddock (2015)

Contributor Notes

Karen T. Craddock, Ph.D., is an Applied Psychologist and Principal Researcher whose more than 20 year study and practice concentrates on the socio-cultural context of human development, organizational capacity building, relational frameworks, community-based training and program evaluation research, particularly within the fields of Health and Education. Her exploration of psychosocial functioning, maternal/child health, race/gender disparities, violence prevention, social-emotional wellness and neuroscience focuses on creating healthy relationship, effective partnership and network cultivation. Her interests areas extend into the integration of traditional and expressive healing practices, expanding entrepreneurial opportunities and cohesive systems of support, especially among and for women and ethno-culturally diverse groups, and particularly within her own African-American and Native-American communities. Dr. Craddock is faculty and lead scholar of Relational-Cultural Theory and Social Action at JBMTI Wellesley Centers for Women where she is investigating the ethno-cultural context and connections between relationship and brain science to inform social justice equity platforms and programs, such as co-developer of the S.T.O.P. model—a relational neuroscience frame to understand and counter social pain and exclusion. She is author developer of the Profiles of Resistance to Marginalization an analytical framework examining the impact of societal stressors and varied strategies to resist them. Karen is founder and president of KCollaborative Connections, a relationship-based consultation, training and action research practice informed by collective impact models to provide services across multiple sectors. She is a lead partner and developer of the Sodina project (The Avielle Foundation) a national story mapping initiative developing pathways for healing by engaging a diverse network of people who have suffered loss due to violence. Author and instructor of a range of works on topics including adolescent parents in juvenile justice, personal narrative, mothering and mentoring among Black women in the academy and Native American engagement in STEM, she also holds several editorial and advisory roles, including Harvard University Achievement Gap Initiative's Seeding Success campaign and is chair of the domestic violence advisory for the Wampanoag Women's Center (Aquinnah) of which she is also an enrolled tribal member. Karen is fueled by her desire to collaboratively build bridges between innovative thinking and creative effective action that support and catalyze sharp awareness, vibrant compassion, and healthy networks to enhance and enrich lives across all communities. Dr. Craddock earned her Ed.M. at Harvard University and Ph.D. at Tufts University.

Helen Crump is an Assistant Professor of English at Jackson State University. She earned a doctorate in Feminist Studies, minoring in African American and African Studies, from the University of Minnesota. Her current research includes black women's fiction as theorizing African Diaspora identity, women's resistance writing, and coming-of-age narratives.

Celeste Doaks is a poet and journalist and author of *Cornrows and Cornfields,* published by Wrecking Ball Press, UK, March 2015. In 2012, she received the Lucille Clifton Scholarship to attend Squaw Valley Writers Workshop. Her work has garnered a variety of accolades including the 2009 Academy of American Poets Graduate Prize, the 2010 AWP WC&C Scholarship, and residencies at Atlantic Center of the Arts and the Fine Arts Work Center in Provincetown. Her journalism has appeared in the *Huffington Post, Village Voice, Time Out New York,* and QBR (*Quarterly Black Book Review*). Her poems have been published in multiple on-line and print publications such as *Chicago Quarterly Review, Asheville Poetry Review, Bayou Magazine* and *Beltway Poetry Quarterly.*

Celeste received her MFA from North Carolina State University; she currently teaches creative writing at Morgan State University.

Lisa Elwood is an Associate Professor of English at Herkimer College. She teaches writing and literature courses, including African American Literature. Her research interests include American literature, domesticity and sensibility as represented in different genres, and feminist theory. She was hired at the college in 2003 as an Assistant Professor. She has been teaching since 1999, beginning her career at New Mexico State University (NMSU) as a graduate student. She earned her Bachelor's Degree at Marymount College and her Master's Degree at NMSU. She has also received two National Endowment for the Humanities awards, which brought her to Plymouth, Massachusetts, to study Wampanoag women's history and to Concord, MA, to study transcendentalism and the abolitionist movement. Currently, she is working on her Ph.D. in Literature and Criticism at Indiana University of Pennsylvania in their summer-only doctoral program.

Delphine Fongang is a lecturer in the Department of Languages and Literatures at the University of Wisconsin-Whitewater. Her teaching and research interests include Postcolonial literature/theory, Africana Studies, African Women's Life Writing, and Feminist theory/pedagogy. Her publications have appeared in *African and Black Diaspora: An International Journal, a/b: Auto/Biography Studies* and *Spectrum: A Journal on Black Men*

Tyralynn Frazier is a medial anthropologist working on topics ranging from examining the influences of stress on maternal health and reproductive outcomes to the effects of stress on adolescent health and development. Through this work, her primary focus is to better understand how the social environment influences early emotional development, and the long term health effects early emotional self regulation has on adult well-being.

Emilie Gangnat, Ph.D., focuses on photography in Christian missions. She is particularly interested in the use of images by christian organizations and the construction of stereotypes and identities in missionary photography. In 2013, she co-edited the book *Cinema et mission*, published by Karthala. Her current project explores family photographs taken by missionaries.

Florence Kyomugisha is a Professor in the Gender and Women's Studies Department at California State University – Northridge. Kyomugisha has a Ph.D. in Urban Studies and a Graduate Certificate in Women's Studies. Her research focuses on health issues in women and minority populations, and families in the African Diaspora.

Marva L. Lewis is an Associate Professor at Tulane University School of Social Work with a Ph.D. in Sociocultural Psychology. She is a Visiting Professor at the Merrill-Palmer Skillman Institute and Wayne State University School of Social Work. Her scholarship uses a cultural practices approach centered on attachment and hair-combing interaction as a context for research, assessment, and intervention. She is Founder and Director of the Natural Connections Center for Research and Training with initiatives designed to address the impact of race and culture on parent-child relationships. In 2011, the National Zero to Three Safe Babies Court Teams commissioned her to conduct a series of workshops titled, "Healing from the Historical Trauma of Slavery" to address racial disparities in the child welfare system. She is a member of the National Leadership Team with the Quality Improvement Center for Research-Based Infant-Toddler Court Teams, a partnership funded by the Administration on Children, Youth and Families (ACYF), Zero to Three Center for the Study of Social Policy, the National Council of Juvenile and Family Court Judges, and RTI, International.

Regina McCoy, MPH, is a academic professional Professor of Public Health Education at the University of North Carolina-Greensboro. Her teaching and research interests focus on healthy sexuality in communities and school, maternal and child health promotion, and community-based participatory research.

Tracy R. Nichols, Ph.D., Dr. Tracy R. Nichols is an Associate Professor of Public Health Education and Women and Gender Studies at the University of North Carolina-Greensboro. Her expertise is in developmental issues for adolescent girls; mother-daughter relationships; intervention development and evaluation; and the construction of gender-based analytical frameworks for women's health and wellness.

RaShell Smith-Spears, Ph.D., is Associate Professor of English at Jackson State University in Jackson, Mississippi . She earned her undergraduate degree from Spelman College and her Ph.D. from the University of Missouri-Columbia. Her areas of interest are African American Literature, identity politics, and popular culture studies. She has published academic essays and creative works in *Pearl Cleage & Free Womanhood*, *Icons of African American Literature*, *South Atlantic Review*, *Encyclopedia of Hip Hop Literature*, *Short Story*, *Black Magnolias*, and *A Lime Jewel*, among others.

Tracy Robinson-Wood, EdD., is a professor in the Department of Applied Psychology at Northeastern University. She is author of *The Convergence of Race, Ethnicity, and Gender: Multiple Identities in Counseling*. The fifth edition, to be published by SagePublications, is anticipated in 2016. Her research interests focus on the intersections of race, gender, sexuality, and class in psychosocial identity development. She has developed the Resistance Modality Inventory (RMI), a psychometrically valid measure of resistance, a theory she co-developed for black girls and women to optimally push back against racism, sexism, classism, and other forms of oppression. Her research is also focused on parents' racial socialization messages within interracial families, and the relational, psychological, and physiological impact of microaggressions on highly educated racial, gender, and sexual minorities.

Theresa Craddock (cover artist) is a retired art educator who received her training and degree from Emmanuel College and Massachusetts College of Art in Boston. For more than 28 years she taught in the Boston Public School system at Boston Latin School instructing the Advanced Placement level courses and developed the existing art program that expanded and grew tremendously under her leadership. Through a Getty Foundation funded grant, she co-developed the 8th grade interdisciplinary art curriculum, which was cited by the National Art Educators Association in 1994 as a "national model." Theresa was named the Massachusetts Art Educator of the year in 2000 for her exemplary contribution and gifts, and in 2001, she was honored as the Eastern Region Art Educator of the year for the entire Northeast region of the U.S.A. She was a member of the Boston Globe Scholastics Advisory Board on which she had served for over 26 years. In 1998, Boston Mayor Menino and then Boston school superintendent, Dr. Payzant, presented her with an award for her concept and direction of the two 25ft. long murals that deck the walls of the then named Boston Garden. She was the first recipient of the Boston Public Schools Art and Music departments Starfish Award awarded to her for promoting, developing and continuing a program at a time when there was no central direction. Theresa has been selected to participate in a number of local and national art and education institutes over the years and her work is often commissioned for private collections and local shows. Her work has been featured, sold and exhibited at several venues including the Cousen Rose Art Gallery in Oak Bluffs, MA (Martha's Vineyard), and the Massachusetts Audubon Society. In 2009, she and her daughter, Karen Craddock (also the editor and author of this volume), collaborated for an art salon and exhibition, *Cairns,* at Brandeis University Women's Studies Research Center featuring Theresa's art work and Karen's poetry in a collection entitled *Of You I Am*: *Stones within the Circle of Black Mother-Daughter Relationship.* Theresa lives in Sharon, MA, and is a member of art associations Along with her art, she enjoys reading, gardening and spending time with her family, which include her husband, three adult children and seven grandchildren. Her depth of insight regarding the importance and breadth of art and expression branches out beyond the art studio and into the realms of relationship, self-discovery, culture and spirituality.